Sunsets: Reflections for Life's Final Journey strikes a delicate balance in the treatment of an exceedingly sensitive subject. Most conspicuously, its intense emotional impact is complemented by commendable controls of fact coming from both medical science and the Scriptures.

The book is very well written. For example, Howard's primary case scenario is recounted in historical increments so as to provide an organizational framework for the book, not an arbitrary one but one that corresponds to the common stages of dying and death. This development serves as a natural vehicle for not only describing the signs of each of these progressive stages, but also for illustrating how the patient, the family, and caregiver often respond. At these junctures Howard, speaking from knowledge and experience, delicately, lovingly, and humbly suggests how they should respond based upon medical and scriptural realities.

This book will be of help to a wide-ranging readership, from physicians and nurses to families facing an imminent loss. I am particularly recommending it to pastors, counselors, and serving saints. Howard's use of the Scriptures is quite commendable. She is hermeneutically careful and theologically credible.

GEORGE J. ZEMEK, TH.D., professor and author

Deborah Howard has . . . shown in a discerning, lovely way that the grim realities of disease and death, the dreaded consequences of sin, can be faced with dignity, peace, and hope through faith in Jesus Christ because of the love of God. I know of no other book that so ably brings the reader intimately face to face with the helpless agony of families confronted by a loved one dying and by the ordeal of the one who senses that his own life is ebbing unalterably away. Here we find sobering sadness. But above all, we find the joy to be had in the One who said, "I am the way and the truth and the life." This is a book for everyone who loves anyone who may die, for everyone who someday will himself be confronting death.

BILL SIMMONS, Political Editor, *Arkansas Democrat-Gazette*

In *Sunsets: Reflections for Life's Final Journey*, Deborah Howard has written a book that I wish I had read early in my ministry, particularly before my family, friends, and church members began to die. Knowledge of how to handle terminal illness is not something we are born with. As a result, most of us have stumbled around trying to do and say the right things.

Yet Deborah knows what she is writing about. As a hospice nurse who daily attends to dying people and their families, she has the hands-on experience, coupled with a rich theological understanding, to give us an insightful and thoroughly readable manual of things to do and to avoid (and the proper way to think) when a person is dying. Her deep well of sound biblical convictions is amazing for someone who has had no formal theological training.

Actual case studies make this book come alive for the reader. You will grieve, laugh, and be thoroughly challenged to think through a whole range of matters relating to death. At some point all of us will be involved with death— of our loved ones, our friends, ~~our own~~. Get a copy of this book, live with it, and you will be better prepa~~red~~ ~~when it does~~ come.

CURTIS C. THOMA~~S~~

[Here is] firsthand experience and insight with true spiritual discernment for the here and the hereafter. A comfort, a support, and a guide for the saint and the sinner alike as "the shadow of death" closes in. The glory of God and the truth of the gospel permeate these pages. The Lord will surely use them in many lives—and many deaths.

DAN SHANKS, missionary to Dominica

Deborah Howard brings us a work about caring for the dying from the perspective of a Christian hospice nurse. Her book is about sharing the mystery, the suffering, the spiritual growth, the beauty, the intimacy of the dying process with those at the end of their lives. With touching case histories powerfully written, she brings the stories of her dying patients to life, illustrating the points above, and acknowledging the privilege it is to attend one who is dying. This is a book about being a Christian, but it is more than that. And it is a book about being a hospice nurse, but it is more than that too. Ms. Howard uses her thorough knowledge of Scripture to discuss and defend her ministry to the dying. The book is so comprehensive that it very nearly becomes a Christian apology for hospice nursing. Her prose is clear, smooth, and engaging. Her thoughts are well organized. She has a gift for the written word that makes her book very readable, and a gift for nursing that makes her a healer even at the time of death.

A. REED THOMPSON, M.D., Director, Palliative Care Service
University of Arkansas for Medical Sciences
Medical Director, The Arkansas Hospice

I found myself facing the reality that a man who is eighty-two years old, with a recent history of surgery for a malignancy and a long-standing history of metabolic disease, might soon face the "inevitable becoming actual." I found comfort and reassurance for me and for my family when, in the benevolent sovereignty of a loving Father, we experienced the scenario described in this book.

CARL E. WENGER, M.D.

Deborah Howard, a long-time, faithful member of our church, has done the body of Christ a great service in writing this excellent book on death and dying. She writes, not from the perch of a distant and detached observer, but rather from years of uniquely hands-on and intimate service as a hospice nurse. Much more than that, she has ministered as a committed Christian whose heart of love is evident as you read these reflections. She cares enough about her patients (and their families) to both comfort them in their dying and to speak God's Word to them when appropriate. May God grant a wide audience for this book's timeless and transcendent message that our only dying hope is in Jesus Christ.

LANCE QUINN, pastor, Bible Church of Little Rock, AK

REFLECTIONS FOR LIFE'S FINAL JOURNEY

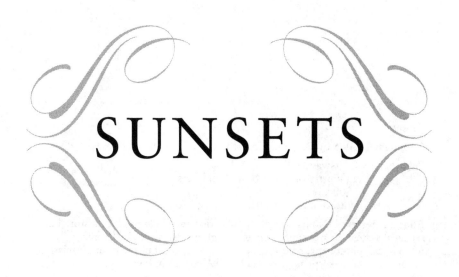

SUNSETS

DEBORAH HOWARD, RN, CHPN
FOREWORD BY D. A. CARSON

CROSSWAY BOOKS

A MINISTRY OF
GOOD NEWS PUBLISHERS
WHEATON, ILLINOIS

Sunsets

Copyright © 2005 by Deborah Howard

Published by Crossway Books
        a ministry of Good News Publishers
        1300 Crescent Street
        Wheaton, Illinois 60187

All of the italicized words in the Scripture verses and other quoted material indicate the author's emphasis.

Scripture verses are taken from *The Holy Bible, English Standard Version.* Copyright © 2001 by Crossway Bibles, a ministry of Good News Publishers. Used by permission. All rights reserved.

Scripture verses marked NIV are taken from the *Holy Bible: New International Version*™ Copyright © 1973, 1978, 1984 by International Bible Society. Used by permission of Zondervan Publishing House. All rights reserved.

The "NIV" and "New International Version" trademarks are registered in the United States Patent and Trademark Office by International Bible Society. Use of either trademark requires the permission of International Bible Society.

Cover design: Jon McGrath

Cover photo: Getty Images

First printing 2005

Printed in the United States of America

Library of Congress Cataloging-in-Publication Data
Howard, Deborah, 1952-
Sunsets : reflections for life's final journey / Deborah Howard.
    p. cm.
Includes bibliographical references.
ISBN 1-58134-645-X (tpb : alk. paper)
1. Death—Religious aspects—Christianity. I. Title.
BT825.H79   2005
248.8'6175—dc22   2004013371

ML		15	14	13	12	11	10	09	08	07	06	05
15	14	13	12	11	10	9	8	7	6	5	4	3	2	1

*This book is lovingly dedicated
to my brother,*

JOHN DAVID KOON

*John accepted his challenge
with courage and faith.
His attitude of sweet submission
to the will of our sovereign Lord
has provided a godly
example for all to follow.*

CONTENTS

ACKNOWLEDGMENTS

To my husband, Theron—my partner in grace and my friend for life. Thank you for the patience and understanding you've shown me during the writing of this book. You were the first person who believed it would be published. You have encouraged me every step of the way and never complained about all the time you spent alone while I was perched at the computer. I love you.

To my "readers" (who have evaluated my efforts on the book):

Bill Simmons—Thank you so much for freely giving of your time and talents in order to keep me honest and balanced in my writing. You have been such a good friend and a valuable asset to me during this time.

Dr. Mark Rens—Thank you for the time you spent reading these chapters, for checking my medical accuracy, and for the good suggestions you contributed. This is a better book because of you.

My mother, Glen Koon, Dr. George Zemek, Curtis Thomas, Judy Howe, Bob Lepine, Lance Quinn, and Larry White—Thanks for allowing me to use you as sounding boards for ideas. Your feedback has been enormously helpful and encouraging.

My friends and family—Thank you so much for believing in me and supporting my efforts to put these ideas and experiences down in writing. You have challenged me, listened to me, and encouraged me every step of the way.

Arkansas Hospice, Crossroads Hospice, and VNA Hospice— Thank you for allowing me the privilege to work in a field so rich in rewards.

Jerry Bridges, D. A. Carson, John MacArthur, Erwin Lutzer, and Loraine Boettner—The rich words of your quotations provided the framework around which I constructed my book.

David N. Steele, my teacher and my friend—Thank you for teaching me that, though flawed and sinful, we can be used by God in a mighty way to change the hearts and lives of his people. You were the tool God used to change my life forever.

I'd like to thank my editor, Lila Bishop, for her excellent work on this book, and for making the editing process as painless as possible.

Last, but certainly not least, I thank God the Father for choosing me in spite of my wickedness, Jesus Christ for making my salvation possible by giving His own precious life to pay the penalty for my sin, and the Holy Spirit, my Comforter, for dwelling within my heart and mind and leading me down the paths of righteousness.

FOREWORD

by Dr. D. A. Carson

OF THE BOOKS ON SUFFERING and dying there is no end. So why should I endorse yet another one? Would I not be wiser to tell Deborah Howard that there are enough volumes in print on this subject?

That kind of facile response presupposes that the many books on this subject are all so much alike that there really isn't space for another. But books on this subject are extraordinarily diverse. Some belong to the genre of theodicy—the attempt, in Milton's words, to "justify the ways of God to man," to make sense of suffering and death. Others take precisely the opposite tack: Suffering and death are so outrageous, they argue, that either the existence or the goodness of God must be called into question. Some of these books are subsets of the philosophy of religion; others come from the pens of theologians; still others present themselves as serious Bible studies. The books are written at different levels: Some are highly technical works; some are driven by clichés; still others evoke strong emotions but without rigorous thought—the polar opposite of cerebral books on this subject that can discuss, for example, the Holocaust in dispassionate terms. Some are designed to help Christians; some aim to destroy Christians; still others try to lead people to become Christians. Most of these books have their place, their own niche.

What does Deborah Howard bring us?

In some ways her book is more focused than many in this arena. Her subject is not suffering in general, but death—the death of your friends and loved ones (in which case you will be bereaved), and your death (in which case you may suffer, and you will probably bereave others). Nor has she written this book for unbelievers (though they are certainly welcome to listen in). This is a book to help Christians come to grips with death—their own and that of others. And for four reasons, I am glad that Deborah wrote it.

First, unless the Lord Jesus comes back first, we are all going to die. Yet for various reasons we live in a culture that focuses on the present, on the unending "now," not on the one thing that is more certain than taxation. Today death is not a popular subject for sermons: We expect to be healed, medically or miraculously. So when death arrives, as it inevitably does, it almost always seems too early. But considering how often the Bible looks at death squarely and demands that we reflect on the afterlife, such a stance is at best shortsighted, and at worst dangerous. So books that dare to bring up the subject of death and reintroduce it to the "naked public square" of Christian discussion are doing a valuable service, quite apart from the concrete help that they give to individual readers.

Second, Deborah Howard has managed to link narrative and exposition. Most of the narrative books in this area tell a story, or tell a lot of stories, and nothing more. Many other books provide doctrinal structures, but they are rather abstract. This book combines narrative and doctrinal exposition. Of course, that makes the book a little long; for many readers, however, the combination also makes the book more memorable. And apart from all the little stories, the ongoing narrative of Bachman is not one you are likely to forget.

Third, while some books are evocative and perhaps sentimental, and others aim at faithful exposition of Christian truth, this volume seeks to capture both your affections and your mind. For those who want nothing more than a stirring of their emotions, it may prove too abstract and doctrinal; for those who want orthodox exposition but who are afraid to love and laugh and cry, this book will be thought too sentimental. But for those who have witnessed loved ones walk through the valley of the shadow of death, or who are beginning that lonely journey themselves, this book will appeal to the whole person. If it does not address all the hardest problems in theodicy, it turns again and again to crucial biblical passages and to central Christian themes and works out their practical value: God's sovereignty, the nature of Christian hope, the purposes of suffering in a fallen world, the glory of the salvation won by Christ.

Fourth, this book is written at a more popular level than many pastors and scholars can achieve. If that means that it is poised to reach a large number of people who may not read narrower or more technical literature, that can only be a good thing, for Deborah Howard is as surefooted as she is compassionate, as biblically faithful as she is tenderhearted. The combination is rare, and always to be cherished.

D. A. Carson,
Trinity Evangelical Divinity School

PREFACE

Truly, I say to you, as you did it to one of the least of these my brothers, you did it to me.

MATTHEW 25:40

IF EVER THERE WAS A motivator for service to others, the truth contained in this verse is the one for me. I can't always rely on my heart to be big enough, tender enough, to care deeply enough, to be reliable enough to show me when and how to care for those around me. But when I view my life and my service to others in the light of this wondrously sweet verse, my direction becomes clearer. This truth can overcome obstacles that would otherwise shipwreck my desire to serve. So I thank God for giving me this passage and the calling to which He has led me.

What motivates nurses to do what they do? Sometimes it is the "bigness," the tenderness of their hearts. Other times it is their value system. For me, however, and for many other nurses, it may be a combination of reasons. For Christian nurses, the overriding motivation comes, in many instances, in the desire to live a life pleasing to Christ, who loves us and gives us eternal life with Him. We may not have enough personal, tender love for patients to seek their highest good and to care for them. But we do have that personal, tender love for our Lord. In light of the above passage of Scripture, if we view our service to each other as rendering service to Christ, that's all the motivation we need, isn't it?

Ephesians 1:3-8 says, "Blessed be the God and Father of our Lord Jesus Christ, who has *blessed us* in Christ with *every* spiritual blessing in the heavenly places, even as *he chose us* in him before the foundation of the world, that we should be holy and blameless before him. In love he predestined us for adoption through Jesus Christ, according to the purpose of his will, to the praise of his glorious grace, with which he has *blessed* us in the Beloved. In him we have redemption through his blood, the forgiveness of our trespasses, according to the *riches* of his grace, which he *lavished* upon us, in all wisdom and insight."

Service to the one who has done all that for us is a privilege. With hearts of gratitude, we should seek to please Him by honoring and obeying His Word. First John 5:3 says, "For this is the love of God, that we keep his commandments."

One of the ways we obey his commands is found in 1 John 3:16-18: "By this we know love, that he laid down his life for us, and we ought to lay down our lives for the brothers. *But if anyone has the world's goods and sees his brother in need, yet closes his heart against him, how does God's love abide in him?* Little children, let us not love in word or talk but in deed and in truth." Then in 1 John 4:11, John writes, "Beloved, if God so loved us, we also ought to love one another."

That's how we can serve others—how we can put their needs before our own. By our love and service to them, we are loving and serving Christ Himself.

> *In his hand is the life of every living thing and the breath of all mankind.*
>
> JOB 12:10

INTRODUCTION

FOR ME, BECOMING A hospice nurse was surrendering to a "tugging" at my heart. A friend with whom I'd worked on the oncology floor left the hospital to become a hospice nurse. She loved it and urged me to come talk to her about the job. Finally I decided to give it a try. I didn't expect to fall in love with this specialty or with the patients I would come to know. But that's exactly what happened.

After I experienced the joy and sorrow of caring for and losing my first several patients, I began to sense another tugging—to put into writing those intense experiences. I wanted to try to help others deal with the pain of losing a loved one or make sense of their own impending death. Thus the idea of this book was born, and through circumstances given to me by the grace of God, I have now been given the opportunity to write it.

You will find several elements in this book. *There is my own personal experience as a hospice nurse.* Part of my job description is serving as a coach, of sorts, for this "death experience."

Dealing with those who are dying is not an easy job. Though our hearts are broken many times, we are *willing* to have our hearts broken for such a good cause. And that cause is what hospice is all about: *We lovingly care for patients who have a terminal illness and give them the support they need to die at home with as much dignity as possible—without suffering and surrounded by those they love.*

Through hospice I have encountered many situations, have been inspired by wonderful people, and have been touched emotionally by their stories. Now I want to share some of those stories. All the ones under the heading "Case Study" are true. I have changed the names in most to protect patient confidentiality. I hope these stories give you a glimpse into what hospice is all about.

Another element you'll find is the Christian perspective that brings comfort and acceptance through the very words of God to His peo-ple. I believe the only way we can truly know God and know what He expects of us is to study His Word. I have been pleasantly surprised at the number of Bible texts on death and dying and offering comfort to those afflicted with the anguish of loss. I want to share some of those verses with you and spread the news that God is a God of comfort and restoration. He can heal broken hearts and put hope into lives touched by the sorrow of death.

Much has been written on death and dying over the years. Few subjects have undergone more transition in the eyes of society, and few are as controversial. Even a hundred years ago, death and dying might have been considered matter-of-factly as just another part of the life cycle—people lived and they died.

Before modern medicine moved the process of dying to hospitals, people died at home in their own beds. Inevitably they would find themselves surrounded by friends and relatives. Even as they lay dying, the comings and goings of the concerned and grieving (or even the avaricious) made their bedrooms resemble Grand Central Station.

Later death became a taboo subject. If you had the bad manners to speak of it at all, you certainly would not talk above a whisper. People thought that if you mentioned death, you would somehow be responsible when it happened. Believe it or not, I still see evidence of that superstition at work today. But more and more it seems that we are honestly and realistically trying to deal with some of the toughest issues facing us today. Death is one of those issues.

Not only should we learn about death, but we must also prepare for it. Since no one knows the day or hour of his death, it is best, in the words of the Boy Scout motto, to "be prepared." I hope this book will help us learn more about death and give us the proper motivation to prepare ourselves financially, physically, emotionally, and spiritually for this inevitability.

I want to be absolutely clear when I say that I do not know all the answers to the tough problems that arise with death and dying. I in no way want to portray myself as an "expert" on the subject. I'm a sojourner myself. But the more I learn about this subject, the more I want to share the information with others in hopes that it may be helpful.

One of the best books I've read on finding peace and acceptance in the face of adversity is *Trusting God Even When Life Hurts* by Jerry Bridges. His beautifully expressed thoughts and feelings on this subject are exceedingly helpful, convicting, and comforting to those who are hurting. I wish I could quote the whole book for you but will settle at this point for his statement of purpose:

> I sincerely hope that none of the statements I make in the following chapters come across as glib and easy answers to the difficult problems of adversity and suffering. There are no easy answers. Adversity is difficult even when we know God is in control of our circumstances.[1]

I would like to adopt this statement as a disclaimer for my own work. I certainly don't have all the answers to the difficult questions I'll introduce. But it is my hope that I can help other people, using the biblical and practical answers that I do have.

I have had the privilege to love and comfort many who have gone through this difficult time. A lovely truth is that no matter how much I try to give, I always seem to get back more than I have given. It is my prayerful desire to comfort, enlighten, and encourage many others.

This is not a book just for Christians. Rather, it is for anyone who is dying, anyone who knows someone who is dying, or anyone who wants to learn how to help and comfort those who are dying. May God, who is the God of comfort, comfort and bless those who read this book, giving them the eyes to see His truth and the mind to comprehend what He has to say about this important topic.

> *Blessed are those who keep his testimonies, who seek him with their whole heart.*
>
> PSALM 119:2

1

DENIAL

If we are in a battle with this enemy called Death, I believe we should learn about it, in order to know how to confront the dying experience. We need to know how to face that enemy on our own behalf and how to deal with the inevitable death of loved ones and friends.

BILLY GRAHAM

THIS CAN'T BE HAPPENING

Big Bachman McNair III sat in the doctor's office with his slender wife seated apprehensively on the edge of her chair beside him. He'd always been a big guy—a talented football star in high school and college. But football wasn't his only claim to fame. He was a big man in the business world as well and had provided a safe and comfortable life for his family.

For the thirtieth time, he shifted his six-foot-four, 234-pound frame in the chair. Seemed he just couldn't find a comfortable position anywhere anymore.

"This blasted chair is way too small," he grumbled to his wife. "Why doesn't he get some sturdy furniture in here? I'm sure he can afford it. For what we've shelled out, he could refurnish this whole place."

Penny smiled at him. "Patience, darling. He'll be in soon." She reached for his hand. They both turned as Dr. Tanner opened the door and sat down behind his desk. He put a folder on the desktop in front of him and looked at both of them for a moment before he spoke. Penny's breath caught.

"Mr. and Mrs. McNair, I have the results back from all the tests now." Peering squarely at Bachman, Dr. Tanner said, "You do not have a pulled muscle in your back. We discussed that last time, you recall. What we've found is that you have cancer. We believe the cancer started in your left lung but has now spread to your liver and spine. The cancer in your spine is likely the primary cause of your back pain."

Getting no response from his patient but a slack-jawed stare, he continued, "Perhaps if you had come in when you first noticed the pain, we might have had a better chance of helping you."

Bachman had put off going to the doctor until he couldn't stand the pain. He had thought he just needed some kind of painkiller or muscle relaxant. After two months of pills with almost no improvement, he had gone in for something stronger. His doctor had referred him to Dr. Tanner.

Penny turned worried eyes to her husband, who was red-faced and looked ready to explode. She'd seen that expression too many times not to realize what was coming.

"You're crazy," he raved. "Cancer. Why, I don't believe that for a second. I'm healthy as a horse. If it weren't for this back pain, I'd be as fit as I was in high school. I've lost down to my college weight already. I just overdid the exercise and pulled my back. That's all." Looking over at Penny, he asked, "What's your chiropractor's name? Maybe I should go to him after all."

Ignoring him, Penny asked Dr. Tanner, "Where do we go from here? Will he need chemo or something?"

Dr. Tanner looked down, sighed, and raised his troubled eyes back to Bachman. "We can go ahead and try chemo and possibly even consider radiation therapy, but I have to tell you that with the disease this advanced, the odds are against a full recovery."

"What does that mean?" Bachman blustered. "'Full recovery.' Do you think I can lick this thing or not?"

"We'll do everything we can. But you should also set your affairs in order if you haven't already, just in case."

"Just in case what, Doc?"

"In case you don't make it, Mr. McNair. That is a definite possibility."

Straining to stand, Bachman stormed out of the office, muttering, "This is absolutely ridiculous. I don't believe this stuff for a second."

Penny stood slowly and held her hand out to Dr. Tanner. "I'm sure he'll be more reasonable later. Please just let us know what we need to do and when."

"I wish I could be more optimistic, Mrs. McNair. I promise I'll do everything I can to help your husband. We'll be in touch with you regarding the schedule for his treatments."

"Thank you, Doctor. This will take some getting used to. Can you tell me how long you think he may have?"

"One can never accurately predict that kind of thing. I would say anywhere from four months to a year, depending on how he responds to treatment."

Placing her trembling fingers over her lips, she managed to breathe, "I see. Thank you." Choking back the tears, she resolutely followed her husband.

She found Bachman standing at the elevator, muttering to himself, "I'm not used to being sick. I can't be that ill. Sure, I've been losing weight. Appetite's not as robust. But I look so much better in these loose-fitting clothes. And I know what pain is. I learned in my football days to ignore it, to move along with life in spite of it." He set his jaw. "All right. I'm not about to let a doctor tell me I have cancer. I'll just get a second opinion. This guy's wrong. I should never have come to him in the first place."

WHAT IS DENIAL?

Bachman McNair is a fictional character but one I created as a composite of several patients I've known. The experiences he faces in this book reflect actual situations in the lives of those who have shared their stories, their lives, and their deaths with me.

Bachman's thinking and behavior are predictable and understandable. He experienced one of the first reactions common to those confronted with shocking or heartbreaking news—denial.

At the crucial moment of revealed truth, the situation may be too horrible for us to face; so in our minds we change it into something we *can* handle. "The doctor is wrong. We'll just get a second opinion." "He's not dead; he's just sleeping." "That can't be true. You look so healthy." "If we can just get Daddy to eat, I know he'll get better."

Those who make these kinds of statements may not want to look at the fact that their loved one is fading before their eyes and that death is imminent. Some even deny the patient the comfort and benefit that hospice services can provide because they don't yet believe their loved one is close to death.

WHOM ARE WE REALLY PROTECTING?

Denial protects us *from the full impact of emotional pain.* Denial *doesn't* protect our loved one. Denial allows us to pretend for a little while. The problem is that some people never progress beyond denial, and nothing constructive can come from this kind of thinking. These people believe that everything will be okay, that the medical experts are all wrong, that nothing in their life has really changed. In order to *help* the situation, they *must* face their circumstances. They *must* come to grips with what they're dreading the most. *Denial* must be replaced with *reality*.

Philippians 4:8 says, "Finally, brothers, whatever is true [or real] . . . think about these things." None of us can take steps to make positive changes until we start dealing with *fact* instead of *fantasy* or *feelings*. We are of no use to anyone otherwise. *We're part of the problem, not the solution.*

In my hospice experience, I have often heard patients say in a quiet, accepting tone, "I don't think I'm going to be around much longer, but I'm ready to go." Suddenly a well-meaning family member in denial jumps up and says, almost hysterically, "Now don't you talk like that, you hear? You're going to get well yet. We all just have to be positive." The patient usually remains silent, lacking the energy to argue, but when his eyes meet mine, we share an unspoken understanding that seems comforting to him. He knows that I know.

In situations like these, that family member has missed a precious opportunity to share with the loved one in a way that can only bring them closer. The person in denial closed the door to genuine participation in one of the most important events in the loved one's life—death. Denial can be a monstrous foe.

Patients have told me in quiet talks when we're alone, "I know I'm dying, but don't tell my daughter. She's not handling this very well right now." Then there's the other end of the spectrum, when the children want me to keep a secret from Grandma, saying, "We don't want her to know she's dying. We don't think she could handle that right now."

To be quite blunt, if I went in the room and asked Grandma, "What do you think is happening with you right now?" she would most likely say matter-of-factly, "I'm dying." She knows. The actual truth may be that the grandchildren can't or won't face that fact yet, or they don't know how to talk to her about it; so they're postponing the inevitable. I make note of these requests. They indicate a need that should be addressed later.

DENIAL: FRIEND OR FOE?

Early in a relationship with a dying patient and the family, I allow them to express denial without challenging them. I realize that even though denial is, at worst, destructive and, at best, a procrastination, these people may feel the *need* to believe such things at first. It wouldn't be the most effective time to address the issue. But as our relationship deepens through more and more contact, and trust builds between us, I try to, as they say in nursing lingo, "orient them to reality" in a most gentle and nonthreatening way.

In helping people move past denial, I am in no way trying to take away their hope. There is a huge difference between hope and denial.

Denial **hurts** the situation and is unhealthy. Denial eventually leads to regret.

Hope always **helps** a situation. It takes a good, long look at the facts and then gives people wings to soar above the difficulties. People don't have to bury their heads in the sand to have real hope.

A REALLY INCREDIBLE JOURNEY

One of the duties of a hospice nurse is to help people confront what's going on in their lives so they can eventually find peace and acceptance of their circumstances. We assess not only the health of their thinking and the strength of their spiritual faith, but we try to pinpoint exactly where they are in the process leading to acceptance. The pace at which they move through that process is different in every situation. Some people embrace reality quickly. Some take a long time to journey from denial to acceptance. Regardless, they should all be treated with the utmost respect, understanding, and tenderness.

Denial is the most common reaction to a shocking experience or to shocking news. Simply defined, denial is a refusal to acknowledge a threat of some kind. It is a shock absorber, of sorts, that can *temporarily* insulate us from the full impact of a traumatic situation. But denial also leads us away from finding healthy solutions to the problems that confront us.

What are we denying when we are in denial? Whatever circumstances we find ourselves in, right? And who has brought those circumstances into our lives? God has, or at least He has allowed them. So what we are actually denying is the *providence of God*. And that is *never* a healthy response to trial.

None of us has attained perfection. So when we face something that brings us pain, we may have this natural tendency toward denial. Don't kick yourself if this has happened to you. Just recognize it as what it is—an obstacle that needs to be removed, and move past it as quickly as you can. Most people are able to do this after a *short* time and do a beautiful job of preparing for what lies ahead.

CASE STUDY

A patient was referred to hospice from the hospital. She had been told nothing else could be done for her medically, and the family wanted to take her home. At sixty-one she was dying of a brain tumor. When I first met her, I immediately noted that she was in significant respiratory distress. Her color was pale to gray, with slight cyanosis (blueness) in her nail beds and around her mouth. Though the head of her bed was elevated, she was gasping for breath and unable to speak because she couldn't take in enough air. But her eyes held mine and told a story in their glance. She knew she was dying and accepted it.

If I had been working in my old capacity as an ICU nurse instead of a hospice nurse, I might have suggested she be placed on ventilator support. But I knew that would go against her wishes.

I walked with her husband to a Quiet Room and went through the admission paperwork after he assured me they wanted no heroics, that she just wanted to be at home when she died. I asked if the doctor had told him how long she expected his wife to live. He said, "She said it could be six weeks or six months. But Mama's pulled through this thing before. She just might surprise everybody." What I didn't say was that I thought a more realistic prognosis would be six hours. But I didn't believe that was the time for such news. It was important for him to hang together long enough to get her home and taken care of. So I allowed him his delusion, knowing he would realize soon enough how sick she was.

He was in denial.

When we walked back to her room, her daughter was packing for the trip home. I ordered all the medical equipment I thought would be appropriate and was assured by the equipment company that it would be delivered and set up before her arrival. I called the pharmacy to order the prescriptions. They would be ready that afternoon. Hospice tries to anticipate every need every step of the way.

That afternoon I drove to their house in the country to ensure that they had everything they needed. They had placed her hospital bed in a wonderful room with an entire wall of glass through which she could view the glories of nature—their pond, the red barn, the horses grazing lazily across their pastureland. The sun shone on trees lustrous with the brilliant reds and golds of autumn. The sky was clear and blue-white above the horizon. Gathered around her were family members ready to provide comfort and love.

Her husband was still talking about how she was going to get better, but the patient shook her head and said, "Not this time." Her breathing had improved enough to allow her to speak quietly.

He patted her hand and said, "You don't think you're going to make it?"

She looked into the same eyes she'd gazed into for forty-three years and said, "No, honey. I'm ready to go now. It won't be long."

To his credit, he didn't argue with her about it. He asked if she wanted him to call her minister, and she nodded. Her husband had finally moved past his denial and, looking realistically at her condition, was now truly able to help her. He supported her in her last wishes—to be at home with her family in her own familiar surroundings. He waited with her for the Lord to take her to her heavenly home.

Her husband rarely left her side from that time on. He told me once that he never really knew what to say to her. He just sat holding her hand and telling her how much he loved her. Though she was bloated with excess fluid and bald from radiation and chemotherapy, her soft brown eyes watched his face lovingly as he told her how beautiful she was to him. I thought, whether he realized it or not, he knew exactly what to say.

She didn't die that night or the next. But early in the morning of the third day, she quietly slipped away, with her husband sleeping on a cot beside her. She had been ready to meet her Lord.

Hospice was not there to save her life but to support her wishes by enabling her family to care for her at home. As part of that support, I taught them what to expect each step of the way so they would know what to do. They knew we were a phone call away. Knowing that, and armed with the right information, they calmly faced death without panic. Afterward, I got there as soon as I could and found the family sitting in the room with her, sipping coffee and telling lovely stories about what she had meant to them. They had indeed reached acceptance. They were glad she didn't have to struggle anymore. They knew where her soul was, and they rested in that assurance. It was an honor to be there for them and to have gotten to know this lovely family.

ARE THERE STAGES OF GRIEF?

Many of us have read or studied Elizabeth Kubler-Ross's Five Stages of Grief:

1. Denial
2. Anger
3. Bargaining

4. Depression

5. Acceptance

All people do not experience each of these steps every time. Some go through the steps but not in this particular order. Others skip steps entirely. However, many people do go through these steps in varying degrees, and in most cases they proceed in this general order.

According to *the* manual for living, the Bible, there are no universal steps for grieving. God's people are supplied with enough strength, faith, and power to get through any crisis, knowing that our Lord is with us—comforting us, loving us, and reminding us that all things are under His divine control and will eventually work for our good.

I've seen over the years that the more we understand the way God works in our lives and the stronger our faith in Christ, the better we are able to find the sweet acceptance that proves so elusive for others without that personal relationship with Him. I'm not saying there is no pain. It always hurts to lose someone you love. I'm saying there is never a reason for despair, bewilderment, or feelings of abandonment when we experience His lovingkindness and understand the truths of His Word.

HOW CAN WE GET PAST DENIAL?

What is the first step in dealing with death? *The first and most crucial step is to get past your own denial.* How can you do that? The answer is simple though the task itself can be tough. First, you must ask yourself if you could be in denial. This recognition is more than half the battle. Ask God to help you see the situation clearly and to give you the strength and wisdom to handle it. After that, take a realistic look at your situation and learn all you can about it (physical, emotional, and spiritual aspects). Soon you'll be able to replace *pretending* with *fact*. In that way, you can move past the paralysis of denial to acceptance of the task at hand—whether that is addressing your own approaching death or that of a loved one. It is only then, when you are grounded in reality, that you can truly be an effective help and comfort for someone who needs you.

DENIAL IN OTHER ASPECTS OF LIFE

I also see evidence of denial in the spiritual realm. One of the questions I ask my patients or their family is, "What do you believe about life after death?" Some don't have a clue about what I mean. Some believe I'm talking about near-death experiences. But most know that I'm talking about a spiritual existence after physical death.

Their answers can be startling. Some believe that there is no literal heaven or hell. Some believe in reincarnation. Others believe that when you die, you cease to exist in any state. Then there are those who believe that faith in life after death is for the weak and unintelligent—those who need to create a Supreme Being in order to make themselves feel better. Even Christians have a lot of mixed thoughts on the subject. Many do not fully understand what the Bible teaches about life after death.

Some even differ on what it means to be a Christian. The simplest way to discern if you are truly a Christian is this: Unless Jesus Christ is your Lord and a very real part of your life, your thinking, and your attitudes, you are not a Christian. Or as the apostle John writes in 1 John 2:3-6, "And by this we know that we have come to know him, if we keep his commandments. Whoever says 'I know him' but does not keep his commandments is a liar, and the truth is not in him, but whoever keeps his word, in him truly the love of God is perfected. *By this we may be sure that we are in him: whoever says he abides in him ought to walk in the same way in which he walked.*"

One of the most common things people say to me is that they have no fear of going to hell. When I ask them why, they usually say something like, "Well, I've always tried to live a good life. I've never really hurt anybody, and I've tried to be a good person. Of course, I haven't been as good as I could have been, but I've done all right." Others give church membership as the basis for their confidence.

Their answers have something in common. There's no mention of Jesus Christ. They focus on their *own performance* in life. How can they be sure about their eternal destiny and call themselves Christians if Christ doesn't even enter into the picture?

The Bible makes it clear that there are genuine Christians, and there are "professing" Christians. Professing Christians say they are Christians but do not have a genuine, saving faith in Christ. They may attend church, but that doesn't make them Christians. Corrie ten Boom used to say, "A mouse in the cookie jar isn't a cookie."

The Bible says that there is nothing we can *do*—no *performance* is good enough—to merit the kingdom of heaven. It is only by the grace of God through Jesus Christ, His Son, that any of us can enter that kingdom. Therefore, our security is based, not on our own works (performance), but on the righteousness of Christ and His substitutionary death on the cross as a payment for the sins of His people. "For *by grace* you have been saved *through faith*. And this is *not your own doing; it is the gift* of God, *not a result of works*, so that no one may boast" (Ephesians 2:8-9). *We* cannot generate faith. Saving faith is *generated by God*. In other words, He actually *gives* us our faith.

When we say we don't need a Savior to go to heaven, we are in denial—denying the very Word of God. Some would argue that this statement does not really reflect denial but ignorance. In some cases, I believe that is true. There are men and women across the globe who have yet to hear of Jesus Christ and His atoning work for sinners. I would agree that those people are in a state of *ignorance* rather than in *denial* of their need of a Savior.

In most cases, however, unbelievers are considered to be those who have been told the truth and refuse to believe it. If the doctor tells you that your mother is dying, and you refuse to believe it, you are considered to be in denial. If a Christian tells you that you *cannot* attain a righteousness on your own that will make you deserving of heaven, and you refuse to believe it, you are in a state of denial—denial of the truth of the living God.

When we think our own good works are adequate to merit heaven, we are in denial. When we say that there is no literal heaven or hell, we are most definitely in denial, and that is a very dangerous place to be.

Remember the words of the Lord as He reminds us of who He is and who we are: "See now that I, even I, am he, and there is no god beside me; I kill and I make alive; I wound and I heal; and there is none that can deliver out of my hand" (Deuteronomy 32:39).

And yet we are told repeatedly throughout the Bible how very much this all-powerful, all-knowing God loves and cares for His people. One beautiful example of the tender way He protects and shelters us is found in Psalm 91:4: "He will cover you with his pinions, and under his wings you will find refuge; his faithfulness is a shield and buckler."

The only truly secure place any of us will ever find is in the embrace of God the Father, who sent His Son, Jesus Christ, to pay the price for the sins of His people. May we be found in Him.

How we deal with death and tragedy says a lot about what kind of people we are.[1]

BILLY GRAHAM

2

WHY ME?

*My God, my God, why have you forsaken me? Why are you so far
from saving me, from the words of my groaning? O my God, I cry
by day, but you do not answer, and by night, but I find no rest.*

PSALM 22:1-2

WHY ME?

Bachman stared intently at the TV screen, seeing but not perceiving as
Tiger Woods made a seven-foot putt into the cup on the fourteenth
green. The fans exploded with cheers as Tiger smiled that smile, holding the ball up in a brief but triumphant gesture. Bachman stared
expressionlessly.

Penny called to him again, "Aren't you going to get the door?"

Not receiving a reply, she crossed into the foyer to answer the
doorbell. Alex Ziegler, their worship pastor, stood on the porch.

"Alex. It's good to see you. Please come in."

"Hi, Penny. I was really concerned last Sunday when you told me
about Bach's depression, that he's withdrawn into himself and won't
talk. He's stayed home from church almost three months now."

"Yes, I'm very worried about him."

Alex entered the den and sat across from Bachman on the soft,
dark brown leather sofa. He'd sat there many times in the past when
he and his wife, Destra, had been invited over for dinner or to watch
a ballgame on TV. But this time Bachman wasn't looking at him,
hardly registering his presence. Just a "hey" when he'd first walked in.

"What's going on, man?" Alex asked jovially.

"Not much going on around here, Bud."

"Well, how're you doing these days? Missed you Sunday."

"Yeah, well, I just haven't felt much like going out lately."

"How are you feeling today?" Alex looked closely at his friend with genuine concern.

"Not too bad. Got through with that last chemo without getting too sick. Just washed out. No energy."

"What's going on in your head, Bach?"

"Don't ask. Believe me, you wouldn't want to know."

"What's the matter? You think I couldn't handle it? Think I might hear something I've never heard before?"

Bachman kept gazing silently at the TV, his mind sorting through the options of what to say next. He decided not to say anything at all.

Alex pressed a little from a different angle. "I can imagine you'd be pretty down about this whole situation about now. But I want to be there for you, to help you get through this thing if I can. You've gotta talk to me though. I can handle it. I promise. Don't you know you can trust me?"

Bachman looked into the worried eyes of his friend. Suddenly he couldn't keep it back anymore. "Alex, where is God in all of this? Why did He allow this to happen to me? What did I do to deserve this? What did Penny do to deserve being a widow before she's even fifty years old? It's just not fair. Nothing's fair anymore. I'm sick and tired of sitting around here with nothing to do, getting weaker all the time. I can't be a husband to Penny. I can't even walk from here to the bedroom without stopping to rest."

Bachman paused, looking down at his hands as if he were deciding whether to go on or not. Softly he continued, "Alex, I can't even pray anymore. And I try. Believe me, I do." His voice broke as the tears sprang unexpectedly to his eyes. "I start with, 'Dear God,' and can't get any further. I just don't know what to say to Him. I feel like He's turned His back on me. What am I supposed to do? . . . I know I shouldn't think like this."

Alex moved over to the chair next to Bachman and put his arm around those big shoulders, feeling for the first time the bones protruding, noticing that the familiar bulk of muscle was fading fast away. He squeezed Bach's shoulder.

"Let it out, Bach. Keep talking to me."

Bach buried his head in his hands, sobbing and mumbling, "I just don't understand. Just don't understand."

Alex said to him softly, "Bach, God hasn't turned His back on you. He's right here with you during all of this. He's here with us right now. Let's talk. Maybe I can help. Okay?"

Silently Bachman nodded his head. Penny, listening from the kitchen, clasped her hand over her mouth as tears ran hot over her trembling fingers. She moved toward the stairs to her bedroom, thankful that Bachman was willing to talk to Alex, even if he didn't feel comfortable talking with her. She knew it was the first step in dealing with the emotional and spiritual disease growing inside his heart and mind, one potentially more harmful than the rampaging cancer cells in his body.

Again what Bachman McNair was experiencing was predictable and understandable. Depression hurts. Whenever Bachman thought of God, his supposedly loving Father, his heart broke. He wasn't used to feeling such emotion, such inner pain. King David expressed similar suffering in Psalm 55:4-5: "My heart is in anguish within me; the terrors of death have fallen upon me. Fear and trembling come upon me, and horror overwhelms me."

Most of us have felt the terrible pain of a broken heart at one time or another. Usually it can't be rationalized away. When your heart is breaking, it hurts even more when someone well intentioned says something like, "Well, it's God's will," or, "You'll just have to keep your chin up," or, "I know exactly how you feel."

The best way to deal with the pain of a broken heart is to arm yourself with knowledge, faith, and trust in God before your heart is broken.

We must have the essential faith and trust in God *before* our hearts are broken. Then we will possess the tools needed to understand and deal with the situation *without being devastated.* In the psalm of David, quoted above in part, notice that the psalmist doesn't leave us at that place of pain and torment. He goes on in verse 22 to speak of his great love and dependence on the Lord: "Cast your burden on the LORD, and he will sustain you; he will never permit the righteous to be moved." The apostle Peter echoes this truth in the New Testament: "Humble yourselves, therefore, under the mighty hand of God so that at the proper time he may exalt you, casting all your anxieties on him, because he cares for you" (1 Peter 5:6-7).

We're told in the Scriptures that heartache and disappointments *will* befall us. One of my favorite passages of hope is John 16:33 where Christ tells His disciples, "I have said these things to you, that in me you may have peace. *In the world you will have tribulation [trouble]. But take heart; I have overcome the world.*" He didn't say there was a *possibility* that we would have trouble or that if we didn't "play our cards right," we would have trouble. He said emphatically that *we will have trouble.* Then He says to take heart. Why? Because He *has overcome* the world. Note that He doesn't say He *will* overcome the world. He speaks in the past tense even though He had not *yet* overcome the world. That's how confident we can be that He will do so. To Him it had already been accomplished. In other words, it's a done deal.

Don't get me wrong here. I'm not saying that loss is not painful. Grief is horrible. Losing those you love can sometimes be a torment too painful for words. But it does not have to defeat us. And *despair* is something that never needs to enter a Christian's life even when we are hurting. "We are *afflicted in every way,* but not crushed; *perplexed,* but not driven to despair; *persecuted,* but not forsaken; *struck down,* but not destroyed" (2 Corinthians 4:8-9).

Understanding God doesn't magically take away all our pain and grief. It doesn't mean we must face the death of a loved one with a smile on our face or whooping with glee. It does mean that we can trust that whatever has been brought into our lives is still under God's control, and, whatever it is, we can trust Him to do what is perfect, right, and for our good. One of my best friends says that trust in God makes any situation more "get-through-able." I like that. He's right.

The Bible also talks about these things. "But we do not want you to be uninformed, brothers, about those who are asleep [a biblical metaphor for death], that you may *not grieve as others do who have no hope*. For since we believe that Jesus died and rose again, even so, through Jesus, God will bring with him those who have fallen asleep" (1 Thessalonians 4:13-14).

We need our thinking transformed more and more into *biblical* thinking. "Do not be conformed to this world, but be transformed *by the renewal of your mind*, that by testing you may discern what is the will of God, what is good and acceptable and perfect" (Romans 12:2).

Bachman asked some tough questions of Alex, his friend and pastor. But the more we study our Bibles, the easier it is to understand and take comfort in the answers to these difficult questions.

One of my favorite Bible commentators is J. C. Ryle, a master of scriptural application. He was a pastor in England in the nineteenth century, but what he wrote then applies also to the times in which we live: "The poorest [man] who understands his Bible, knows more about religion than the wisest philosophers of Greece and Rome."[1] He also wrote, "Knowledge of the Bible never comes by intuition. It can only be got by *hard, regular, daily, attentive* and *wakeful* reading. Do we grudge the time and trouble this will cost us? If we do, we are not yet fit for the kingdom of God."[2]

Acquiring a keen understanding of the Bible is not an easy task. Let me assure you that the knowledge in its pages is not mysteriously "zapped" into your head. It takes time and effort to read, study, learn, and know God's Word. But the reward of doing so is beyond price in what it does for your confidence, your peace, and your acceptance of the truth it imparts.

However, even though one puts forth much effort, it takes something else for us to *understand* what we read. God the Holy Spirit is the One responsible for opening our eyes that we may see the truth, our ears that we may hear, and our hearts that we may understand and love His ways. So we should prayerfully ask Him to bless our study of the Scriptures in order that His truth may be revealed to us: "Make me understand the way of your precepts [laws, commands, word], and I will meditate on your wondrous works" (Psalm 119:27).

Grief is a natural emotion, a normal human response. We see in the Scriptures many of God's people experiencing grief. King David grieved when his child, born of Bathsheba, was dying. In 2 Samuel

12:16-17 we read, "David therefore sought God on behalf of the child. And David fasted and went in and lay all night on the ground. And the elders of his house stood beside him, to raise him from the ground, but he would not, nor did he eat food with them."

In Psalm 42:3 we encounter a vivid description of grief: "My tears have been my food day and night. . . ." In Psalm 22, with which I began this chapter, David cries out in anguish to God, feeling abandoned and alone. But note that the psalm doesn't end there. It culminates with praise for God, who sustains His people. David wrote, "I will tell of your name to my brothers; in the midst of the congregation I will praise you: You who fear the LORD, praise him. . . . For he has not despised or abhorred the affliction of the afflicted, and he has not hidden his face from him, but has heard, when he cried to him" (Psalm 22:22-24).

The New Testament also gives us examples of grief. One of the earliest Christians (Stephen, a man full of God's grace and power) was falsely accused and handed over to the Jewish leaders in Jerusalem. After hearing Stephen's eloquent and powerful defense of his own beliefs, the men were outraged, and they stoned him to death. Acts 8:2 says, "Devout men buried Stephen and made great lamentation over him."

Not only are we given examples of Christ's followers rightly grieving, but we're also told of Christ's grief after the death of His friend Lazarus. The shortest verse in the Bible, John 11:35, says, "Jesus wept."

Those of you with a good grasp of the Bible know that these stories don't end with sorrow. They end in victory. They are only given in this section as examples of biblical grief. We'll pick this subject up again in a later chapter.

Erwin Lutzer's book *One Minute After You Die* wisely states:

Some Christians have mistakenly thought that grief demonstrates a lack of faith. Thus they have felt it necessary to maintain strength rather than deal honestly with a painful loss.

Good grief is grief that enables us to make the transition to a new phase of existence. . . . Grief that deals honestly with the pain is a part of the healing process.

Sorrow and grief are to be expected. If we feel the pain of loneliness when a friend of ours moves from Chicago to Atlanta, why
should we not experience genuine grief when a friend leaves us for
heaven?[3]

CASE STUDY

*One of the hardest parts of being a hospice nurse is witnessing the grief
of the families. It's more difficult to take care of younger patients
because you usually have the spouse's grief, the parents' grief, and
sometimes the grief of their children as well.*

*Ally Simpson was forty-five years old. She was beautiful, vibrant,
intelligent, and loving. She and her husband, Sonny, had two children—a daughter, twenty, and a son, sixteen. Ally had been recently
diagnosed with pancreatic cancer that had spread to her liver.*

*As a nurse, she knew the implications of her disease. She had gone
through chemo and radiation but to no avail. Her doctors had just told
her that she had only a week or so to live. Ally was very self-possessed
and organized. She had made all her arrangements, counseled with her
family, and made the difficult decisions for the life she had left to live.
Hospice was there to support her decisions and help her manage pain.
She wanted to die at home with her family present.*

*Ally waited until the pain became unbearable before she allowed
us to bring in an IV morphine pump. The Dilaudid she had been taking for pain was ineffective at that point, and she could no longer swallow the pills without choking. A morphine pump is considered
"bringing in the big guns." It was her decision, with her doctor's agreement. So she was given the lowest effective dose of morphine (the
amount high enough to ease her pain and low enough that she could
still function) on a continuous rate. She also had a bolus dose—an
extra amount of morphine that she could administer herself by push-
ing a button on her pump. It had a lockout feature so she could not
give herself more than a safe dose. But that really wasn't a concern for
Ally. She wanted the lowest dose possible so she would still be able to
function until the end.*

I received a call two days after starting her on the pump. She had suddenly taken a turn for the worst. I rushed to her house and found her sitting on the bedside. Her skin was deep yellow, her beautiful blue eyes were glazed, and her thick, blonde hair had been pulled back from her gaunt face. Since Ally was too weak to support herself, her sister was next to her, holding her upright so she wouldn't fall back. Her sister explained, "She kept saying she wanted to sit up."

I sat down next to Ally and held her upright. She put her head on my shoulder and went totally limp. I held her like that for several minutes. She was still breathing, but there was no response from her anymore.

For the first time in three weeks, Sonny had left her side to go to the bank. Her children were there, watching over her. Her daughter was "being the mom," doing household duties and straightening up. Her son sat on the foot of the bed, looking desperately at his mom.

I lowered her back onto the bed and covered her to the waist with her sheet and blanket. Her breathing was very slow, very labored— about eight breaths per minute. She didn't show any signs of pain. I checked her vital signs again. I couldn't get a blood pressure. Her breathing slowed to only four or five breaths per minute. I stepped back to allow her sister to take my place at her side. Donna held Ally's hand and looked into her face as if she was trying to memorize every detail. Ally's son Jeff gingerly placed his hand on her leg and fought back tears.

Holding Ally's hand, stroking her arm, Donna spoke to her softly, tears spilling over onto the covers: "It's okay, Ally. If you need to go, you go. We'll be fine. We love you. We'll miss you."

I stood behind her, watching as the scene unfolded, trying to maintain my own composure.

Donna continued, "Ally-girl, I'm so proud of you. You fought so hard and did so good. We're all so proud of you. Oh, Ally, we love you so much."

Jeff spoke up, his voice breaking, "Mom, don't go. Please don't go. I love you, Mom." Ally's daughter came up behind him and held him close. "No, Jeff, it's time. But you know she'll always be watching out for us."

Ally stopped breathing. We all looked at her, and then they all looked at me. I merely whispered, "She's gone now." They cried and clung to her for several long minutes.

That's when Sonny walked through the door. Donna called out to him, "Sonny, she's gone."

"No," he cried. "I wasn't even gone thirty minutes. What happened? Ally. Ally."

Donna moved aside as Sonny rushed to the bed. He bent down over her. "Ally, can you hear me? I love you, Baby. I love you." Then he bent lower and kissed her forehead tenderly, lingeringly, and collapsed in a heap over her.

I motioned for the kids and Donna to come out of the room to let him be alone with her for a few minutes. I made the phone calls to the police and the doctor. Then we walked quietly back into the room. He had composed himself by this time and just sat beside her, holding her hand. He said, without looking away from her, "I wasn't here. I'll never forgive myself."

I walked over to him and placed my hand on his shoulder. "You know, Sonny, I believe that all things happen for a reason, that God is in control of everything. You and Ally believed that too, didn't you?"

"Yeah, but I've been right here all this time, and then she dies the first time I leave the house. I wasn't even here for her."

"You've been right here for her all along. You've been here for her when it really mattered. If it had been meant for you to be here at the very end, nothing in the world would have prevented it. She might have even been waiting for you to leave. Sometimes people will do that, you know. She might have been worried about you."

"Yeah, she was always worrying about me, wasn't she?" He sniffed.

Loss Hurts

A grieving person must first come to accept the *reality* of the loss. The next realization is that grief is painful. That seems to go without saying, doesn't it? Then why are we so surprised when we feel the intensity of the pain of grief? We realize, "Hey, this really hurts."

Though this book is devoted to expressing Christian truths, I am reminded of what Kahlil Gibran wrote about joy and sorrow in *The Prophet*: "When you are joyous, look deep into your heart and you shall find it is only that which has given you sorrow that is giving you joy. When you are sorrowful look again in your heart and you shall see that in truth you are weeping for that which has been your delight."[4]

Another difficulty for a grieving person is adjusting to an environment that no longer includes the person who has died. This can be an overwhelming time. Perhaps the wife has never learned to pay the bills or to handle her own financial accounts. Now she must learn new skills in order to face a life without her husband. A husband may not know how to care for himself or keep order in the house without his wife. He must acquire these skills.

Such learning is tough for many people. They must adjust to living as an individual instead of as a part of a couple. These changes can often bring pain and loneliness that may seem unbearable at times.

Slowly people are weaned from those they've lost. Each person deals with this loss in his or her own way. One widow I know found comfort in wearing her husband's jogging suit around the house. One man refused to do anything with his wife's clothes because they still smelled like her, and he could press a blouse to his face and remember her sweet scent once more.

With the passage of time he or she will experience a decrease in the degree of emotional energy invested in the deceased person and will begin to reinvest that energy into other relationships. This may happen quickly for some, more slowly and gradually for others. They must come to realize that they will survive—that life does go on. Their recovery is at hand. Some people deny that they will ever be able to love again, but in time many find the surprising ability to do just that.

PHYSIOLOGICAL SIGNS OF GRIEF

We tend to think of grief as a deep emotion, but it can manifest itself physically as well. Some people report a significant drop in their energy level. They don't seem to have the strength or desire to do anything or go anywhere. I hear from some that mealtimes are especially hard. Though they may feel a little hungry or empty inside, nothing really tastes good. Nothing smells good. Others complain of a feeling of tightness in the throat, shortness of breath, panic or anger. Some say that they are so preoccupied and distracted that it's hard for them to concentrate. Most confess a vague feeling of misery throughout their bodies but nowhere in particular.

What can we do to help those experiencing grief? First we must be where we can see the problem—in contact with those we suspect are hurting. One of the most important things we can do is just to be there. Our presence speaks louder than words. There are two things we need to take them every time we go—hope and a tender, listening heart. We don't have to come up with flowery phrases. Sitting quietly with them is more comforting than preaching sermons to them. And sometimes we can gently direct their thinking toward the faithfulness of God.

When I'm spending time with those who are hurting, I don't force Scriptures on them or force them to pray. But I do offer both during the course of the visit. Many people have told me they didn't know how to get started even though they felt the desire and the need for Scripture or prayer. "May I?" is a simple way to begin when the reading of a passage is in order. "Would you like to pray together before I go?" is another easy way to meet this need.

The emotion causing us to ask, "Why me?" is powerful and painful. If we don't understand the answer to the question, we can become bitter and discouraged. Being a Christian doesn't exempt us from the pain, but it frees us from its *power*.

Though we'll never be able to *fully* comprehend the greatness of God and the workings of His mind, He allows us to glimpse His perfect and holy character and His lovingkindness to us through the pages of the Bible. Beginning in chapter 4 of this book, we will explore the biblical evidence for God's sovereignty. With a better understanding of this aspect of our heavenly Father, we can begin to find the comfort and understanding we seek.

Oh, the depth of the riches and wisdom and knowledge of God. How unsearchable are his judgments and how inscrutable his ways. "For who has known the mind of the Lord, or who has been his counselor?" "Or who has given a gift to him that he might be repaid?" For from him and through him and to him are all things. To him be glory forever. Amen.

ROMANS 11:33-36

3

OPTIONS

You matter to the last moment of your life, and we will do all
we can, not only to help you die peacefully, but to live until you
die.

DAME CICELY SAUNDERS,
(FOUNDER OF THE FIRST MODERN HOSPICE)

TELL ME ABOUT MY OPTIONS

Bachman and Penny sat facing Dr. Tanner again across the big desk.
Bachman didn't seem to be the same man anymore. His continued
weight loss had left him a tall, gaunt version of himself, with his skin
hanging loosely over the framework of his big body like a shirt hung
carelessly over a wire hanger. His muscular roundness had changed
into angles and lines. He had discovered cheekbones, ribs, and pelvic
bones he'd only assumed before, and he didn't like them—not at all.

But the most drastic transformation had been the way his illness
had changed his very identity. No more the blustery, self-assured businessman, this subdued version of Bachman McNair sat in meek submission, leaning forward and straining to hear the next words out of
Dr. Tanner's mouth. Penny sat quietly, her hand gently resting on her
husband's arm.

Dr. Tanner dropped the sheets of paper to the desk, sat back in his
chair, and with a low and quiet voice affirmed their worst fears.
"Bachman, I'm sorry. The tumors have not been significantly reduced
by the chemo or by the radiation. While a couple of the lesions seem
smaller, several new ones have appeared since your last scan."

"What are you saying? Am I going to have to do this whole thing
all over again?"

"No. That's not what I'm saying. I'm trying to tell you we're losing the battle. I think it's time to explore other options."

"What other options? New treatments? Experimental drugs? I'm willing to try anything." Bachman's eyes reflected the desperation in his heart.

"We've done everything we can do, Bach. I'm afraid there's nothing else we can try at this time. What I'd like to suggest is for you to go home and try to live your life to the fullest. Spend time with your family and friends. Do things you've always wanted to do. Without the chemo, you may even feel a little better and stronger for a while. We'll do everything we can to keep you comfortable."

Bachman spoke in a weak, defeated tone with his eyes downcast, staring at nothing. "You want me to go home to die, you mean. That's real great news, Doc."

Dr. Tanner fixed his gaze on his fingers as he fiddled with the pen on his desk. The ticking of the brass clock on the corner of the desk was deafening.

"How much time do I have?"

"I honestly don't know. It could be weeks or months at this point. But I do have a recommendation for you. I want you to talk to the people from hospice."

"Hospice! I'm not on my deathbed *yet!*"

Dr. Tanner smiled and shook his head. "No, Bach, you don't have to be on your deathbed to qualify for hospice benefits. The fact that you have a terminal disease and that we've exhausted all curative medical treatments makes you a candidate for hospice. I think being a part of the hospice program can really make a difference in the quality of the life you have left. If it's okay with you, I'll have them contact you later in the week."

Bachman said nothing, just stared vacantly. Penny spoke up. "We'll at least talk to them, Dr. Tanner, and make a decision after we hear what they have to say. That okay with you, honey?"

"I guess so."

A few days later, a hospice nurse came by to talk to the McNairs in their home. Expecting gloom and doom, they were surprised by Paula Shaw's bright smile and the twinkle in her eyes. Her energy was evident as she stepped into the room. After the introductions, she sat down next to Bachman, patted him on the hand and started explaining the benefits of hospice.

Unlike most of their family and friends, she seemed confident and comfortable talking about his illness and some of the symptoms he had already experienced. She even talked a little about what to expect in the future. The word *death* was used a time or two, but it didn't sound so bad coming from Paula. They both appreciated her warmth and understanding.

HOSPICE—A LOVING APPROACH TO THE END OF LIFE

Hospice becomes a real option for those terminally ill for whom there is no further curative medical treatment available. Although nothing else can be done for hospice patients medically to cure their disease, that doesn't mean nothing more can be done for them. There are always measures to take for their comfort and peace. That's where hospice fits into the equation.

The primary goal of hospice is to ensure the patient's comfort for the duration of his or her life. The hospice team provides medical management of the disease as well as spiritual and emotional support for the patient and family. In most cases, the patient will never have to go back to the hospital.

It is estimated that 80 percent of deaths occur in hospitals. Hospitals are wonderful places, in general, for diagnosis, treatment, care, and recovery. But they may not be the best places to die. Most hospitals engage in some activities that run contrary to the hospice philosophy.

One such area is the way death is approached in the hospital. In many cases, hospital personnel may be uncomfortable telling the patient that he or she is dying, and subjects pertaining to death are generally avoided. In hospice we believe the patient has a *right* to know the truth about his or her condition. We do not try to conceal the facts. Thus the patient has the opportunity to make plans and preparations for the remainder of life.

That means, in most cases, that patients have an opportunity to say good-bye and to talk about matters of concern regarding their death and its implications. Wills and funeral arrangements are finalized. The opportunity exists to set right those things in their relationships, spiritual matters, or business affairs that may be burdening them. And most of all, this period can be of significant value to family members after the patients are gone. The family will have had the privilege of sharing this most intimate and bittersweet period of life, without pretense, without stepping around subjects important to all of them.

Another contrast to the hospice philosophy is the practice in most hospitals of isolating the dying patient from family and friends at the very end (unless they have requested a "Do Not Resuscitate" order). That used to bother me when I worked in the ICU/CCU. At the moment when the family should have been at a patient's bedside, holding his hand and telling him they love him, we were ushering them quickly into the waiting room so we could "work with the patient." The family was totally dependent on one of us periodically coming out to let them know what was going on with their loved one. So sometimes the patient died surrounded by a team of hospital professionals instead of the people who loved him the most. That seemed unnatural to me even then.

Since I've been in hospice, I've seen a gentler, kinder, more peaceful and loving approach to death. Hospice enables families to take care of their loved ones in a home setting—with familiar surroundings, their pictures on the walls, and the family right there next to them. It can actually be a sweet experience.

The hospice nurse tries to attend each death. Trained to assess the subtle changes that typically occur preceding death, we can usually recognize when a patient moves toward the end. Then the patient's hospice status may change from "routine" to what we call "continuous care." At this level hospice provides twenty-four-hour care in order to intervene if needed to make the patient more comfortable and to teach and support the family during the dying phase. Near the time of death many questions are raised, emotions can run high, and it sometimes helps to have an "expert" on hand to add calm reassurance.

Sometimes the patient dies without those warning signs, and hospice may not be there at the exact time of death. In that case, the family calls hospice, not 911, and the hospice nurse (available twenty-four hours a day, seven days a week) responds as quickly as possible.

The last thing the family needs to worry about at an emotional time like this is the "business" part of the death. Hospice takes care of those things as a courtesy. We call the police, the coroner, the doctor, and the funeral home. The nurse or other hospice staff member(s) stays with the family until the body has been collected by the funeral home and the family is coping appropriately with the death.

However, even though we are usually present at the death, our greatest benefit is to the patient and family *while the patient is living*. Hospice is about living a quality life for as long as possible. One of the most common expressions we hear from the families is, "I only wish I'd known about hospice sooner."

Writer Philip Yancey commented on the role of hospice:

I once interviewed Dame Cicely Saunders, founder of the modern hospice movement, at St. Christopher's Hospice in London. A social worker and nurse, she was appalled at the way the medical staff treated people who were about to die—in essence, ignoring them, as tokens of failure. This attitude offended Saunders as a Christian. . . . Since no one would listen to a nurse, she returned to medical school and became a doctor before founding a place where people could come to die with dignity and without pain. Now hospices exist in 40 countries including 2000 in the US alone—about half of which have a Christian base. Dame Cicely believed from the beginning that Christians offer the best combination of physical, emotional and spiritual care for people facing death. She holds up hospice care as a glowing alternative to Dr. Kevorkian and his "right to die" movement.[1]

There are many myths related to hospice. One of the most common is that the time to think about this service is when someone is on their deathbed. That's not true. Ideally hospice is called when the prognosis for a patient is less than six months and other curative treatments have been exhausted. The patient may be up walking and talking, eating, traveling, socializing, working in the garden, and doing any number of other daily activities.

Unfortunately, many doctors wait until the patients are already bed-bound and showing signs of imminent death before referring the family to hospice. That doesn't have to happen though. Hospice referrals can come from a physician, a nurse, a family member, a friend, or even the patients themselves. It is true, however, that for admission to the hospice program, a physician must sign a certification that the prognosis is in all likelihood less than six months.

So what happens if six months pass and they're still living? Many people think we have to "kick them out" in that case. That is also a myth. As long as we can document a decline, even a slow but steady one, in the last sixty to ninety days, patients still meet the criteria for hospice. There are other cases where people have actually gotten better with hospice care and had to be discharged because they no longer met the criteria. However, they can always come back to hospice if and/or when they begin to decline.

One of the values of the hospice program is the socialization it offers the patients. Many times patients become more and more socially isolated long before they die physically. Many of their friends, and even some of their family, may feel uncomfortable around them. People may not know what to do or say. So they stop coming around as much. The patient begins to spend more and more time alone. Loneliness is an issue hospice tries to address.

(For more detailed information about what hospice is all about, please see the Appendix.)

CASE STUDY

I was called to a home once to talk to a son and daughter about placing their mother under hospice care. Imagine my surprise when I got there, and the son and daughter were seventy-three and seventy-five years old. Their mother was in her late nineties. After talking to them briefly, asking them questions, and watching them with their mother, I realized their whole lives were devoted to caring for her. They weren't going to church anymore. They never left the house except for quick trips for food or supplies or to take their mother to the doctor or the hospital.

The patient (we'll call her Mrs. Chambers) had end-stage Alzheimer's and significant cardiac disease as well. She was deaf, and she couldn't speak, walk, dress herself, or bathe. Although she was a big woman, her son had been picking her up and putting her in her wheelchair and transferring her to a chair in the living room or kitchen.

The reason the doctor had recommended hospice was that now Mrs. Chambers was losing the ability to swallow, and they had to decide whether to insert a feeding tube. The effort they had been putting into feeding her was admirable but pitiful. My heart went out to these two sweet people who were trying so hard to keep their mother with them.

After the son told me the patient's history and what they'd been doing for her, I said I'd like to talk to them a little about hospice. At that point the sister, Johnnie Sue, got up and left the room, dabbing eyes already spilling over with tears. I turned to the son and asked how much he already knew about hospice.

"Enough to know that the very word is objectionable to me," he said, holding his head high in defiance.

"I'm so sorry. I hope this talk won't be too uncomfortable for you." Then I said something that surprised him and got his attention. "First let me say that I really don't think you and Johnnie Sue are ready for hospice for your mother yet. I don't think you're appropriate candidates at this time. You're just not ready to let her go and to let nature takes its course. And I understand that. But," I continued, "I believe there will come a time when you are ready, and I want you to have all the facts when that time comes. So let me tell you about hospice now so you'll have the information when you need it."

He visibly relaxed and suddenly was open to talking about it. He listened, even asking questions and expressing his opinions and feelings. We talked for over an hour. When I stood up to leave, he grasped my hand and told me how nice it was to meet me, that he'd consider what I said and talk to Johnnie Sue. He would call if he ever decided to put his mother under hospice care.

I called the office from my cell phone as I drove to my next visit. I told them that the Chambers family was not ready for hospice, and we needed to follow up with them in a few months. It was sad, though, because I knew they needed our services. They needed someone to relieve them, someone to come in and say, "It's okay—we're here now. Let us take some of this burden for you." Both of them were obviously exhausted.

About an hour later, I received a page from the office. I called to find out that Mr. Chambers had already called and was ready to sign his mother up with hospice. Tears filled my eyes as I realized what had happened. Once armed with the facts, he had been able to make the difficult decision to let his mother go and allow someone else to help them.

That proved to be one of the most meaningful relationships I have ever had with a family. Their mother received much-needed care from us. We provided encouragement, supplies, information, and tips on caring for her and keeping her as comfortable as possible. We assisted with feeding her with a syringe until she couldn't swallow anymore without aspirating (breathing the food into her lungs) and choking. Her condition was steadily declining to the point that she was no longer able to get out of bed. She began sleeping for longer and longer periods of time, until early one Sunday morning she didn't wake up at all. She had died peacefully in her sleep.

I was so proud of them. Instead of being in a panic, they were calm and accepting. I had told them on my last visit that the end was in sight, preparing them for what might happen. I had hoped to be there when she died, but in God's providence it didn't happen that way.

As soon as they found she wasn't breathing, they called me. I went there immediately to support them, comfort them, and to take care of the situation. I made all the appropriate calls to police, coroner, and funeral home and readied the patient for transfer to the funeral home. The son and daughter were free to grieve without having to worry about those responsibilities. I stayed with them for quite some time after the funeral home people left to make sure they were coping and would be all right without me.

Those two people are precious to me even now, years later. I still keep in touch with "the kids," as I call them. They call or write occasionally. When we see each other, we're like family.

Being a hospice nurse is not an easy profession. It takes a loving heart willing to be frequently broken and a genuine desire to minister to others during a time of great pain and chaos. But the rewards of this ministry are so richly fulfilling. It is a great privilege to work in a field where at the end of each day, we know we have made a real difference in the lives of the people. That's the primary reason we became nurses in the first place.

> *We can do great harm by attempting to do more than we are equipped to do. Yet we can all be comforters—we can be there for the hurting person, and we can share with them the comfort we have received from God.[2]*
>
> SUSAN HUNT

4

THE SOVEREIGNTY OF GOD

And he is not served by human hands, as if he needed anything, because he himself gives all men life and breath and everything else. From one man he made every nation of men, that they should inhabit the whole earth; and he determined the times set for them and the exact places where they should live. God did this so that men would seek him and perhaps reach out for him and find him, though he is not far from each one of us. "For in him we live and move and have our being."

ACTS 17:25-28 NIV

WHO'S IN CHARGE ANYWAY?

Alex was surprised to find Bachman sitting up at the breakfast bar in the kitchen. He hadn't seen him in a couple of weeks, but on the last visit Bachman had seemed withdrawn and depressed. This time he was smiling and welcomed his friend with a handshake.

Alex pulled up a stool next to Bach and watched him eat his oatmeal. The newspaper Bach had been reading was spread out before him.

"Care for some delicious gruel?" Bachman asked mischievously.

Alex eyed his bowl suspiciously and scowled. "No, thanks, man. I'm trying to quit."

"All right, you two," Penny chimed in. "This is excellent. Bach loves this stuff. Maple and brown sugar flavor. Mmmmm."

Bachman looked over at Alex and shrugged his shoulders.

"Now quit it. You know you like it." Penny smiled.

"Yes, dear. It's delicious."

"Hey, I'm just glad you're eating." Looking at Alex, she explained, "His appetite has almost vanished these days. He's *never* hungry anymore, are you, sweetie?"

"Just for you, my love." His twinkling eyes softened.

"Hey, guys."

Alex beamed at Bachman's youngest daughter as she bounced energetically into the room.

"Laura, don't you ever just *walk* into a room?" Penny asked.

"Not unless I have to." Laura nudged her dad's arm until he placed it around her shoulders and hugged her as tightly as he could. "Do I *have* to walk into the room, Daddy?"

"No, princess, you come in any ol' way you want to, okay?" He planted a kiss on her head and playfully reached out to touch her nose.

Laura scrunched her nose in her mother's direction.

"Hey, Alex. Long time, no see."

"Yeah, what have you been up to, squirt?" Alex had been her choir director when she was in the young people's choir at church years before. He remembered her lovely voice.

"Well, I'm a sophomore now at Hendrix College in Conway. Math."

Alex let out a long, low whistle. "Wow. I'm impressed. I didn't know you were a brain."

"Well, she is," Bachman bragged. "She made a 3.9 last semester, didn't you, baby girl?"

"Yeah, I would have had a 4.0 if my history professor had given me an A on my essay exam like I deserved. He gave me a B instead and then wouldn't tell me why. I was robbed. So it brought my overall GPA to 3.9. I'll have to try to pull that up this semester. So far, I'm doing just fine. Wouldn't it be cool if I graduated cum laude from Hendrix College, Daddy? You'll be taking pictures like crazy of that cap and gown and all those ribbons and stuff. I can see it all now." She giggled and kissed her father on the cheek.

As she plopped down on the bar stool across from Alex, her face dropped its carefree smile, and sudden tears flooded her eyes. Her pretty little mouth formed an "O" as she remembered that her father wouldn't be there for her graduation.

Bachman was studying his oatmeal with renewed interest. His nose had started running a little too. They could hear a sniffle or two coming from his direction.

"Oh, Daddy, I'm so sorry. Man. It's just so unfair."

"Laura!" Penny scolded.

"Well, it is. Why did this have to happen to Daddy? He's the sweetest person in the whole world. He didn't deserve this. Alex, where is your God in all of this? Is this the kind of God I'm supposed to love and praise? Sorry. Can't do that anymore."

"*My* God?" Alex looked her squarely in the eyes. "I thought He was *your* God too, Laura."

"He used to be. But I'm so mad at Him right now I could just spit."

Penny moved next to Laura and put her arms around her.

"Why, Alex? Why is He letting this happen to Daddy? Can you answer that? I'm praying and praying, and nothing is happening. He's not getting any better, and now those hospice people are hanging around. I hate them."

"Hey, now. Don't talk about my girlfriend like that. I actually don't know what we'd have done without her. She's helping me. Are you going to hate someone who is really helping me?"

"No, I guess not. I just hate the situation—that's all." Then turning to Alex, she asked, "Well, why isn't He answering my prayers?"

Alex set his coffee cup on the table for a refill, and as Penny poured a second cup, he asked, "Who says He isn't answering your prayers?"

"Well, Daddy's still sick."

"Then there's your answer. The answer is not always yes, Laura. Sometimes the answer is no. You seem to be losing sight of some things that I think you know. The first is that God is not absent here. He is present. He is in control of everything that happens."

"Humph." She snorted as she rolled her eyes at Alex.

"Don't be rude, girl," Bachman admonished. "Listen to him."

"I'm listening."

Alex continued, "Do you want a God who's like some kind of

genie in a bottle? You rub your hands three times, and He grants all your wishes. He's *all-powerful* but subject to *your* whims and desires. A God who's under *your* control. Do you want a God who only does what *you* tell Him to do? In that case, who's God?"

Laura said nothing. She just looked at him through eyes brimming again with tears. Her lower lip trembled. She started to say something, then thought the better of it, and finally looked down at her hands.

"Laura, is that the kind of God you want? I don't. I'm glad I have a God who is SO BIG that sometimes He does stuff that I might not even understand. We have faith that what He does, He does because He loves us. We are told that whatever He brings into our lives will ultimately be for our good. *Even* when we don't understand. *Even* when we don't like it. That's what trust is all about."

"But how can this possibly work to our good?" Laura asked in a weak, fragile voice.

"That's not for us to know, baby girl." Bachman joined in the conversation. "I've been thinking about this a lot as you might imagine. Yeah, at first I was pretty mad too. But I've been reading some good books and studying my Bible again, and all through the Bible we're told that God is in control and has a purpose for everything. I don't know why this is happening, but it is. We have to accept that."

He motioned for Alex to help him back into his wheelchair. As Alex held it for him, he sat down heavily and grunted. "Besides, everybody's got to die of something. Even you, baby girl, will die someday of something. Death is just a fact of life, isn't it, Alex?"

Alex quoted, "'Man's days are determined; you have decreed the number of his months and have set limits he cannot exceed.' Everyone has a certain length of time to live, Laura. So there is a certain time for your daddy to die. But he won't die one moment before he's supposed to. You can rest assured of that. And the second a believer dies in this life, he'll be right there in the presence of God in the next."

Laura sat in silence for a moment. Then her defiant glare turned into a painful grimace as the tears filled and then spilled out of her soft brown eyes. She held her mother's hand and sniffed. "I just don't know if I can stand it, Alex. I don't think I can live without Daddy."

Softly Bachman said, "Yes, you can, baby girl. It might be tough at first, but you'll make it. Whenever you feel like breaking down, just think about how much I love you and how much I want for you. You'll be fine because you'll know that I want you to be happy. Besides, you have to try to be strong for your mother."

"I can't be strong." Laura got up and ran from the room. In shocked silence they listened to the muffled sound of her socked feet padding quickly up the stairs to her room. Then they heard her door slam shut.

Bachman and Penny looked at each other for a long time. Alex spoke up first. "I think she'll be okay, Bach. It's just going to take some time. We'll all be here for her. You know that, don't you?"

"Yeah. I know that. Thanks."

Alex pushed the wheelchair into the living room and helped Bach into his chair. Bach lay back in the heavy recliner and closed his eyes. "I'm exhausted, Bud. Don't mean to be a party pooper, but I think I'm going to take a little nap. Okay?"

"Sure, Bach." Alex patted his shoulder. As he hugged Penny, he whispered to her, "Don't worry too much about Laura. You think I was too rough on her?" They walked slowly to the front door.

"No, you were great. Actually I think I needed to hear that almost as much as Laura. It was encouraging. I'm sure she'll come around."

"We're praying for you guys every day."

"I know you are. Thank you. And thank Destra for me too. Okay?"

"Sure."

The house settled into quiet after Alex left. Penny leaned back against the door with her eyes closed. Then she took a deep breath, looked around the house, noticed the silence, and thought, *I need to start getting used to the quiet. Pretty soon it'll be all I hear.*

Then she looked heavenward and prayed, "Precious Lord Jesus, give me faith and courage. Help me find comfort in Your Word. Let me be what he needs me to be during this time. Give me the words that will help Laura to accept this as Your will. Thank You for giving me the ability to trust You with everything—my life as well as his. I love You, Lord. Thank You for loving me."

WHY SUCH PAIN?

I often hear people ask, "Why is there so much pain and suffering in the world? Why does God allow tragedy to occur? What is the world coming to? How can this happen to such a great person? Where is God in all of this?

I agree that these can be mind-boggling questions. However, the more we learn about God and how He works in our lives, the better we are able to find the answers to those questions. When the answers are understood, they can become our greatest comfort in adversity *of any kind*.

I wanted to write about the purposes of suffering, but I couldn't find a way to do so without first discussing the sovereignty of God. Those subjects are so interwoven that it's difficult to talk about one without understanding the other.

WHAT IS THE SOVEREIGNTY OF GOD?

Let's start out by defining the term "sovereignty." The dictionary says, "1. Supremacy of authority or rule, as exercised by a sovereign or a sovereign state. 2. Royal rank, authority or power."[1] When I say God is sovereign, I mean He is the all-powerful ruler under whose authority we all live and move and have our being.

Jerry Bridges writes, "This is the essence of God's sovereignty; His absolute independence to do as He pleases and His absolute control over the actions of all His creatures. *No creature, person, or empire can either thwart His will or act outside the bounds of His will.*"[2]

In his description of the limitlessness of God's authority, Mr. Bridges wrote, "*If there is a single event in all of the universe that can occur outside of God's sovereign control then we cannot trust Him.*" What a shocking statement. He continues, "His love may be infinite, but if His power is limited and His purpose can be thwarted, we cannot trust Him. You may entrust to me your most valuable possessions. I may love you and my aim to honor your trust may be sincere, but if I do not have the power or ability to guard your valuables, you cannot truly entrust them to me."[3]

However, God *is* all-powerful. Nothing *can* thwart His divine will.

Those powerful truths can be found on almost every page of the Bible.
For example:

> *Worthy are you, our Lord and God, to receive glory and honor and*
> *power, for you created* all things, *and by* your will they *existed and*
> *were created. (Revelation 4:11)*

> *For* by him all things were created, *in heaven and on earth, visi-*
> *ble and invisible, whether thrones or dominions or rulers or*
> *authorities*—all things were created through him and for him.
> *And he is before* all things, *and in him all things hold together."*
> *(Colossians 1:16-17)*

These verses make the point that *God is not created for us. We are*
created for Him. God is sovereign (He rules and has all authority) over
all things. "All things" includes the earth, the weather, the demons,
governments, fame and fortune, sickness and health, mankind and animals, all our lives, and, yes, even death.

I could overwhelm you with examples of each but will settle for
just one or two to make the point. Before we start, please let me
remind you that though I am a *student* of the Scriptures, I am not
a Bible scholar. This chapter is not meant to be a heavy theological
dissertation but my own thoughtful and honest attempt to explain,
as simply as I can, what I have come to believe with complete confidence to be the truth as set forth in God's rich Word to us—the
Bible.

GOD'S AUTHORITY OVER THE EARTH

"In the beginning, God created the heavens and the earth," says
Genesis 1:1. You can't have more authority than that. If a painter picks
up a brush and palette and paints a scene on a canvas, he has complete authority over that painting. He can add color wherever he
chooses, change the slope of the hillside, add some ducks swimming
in the pond, paint a "happy little tree" here or there . . . or he can
decide to paint over it and begin again. Everything is up to him. So it
is with the Lord and Creator of all the earth. He has total power and

total authority over His creation. "Of old you [God] laid the foundation of the earth, and the heavens are the work of your hands. They will perish, but you will remain; they will all wear out like a garment. You will change them like a robe, and they will pass away, but you are the same, and your years have no end" (Psalm 102:25-27).

We find evidence of earth's Creator not only in the pages of the Bible but throughout the world in which we live. I have often been awed by God's power in creating this world. On the beach I am speechless as I marvel at the sound, fury, and power of the waves crashing to the shore. Standing atop Pike's Peak in Colorado and looking over the "purple mountain majesties" all around me, I shake my head, slowly contemplating a God so great and powerful to have created such awesome beauty. Sitting on my back porch, watching the trees bend and sway in the wind with the bright blue backdrop of the sky, I am sometimes moved to tears. It reminds me of Isaiah's words: "[A]ll the trees of the field shall *clap their hands*" (Isaiah 55:12). That's actually what it looks like—a mighty audience applauding their Maker, standing tall in their ovation of praise. When I look at the beauty of this earth, I see the beauty of God all around me. And I am not alone. "The heavens declare the glory of God, and the sky above proclaims his handiwork" (Psalm 19:1).

Romans 1:20 says, "For his invisible attributes, namely, his eternal power and divine nature, have been clearly perceived, ever since the creation of the world, *in the things that have been made*. So they are without excuse."

"He stretches out the north over the void *and hangs the earth on nothing*" (Job 26:7). How could Job have known that apart from God's direct revelation?

It is by God's grace that the earth is such a beautiful and *stable* place for us to live. In Charles Colson's book *How Now Shall We Live?* he writes:

How does Earth happen to be so special? Is it just coincidence? Luck? Or was it designed by a loving Creator who had us in mind from the outset?

Consider, for example, Earth's orbit. "The Living Seas" exhibit [at Disney World] is quite right in describing Earth as "a small sphere of just the right size [that] lies just the right distance from its mother star." If Earth were even slightly closer to the sun, all its water would boil away, and life would be impossible. On the other hand, if Earth were only slightly farther away from the sun, all its water would freeze, and the terrestrial landscape would be nothing but barren deserts.

And it's not only the landscape that is affected by the position of our planet. The processes inside our bodies also rely on these hospitable conditions. The chemical reactions necessary for life to function occur within a narrow temperature range, and Earth is exactly the right distance from the sun to fall within that range. What's more, for all this to happen Earth must remain about the same distance from the sun in its orbit; that is, its orbit must be nearly circular—which it is, in contrast to the elliptical orbits of most other planets in our solar system.[4]

What luck! What a coincidence! . . . In fact, it is neither. It is all by the design, creative genius, and *authority* of God.

A little while ago I watched a program on the public television station about the debate over the origin of the moon. I was astonished at the different theories put forth. I found myself thinking, *And some think that* creation *is hard to believe. Good grief. This stuff doesn't make any sense at all.* So the next day I looked up the passage on God's creation of the moon and smiled to myself as I read the familiar words:

> *And God said, "Let there be lights in the expanse of the heavens to separate the day from the night. And let them be for signs and for seasons, and for days and years, and let them be lights in the expanse of the heavens to give light upon the earth." And it was so. And God made the two great lights—the greater light to rule the day and the lesser light to rule the night—and the stars. And God set them in the expanse of the heavens to give light on the earth, to rule over the day and over the night, and to separate the light from the darkness. And God saw that it was good. (Genesis 1:14-18)*

For me, that is much easier to believe than that the moon is a fragment of earth propelled into orbit by a direct meteor hit (and somehow formed of foreign material and completely rounded in shape and just the right distance from the earth to maintain orbit). That is only one theory they identified. (The others were no more believable.) Thank you very much. I'll take the Genesis account. I repeat—it is *all* by the design, creative genius, and *authority* of God.

GOD'S AUTHORITY OVER THE WEATHER

Some people think that nature falls outside God's domain. It doesn't. "He caused the east wind to blow in the heavens, and by his power he led out the south wind" (Psalm 78:26). Even the winds follow His command: "Around and around goes the wind, and on its circuits the wind returns" (Ecclesiastes 1:6). You would think God knew about trade winds and the jet stream even back then. Guess what. He did. He created them. That's why Solomon (who wrote Ecclesiastes under divine inspiration) could write about something unknown to mankind at the time.

"And I [God] will summon the grain and make it abundant and lay no famine upon you. I will make the fruit of the tree and the increase of the field abundant, that you may never again suffer the disgrace of famine among the nations" (Ezekiel 36:29-30). You mean that even famine and plenty depend on the Lord's will and design? Absolutely. These things are under His sovereign control. "I [God] also withheld rain from you when there were yet three months to the harvest; I would send rain on one city, and send no rain on another city; one field would have rain, and the field on which it did not rain would wither" (Amos 4:7).

Notice that even the rain is evidence of His love:

Under the whole heaven he lets it go, and his lightning to the corners of the earth. . . . For to the snow he says, "Fall on the earth," likewise to the downpour, his mighty downpour. . . . By the breath of God ice is given, and the broad waters are frozen fast. He loads the thick cloud with moisture; the clouds scatter his lightning. They turn around and around by his guidance, to accomplish all that he

commands them on the face of the habitable world. Whether for
correction or for his land or for love, he causes it to happen. (Job
37:3, 6, 10-13)

One of the best-known examples of God's control over the
weather is found in Matthew 8:23-27:

And when he [Jesus] got into the boat, his disciples followed him.
And behold, there arose a great storm on the sea, so that the boat
was being swamped by the waves; but he was asleep. And they went
and woke him, saying, "Save us, Lord; we are perishing." And he
said to them, "Why are you afraid. O you of little faith?" Then he
rose and rebuked the winds and the sea, and there was a great calm.
And the men marveled, saying, "What sort of man is this, that even
the winds and sea obey him?"

This incident occurred fairly early in the ministry of Jesus Christ.
His disciples were still learning just how powerful He is.

"Wait a minute," you might ask. "You were talking about *God's*
authority over the weather, and now you're talking about *Jesus'*
authority over weather. What's up with that?" I'm glad you asked.

If you are not familiar with the Bible, you may not have encountered this concept before; so let me try to explain one of God's deep-
est mysteries in the simplest way I can. Jesus *was* and *is* God. How can
that be? Many fine theologians have tried to explain the relationship
between God the Father, God the Son (Jesus Christ), and God the Holy
Spirit. The Bible teaches that they are all God, and yet they are separate persons of the Godhead. This is called the doctrine of the Trinity.

The Bible is divided into two parts—the Old Testament and the
New Testament. The Old Testament, the section of the Bible that covers what happened before Christ's birth, contains many passages pre-
dicting the coming of the Messiah, the Son of God. It chronicles the
history of the Jewish nation. The New Testament deals with Christ and
His church and gives us a glimpse into the future, into eternity. Both
sections teach that Jesus is the Son of God and *is* Himself God. The
Old Testament looked *forward* to His coming. The New Testament

describes His birth, His earthly ministry, and ultimately His death, burial, and resurrection.

John 1:1 states, "In the beginning was the Word [Jesus], and the Word was with God, and the Word *was* God. He [the Word—Jesus] was in the beginning with God. *All things were made through him, and without him was not any thing made that was made.*" Then in John 1:14 we read, "And the Word became flesh and dwelt among us, and we have seen his glory, glory as of the only Son from the Father, full of grace and truth." You see? Jesus Christ is God, and He is also the Son of God.

How could that be? In all the Christmas stories you hear about Mary and Joseph being Jesus' parents. So how can He be Joseph's son and God's Son at the same time? The answer is simple. He wasn't.

Mary, a young Jewish woman, was devoted to the Lord. God blessed her when He chose her to be the earthly mother of His Son, Jesus. He sent an angel to her with the news, and the angel told her that the Holy Spirit would place a seed inside her womb that would be the very Son of God. So, though she was a virgin, she conceived this child without sexual intercourse—the Virgin Birth.

At the time Mary was engaged to a man named Joseph. But she and Joseph had never had a sexual relationship. When the Holy Spirit caused this conception, Joseph was confused and dismayed. He didn't believe that Mary had been unfaithful to him, and yet she was pregnant. He decided to break their contract of marriage because that's what the Law of Moses allowed. Then the angel of the Lord appeared to him and explained that the child she carried was the Son of God, that Joseph was to marry her as planned, and that they should call the baby "Jesus," which means "Savior."

When she gave birth in that little stable in Bethlehem, she bore the Son of God. Joseph raised Jesus as his own, but he and Mary both knew that Jesus was the Promised One of God—the Messiah. That's how Christ became man and dwelt among us. (This account can be read in Luke 1:26—2:7.) In other words, the Father, the Son, and the Holy Spirit have dwelt together from the beginning of time, and they will dwell together throughout eternity. But for a short while (about thirty-three years) God the Son walked upon this earth as a man, and in so doing He changed the world forever. "Christ Jesus . . . though he was in the form of God, did not count equality with God a thing to be grasped, but made himself nothing, taking the form of a servant, being born in the likeness of men. And being found in human form, he humbled himself by becoming obedient to the point of death, even death on a cross" (Philippians 2:5-8).

GOD'S AUTHORITY OVER SATAN AND HIS DEMONS

"But the Lord is faithful. He will *establish* [strengthen] you and *guard* you against the evil one [Satan]" (2 Thessalonians 3:3). The demons listened to Jesus and obeyed:

> *And immediately there was in their synagogue a man with an unclean spirit. And he cried out, "What have you to do with us, Jesus of Nazareth? Have you come to destroy us? I know who you are—the Holy One of God." But Jesus rebuked him, saying, "Be silent, and come out of him!" And the unclean spirit, convulsing him and crying out with a loud voice, came out of him. And they were all amazed, so that they questioned among themselves, saying, "What is this? A new teaching with authority! He commands even the unclean spirits, and they obey him." (Mark 1:23-27)*

There is another passage I've always found interesting, located in James 2:19: "You believe that God is one; you do well. Even the demons believe—and shudder!" Some people have told me they know they are going to heaven because, after all, they believe in God. When I ask if they also believe in Christ, sometimes they falter. This passage demonstrates that it is not enough just to believe there is a God. Even the demons believe that.

They understood very well who Jesus was and that He was the Son of God. There was absolutely no question about His authority over them. But they didn't place their faith in Him or trust in Him for salvation.

Faith is the difference! It is not enough to believe that Christ existed. We must enter into a personal relationship with Him. That intimate relationship of trust, love, and hope will prove elusive to unbelievers but will be cherished by all who draw close to Christ in faith.

The demons will not serve God, and that's why they will share the same destiny marked out for Satan and his followers—the "lake of fire and sulfur where . . . they will be tormented day and night forever and ever" (Revelation 20:10).

Why is this relevant today? Satan is not a big deal. Or is he? Don't rest too comfortably, thinking that we are out of the reach of his influence. Satan is alive and active. That's why it's important to acknowledge God's authority over him. But he is much more subtle these days. He knows just the right buttons to push to lead us astray. He can push the "pride" button here or the "jealousy" button there. The "fear" button is always a good one. The "anger" button is one of his favorites. We are told in 1 Peter 5:8-9a, "Be sober-minded; be watchful. *Your adversary the devil* prowls around like a roaring lion, seeking someone to devour. Resist him, firm in your faith. . . ."

Satan is crafty. He is a master of disguise. In 2 Corinthians 11:14-15, Paul wrote, "[F]or *even Satan disguises himself as an angel of light. So it is no surprise if his servants, also, disguise themselves as servants of righteousness.*" The apostle Paul is cautioning the Corinthians to be on their guard—as we should. However, we have nothing to fear from Satan if Jesus Christ is our Lord and our focus remains on Him. We are His, and He will protect us from the evil one.

The Scripture says, "If God is for us, who can be against us?" (Romans 8:31b). Suffice it to say, if you belong to Him, *He will never allow any action against you that is not in accord with His will for you. And His will is always directed to your good.*

GOD'S AUTHORITY OVER GOVERNMENTS

Have you ever thought about the fact that our government and its leaders, elected to serve us, were given to us by God? And not only in America but worldwide? And not only worldwide but throughout history from the earliest times? Even Saddam Hussein was put in power by the sovereign hand of God for God's own purposes. And he was removed from power the same way—by God's hand.

In his book *Trusting God Even When Life Hurts,* Jerry Bridges addresses the fact that God has placed these rulers where they are and governs how long they are to rule as well as the decisions they make: "God *can* and *does* work in the hearts and minds of rulers and officials of government to accomplish His sovereign purpose. Their hearts and minds are as much under His control as the impersonal physical laws of nature. *Yet their every decision is made free—most often without any thought or regard to the will of God.*"[5] Isn't that awesome?

Look at what the apostle Paul said in his letter to the Romans: "Let every person be subject to the governing authorities. *For there is no authority except from God, and those that exist have been instituted by God*" (Romans 13:1).

When Jesus was on trial prior to His crucifixion Pilate said to Him, "'Do you not know that I have authority to release you and authority to crucify you?' Jesus answered him, 'You would have no authority over me at all unless *it had been given you from above*'" (John 19:10b-11a).

The Old Testament is full of passages where God says He will raise up this kingdom or destroy that one, that He will appoint this man to become king and will replace that one. Wars are won or lost at His discretion. Consider these passages:

> *[God] removes kings and sets up kings.* (Daniel 2:21b)

> *The king's heart is a stream of water in the hand of the LORD; he turns it where he will.* (Proverbs 21:1)

> *[T]he Most High [God] rules the kingdom of men and gives it to whom he will and sets over it the lowliest of men.* (Daniel 4:17b)

Noted theologian R. C. Sproul says it this way: "The study of history is sometimes called 'the study of His story.' This play on words reflects the idea that all of history is the unfolding manifestation of divine providence."[6]

We, in our arrogance, sometimes believe all of these political and military maneuverings depend on us, but in the Scriptures we can clearly see who is actually in control. Praise God for that.

GOD'S AUTHORITY OVER MANKIND

This same arrogance makes us believe we are masters of our own fate, that *we* control our lives and everything in our lives. We don't. God is in control of all we are and all our circumstances. He is in control of fame and fortune, sickness and health, our comings and goings, and even the place where we live. "From one man he made every nation of men, that they should inhabit the whole earth; and *he determined the times set for them and the exact places where they should live.* . . . For in him we live and move and have our being" (Acts 17:26, 28 NIV).

Listen to the words of Charles Spurgeon: "Engraven upon the Father's hand your name remains, and on His heart recorded there your person stands. He thought of you before the worlds were made; before the channels of the sea were scooped or the gigantic mountains lifted their heads in the white clouds, He thought of you. He thinks on you still. . . . You are not cut off from Him. You do move in Him: in Him you do live and have your being. He is a very present help in time of trouble."[7]

A preacher of long ago, Richard Baxter, recognized God's control over his life when he wrote these words in his book *Dying Thoughts*: "His undeserved mercy gave me being, chose my parents, gave them affectionate desires for my real good, taught them to instruct me early in his word, and educate me in his fear; made my habitation and companions suitable, endowed me with a teachable disposition, put excellent books into my hands, and placed me under wise and faithful schoolmasters and ministers . . . choosing every place of my ministry and abode to this day."[8]

Most of us never recognize God's sovereign control over these things, but that sovereignty is our reality nonetheless. Please note the following verses, only a small sample of the many biblical passages that teach us this very truth:

Both riches and honor come from you, and you rule over all. In your hand are power and might, and in your hand it is to make great and to give strength to all. (1 Chronicles 29:12)

The heart of man plans his way, but the LORD establishes [determines] his steps. (Proverbs 16:9)

Who has spoken and it came to pass, unless the Lord has commanded it? Is it not from the mouth of the Most High that good and bad come? (Lamentations 3:37)

I [God] make known the end from the beginning, from ancient times, what is still to come. I say: My purpose will stand, and I will do all that I please. (Isaiah 46:10 NIV)

In him we have obtained an inheritance, having been predestined according to the purpose of him who works all things according to the counsel of his will. *(Ephesians 1:11)*

I form light and create darkness, I make well-being and create calamity, *I am the LORD, who does all these things. (Isaiah 45:7)*

For by him [Christ] all things were created, *in heaven and on earth, visible and invisible, whether thrones or dominions or rulers or authorities*—all things were created through him and for him. *And he is before all things, and* in him all things hold together. *(Colossians 1:16-17)*

You see, God knows each detail of the paths our lives have taken. And He knows what lies ahead for each of us. He has allowed our lives to unfold as they have and has overseen all that has happened to us. He has and always will be present with us and involved in our lives as His plan for us unfolds.

In R. C. Sproul's book *The Invisible Hand,* he wrote, "He [God] doesn't have to wait to see which fork in the road we choose to know which fork we most certainly *will* choose. He knows the future precisely because He wills the future."[9]

GOD'S AUTHORITY OVER LIFE AND DEATH

I hope I've adequately demonstrated from the Scriptures that God is in charge of all things. He directs where we live, whom we marry, whether we're rich or poor, in a position of authority or of service. He brings people and situations into our lives that influence our thinking, and in that way He molds us into the people He wants us to be. I believe He's even in control of whether the traffic light turns green or red as I approach an intersection.

"Are not two sparrows sold for a penny? And not one of them will fall to the ground apart from your Father. But *even the hairs of your head are all numbered. Fear not,* therefore; you are of more value than many sparrows" (Matthew 10:29-31). If God is sovereign over such a small thing as a sparrow, then is He not sovereign over us as well?

He is responsible for giving us life and equally responsible for taking that life exactly when and how He has ordained it. Ecclesiastes 8:8 says, "No man has power to retain the spirit, or *power over the day of death.*"

A psalm that I love and frequently use is Psalm 139. When a person asks why questions, I use this psalm. When family members feel guilty because of what they did or didn't do toward their loved one, I use this psalm. When someone believes that death means a person is out of favor with God, I use this psalm. When he believes death happens *outside* the will of God, I use this psalm. It is one of my favorite tools for dealing with the bewilderment of those who are suffering. Let's take a look at Psalm 139 section by section.

> *O LORD, you have searched me and known me!*
> *You know when I sit down and when I rise up;*
> *you discern my thoughts from afar.*
> *You search out my path and my lying down and*
> *are acquainted with all my ways.*
> *Even before a word is on my tongue, behold, O LORD,*
> *you know it altogether.*

This section speaks of the *omniscience* of God—that is, He knows all things. Every Christmas we hear the familiar strains of "Santa Claus Is Coming to Town." It says, "He knows when you are sleeping, he knows when you're awake. He knows if you've been bad or good; so be good for goodness' sake." While Santa is merely fiction, those words *are* actually true of our God and Father. He knows us inside and out. He knows our thoughts, our actions, our hearts. Before a word comes out of our mouths, He knows it. We can't *fool* Him. We can't *out maneuver* Him. We can't *hide* from Him.

Where shall I go from your Spirit?
Or where shall I flee from your presence?
If I ascend to heaven, you are there!
If I make my bed in Sheol, you are there!
If I take the wings of the morning and
dwell in the uttermost parts of the sea,
even there your hand shall lead me, and
your right hand shall hold me.
If I say, "Surely the darkness shall cover me, and
the light about me be night,"
even the darkness is not dark to you; the night is bright as the day,
for darkness is as light with you.

This section touches my heart because it speaks of the *bigness* of God. It describes His *omnipresence*—that is, He is *every*where at *every* moment of time. He is the only being who is. Satan isn't. The angels aren't. And as hard as I try, I still haven't figured out how to be in even *two* places at the same time, let alone everywhere at once!

The next section is my favorite because it speaks of God, the Creator, *my* Creator and *yours*.

For you formed my inward parts;
you knitted me together in my mother's womb.
I praise you, for I am fearfully and wonderfully made.
Wonderful are your works; my soul knows it very well.
My frame was not hidden from you, when I was being made in secret,
intricately woven in the depths of the earth.
Your eyes saw my unformed substance; in your book were written,
every one of them, the days that were formed for me,
when as yet there were none of them.

Jeremiah 1:5 echoes this truth as God speaks to Jeremiah say-ing, "*Before I formed you in the womb I knew you, and before you were born I consecrated you; I appointed you a prophet to the nations.*"

I praise God for the truth of these passages. My heart rejoices to know He cares that much, that He is the designer of my body, my mind, and my heart. He created my inmost being. Psalm 139 uses the words *knit* and *woven* to describe this creation. Those are intimate terms when you think of being personally formed by God in that way. Yes, He may utilize eggs and sperm, DNA, genes, etc., to do it, but it all happens by His design and special attention to every last detail. Who has never wondered at the miracle of childbirth?

What about birth defects? Does He create those too? My answer would be yes. *Nothing* happens outside His sovereign will.

CASE STUDY

His name was Peter. He was thirty-eight years old, only two feet and eleven inches tall, and weighed about forty-five pounds. He was born with a condition called osteogenesis imperfecta. *By the time I was called in on the case, he was a very sick little guy. His chest heaved with each respiration. His lungs were filling with fluid. He was not con-scious and lay perfectly still.*

Though he could not communicate, getting to know him—and his mother—offered me an experience I shall never forget. His mother, Lani Lollar, had tenderly cared for him for thirty-eight years. At the time of his birth the doctors tried to convince her to put him in an insti-tution, but she refused. She devoted her life to caring for this little one that God had given her.

Whenever he'd experienced a life-threatening crisis in the past, she'd instructed the doctors to do all they could to keep her little boy alive. Lani just wasn't ready let him go.

With this condition, the bones are especially fragile and sometimes break when the person is just picked up or turned over. So he'd had multiple fractures over the years. But the fractures had healed quickly.

Peter was bright and charming. His face was adorned with a wide smile, and his eyes sparkled with delight. He cared deeply for others and also possessed a brilliant sense of humor. Lani showed me pictures of the smiles. She gave me examples of his heart. Through her, I felt I knew him a little.

When Peter was younger, he could ambulate with a special little walker and later had to go to a wheelchair. He wore a smile on his face from morning to night. Life was a delight to him. Then at the age of eighteen, he suffered a cardiac arrest on the operating table. The resuscitation attempt was successful, but it left him paralyzed and unable to speak. He remained this way for the rest of his life. So Lani doubled her efforts in caring for her son.

Some might consider this kind of total devotion a waste of time, a loss of freedom in order to take care of a mistake of nature. But Peter was no mistake. God made him the way he was for a reason. And He'd given Peter to her. Lani was thankful for such a blessing.

Now in her seventies, she had developed significant cardiac problems of her own, and for the first time had come face to face with the fact that she might not outlive her son. Trying to decide what to do with Peter in the event of her death caused her much anxiety. She couldn't bear the thought of his being institutionalized. No one would be qualified to give him the specialized care he needed. Eventually she made the tough decision that the next time he developed a life-threatening illness, she would not resuscitate him. She would only be prolonging the inevitable.

Some time after this decision, Peter developed a chest cold. Lani tried to alleviate the cold the best she could, but it got progressively worse until he developed a form of pneumonia resistant to antibiotics. His systems began shutting down one by one. His little body went into a fluid overload brought on by congestive heart failure. His damaged heart wasn't able to pump the fluid in his system efficiently enough to keep it out of his lungs. It was at this time that she called hospice.

I responded to the call and made a visit to their home to assess the patient. I wasn't adequately prepared for the sight of this little man with a five o'clock shadow on his mature and masculine face when his body looked like that of a three-year-old.

After a physical assessment of his condition and baseline readings, I sat down with his mother outside in the backyard while the aide attended to Peter. Amid the lush spring flowers, she told me the remarkable story of Peter Lollar.

I soon realized that I was dealing with a strong woman. She drew heavily on her faith in God for the strength and comfort she needed every day of her life. She read the Bible, spent hours in prayer, and volunteered her time to help out with projects at her church. Everywhere she went, Peter went too. And everywhere they went, Peter touched lives. Thousands of lives. The lives of the doctors and nurses. The lives of the clergy and fellow church members. He was even the mascot for a ship full of sailors who had been introduced to him by the sovereign plan of God. Peter touched their lives in profound ways, and even the toughest sailor had a soft heart where Peter was concerned.

I remember Lani saying, "Peter has touched more lives and made a difference with more people than he ever could have as a whole and perfect man. God knew exactly what He was doing when He brought my son into this world. People want to feel sorry for me, but I tell them not to. My life has been rich and full and complete because of my son. He has been such a blessing to me in so many ways. Why, I wouldn't even be the same person I am now without him. No, my life has not been wasted. And neither has Peter's."

She told me that every night she would pick him up and place him in the bed next to her. She would utter a prayer for both of them and then lie quietly beside him, reading until she would drift off to sleep.

It was supremely difficult for her to allow hospice to care for him. But we came to her house every day to assess Peter, supplied them with an aide to assist in his care, and supported Lani in dealing with the inevitability of his death.

His condition worsened. Then the day came that Lani suspected might be his last. Her family had come to stay with her to lend their support. They had been present in days past when the harsh sound of his breathing filled the house. Now his breathing was curiously quiet and peaceful.

Lani and her daughter spent the day talking to Peter, stroking his little hands. For twenty years his hands had been contracted into tight fists. But that day, as they talked to him about "going home to Jesus," his tiny fists slowly opened, allowing them to hold his hand one last time. Lani told me she felt God's comforting presence in her house all day long. Others noticed it too. She sensed His everlasting arms around her.

At bedtime Lani carried Peter into the bedroom and placed him beside her just like always. But she knew there was a difference. This would be their last night together on earth. She curled herself around him, prayed with him, and fell asleep.

Awakening in the wee hours of the morning, she got up to go to the bathroom. When she lay down beside Peter again, she kissed his cheek. It was cool. She got up and flipped on the light.

There he lay with the most peaceful expression on his face. There was no pain or fear there—only peace and beauty. She knew he was gone, but she wasn't ready to make any announcements yet. Instead, she held him close while she was alone with him. After a little while, Lani woke her daughter to tell her that Peter had died.

They called the hospice nurse as they had been directed. While waiting for her arrival, Lani shaved Peter, bathed him, and put him in some clean clothes. She had purchased a small sleeping bag for him in days past. She placed him carefully in the sleeping bag and wrote a note to the funeral director, urging him to treat this little body with the utmost respect and care. She wrote that this was the body of someone who was treasured and much loved. "Be careful with him." She pinned the note to the sleeping bag.

When the hospice nurse arrived, she found Lani peaceful and serene. The nurse called the police, the coroner, and last of all the funeral home. When the funeral home personnel arrived, Lani told them she wanted to carry Peter to the van herself. She picked him up in his little sleeping bag and placed him lovingly on the cot inside the van.

Upon reentering the house, Lani walked into her kitchen alone and let out one gut-wrenching cry. Her daughter rushed into the kitchen to comfort her. But that one cry was her only expression of grief. There was no sadness for Peter. She knew that at last he was whole and strong and free, experiencing more joy than he'd ever imagined.

Recently Lani told me in her kitchen over coffee that she would recommend hospice to anyone. She said she had been able to deal with Peter's death in her own way and in her own timing. She wasn't rushed. "Because of hospice, his death was more peaceful," she told me.

She said it wasn't what we did that helped so much—she had insisted on caring for him herself. It was that we came into the situation and "blended in" with their routines and desires for his care. It was just nice to know we were there for her if and when she needed us.

As for those of us in hospice, we got back much more than we gave. Lani Lollar was an example to us. Her faith in God and devotion to her son touched our hearts. Because of her, our lives will never be the same.

You've perhaps heard the statement: "God don't make no junk." Well, if anyone ever believed that with all her heart, it's Lani Lollar. She'll be the first to tell you that God used Peter's life in a very powerful way. He knit Peter's body together *exactly* as it was supposed to be. Psalm 139 doesn't offer any exceptions. We are *all* created by a *loving* God—even those with disabilities. "Then the LORD said to him, 'Who has made man's mouth? Who makes him mute, or deaf, or seeing, or blind? Is it not I, the LORD?'" (Exodus 4:11).

Continuing with Psalm 139, we now come to my favorite verse: "In your book were written, every one of them, the days that were formed for me, when as yet there were none of them" (v. 16). The New International Version translates this verse: "All the days ordained for me were written in your book before one of them came to be." What a *freeing* truth. That sentence tells us so much. Each of us has a certain number of days to live our lives. We will not die *one moment* too soon or too late. We will die *exactly* when God has ordained it.

What are the implications of this fact?

1. There are no "accidents." God is in control of the time of our

death. It is *not* left up to chance or a matter of "being in the wrong place at the wrong time."

2. No one dies "prematurely." I often hear family members tearfully confess, "If only I had taken her to the doctor earlier," or, "If only I had listened when he tried to tell me how sick he was," or, "If only I had been with her instead of talking on the phone." But *nothing* we could have done would have ultimately changed the outcome of *any* situation. So we can just *erase* all that guilt. Events happen just as they're supposed to. We can dismiss all those "if onlys."

In his book *One Minute After You Die*, Erwin Lutzer says:

> Let me encourage you to take those "if onlys" and draw a circle around them. Then label the circle, "The providence of God." The Christian believes that God is greater than our "if onlys." His providential hand encompasses the whole of our lives, not just the good days, but the "bad" days too. We have the word *accident* in our vocabulary; He does not.
>
> Accidents, ill health, or even dying at the hand of an enemy— God uses all of these means to bring His children home. As long as we entrust ourselves to His care, we can be confident that we are dying according to His timetable.[10]

This not does mean, of course, that we can glide through life carelessly, recklessly, or dangerously. We are commanded to live our lives responsibly, soberly, and prudently. We're told in the New Testament of a time when Satan tried to tempt Jesus to throw Himself off the highest point on the temple to prove that He would not be harmed. Luke 4:12 gives Jesus' response: "And Jesus answered him, 'It is said, "You shall not put the Lord your God to the test."'"

3. Our *death* was appointed for us *before we were even born.* Remember the familiar passage in Ecclesiastes 3:1-2: "For everything there is a season, and a time for every matter under heaven: *a time to be born, and a time to die.*"

Aren't these amazing truths? If we could really embrace them, we would find we could get through *anything* with more confidence and trust. We would realize our confidence is not based on *who we are* but on *who God is*. We would be at peace, knowing that all things are under God's control.

Nothing will ever happen to us that is not either allowed or caused by His divine providence.

Ultimately, even adversity and heartache will work to our good as He promises us in Romans 8:28: "And we know that for those who love God *all things work together for good*, for those who are called according to his purpose." We will discuss the purposes of suffering in more detail in chapter 6.

In the final verses of Psalm 139 we see the *result* of believing the truths we've been discussing. King David's realization of God's greatness, sovereignty, love, and power caused him to praise God: "How precious to me are your thoughts, O God! How vast is the sum of them! If I would count them, they are more than the sand."

When we seek to learn more about God and His ways, we often see this very effect on our own hearts. The more we understand about God, the more our gratitude and love compel us to praise Him and rejoice in what He has shown us. We learn to *love* His Word. It is only by His grace that we can understand such lofty things. Left to our own understanding, we find these things foolish and unbelievable: "The natural person does not accept the things of the Spirit of God, *for they are folly to him, and he is not able to understand them* because they are spiritually discerned" (1 Corinthians 2:14). "Whoever is of God hears [understands] the words of God. The reason why you do not hear them is that you are not of God" (John 8:47).

To conclude our discussion of Psalm 139, notice the ending: "Search me, O God, and know my heart! Try me and know my thoughts! And see if there be any grievous way in me, and lead me in the way everlasting!" David, the writer of this psalm, ends it by humbly asking God to search his heart, to examine his anxious thoughts. He asks God to reveal his offenses so David can repent of them.

Obviously, David trusted not in his own abilities but in God, his Father, to lead him and direct his paths in a way pleasing to Him. How many of us ever ask God to show us what there is in or about us that is offensive to Him, so we can get rid of it and live a life pleasing to Him? Instead, don't we just carelessly go about our lives, comfortable in our own "goodness" and not concerned with how we look in the eyes of God?

In case you are still not convinced that God controls our dying as well as our living, here are some additional passages. Of the many I could use, let's just look at a few from the Old Testament and an important example from the New Testament: "See now that I, even I, am he, and there is no god beside me; *I kill and I make alive*; I wound and I heal; and there is none that can deliver out of my hand" (Deuteronomy 32:39). "*The LORD kills and brings to life; he brings down to Sheol [place of the dead] and raises up*" (1 Samuel 2:6).

One of the most amazing accounts of the sovereignty of God over death is the story of King Ahab. He had been warned by one of God's prophets (Micaiah) that if he attacked Ramoth Gilead, he (King Ahab) would be killed in battle. King Ahab did not believe the prophet and went against Ramoth Gilead anyway. But to make sure he wasn't injured, he decided to disguise himself in the armor of a chariot soldier, thus removing himself as the prime target. But he didn't consider the sovereignty of God. This is what happened.

"But *a certain man drew his bow at random* and struck the king of Israel between the scale armor and the breastplate" (1 Kings 22:34). We are not even told the name of the person who killed the king. It was most likely a foot soldier who just fired a shot into the air. He had no plan—no target in mind. But God had a plan for that shot and directed that arrow. It went straight between the two pieces of armor King Ahab wore to protect his chest and abdomen. An inch higher or lower, and who knows what might have happened. But it hit *exactly* at the right spot on *exactly* the right person at *exactly* the right time, and the king died as the prophet Micaiah had predicted.

The New Testament also teaches that God is in control of life and death. Let's take the death of His own Son, Jesus Christ, as an example. When asked what they believe was the worst sin anyone has ever committed, many people will say, "Killing the Son of God." However, even Christ's death was within God's control.

Numerous times in the life of Christ, He was threatened with physical violence, but each time He escaped because "[His] time had not yet come." Then in John 17:1 Jesus prayed to His Father and said, "Father, the hour has come." This was just prior to Jesus' arrest and crucifixion.

Throughout the Gospels Jesus warned His disciples about what was to come—that He would be persecuted, hated, arrested on false charges, beaten, tried, and killed at the insistence of the Jewish leaders. He also comforted them by explaining that in three days He would be resurrected from the dead (although they forgot that part in their grief and fear immediately after His death). But it all came to pass exactly as He had predicted.

So who was in control of the events that took the life of the Son of God? The wicked Jews? The Roman governors? The mob? Or an all-powerful, almighty God who had designed this action from before the creation of the world? In Acts 2:22-24, Peter explains, "Men of Israel, hear these words: Jesus of Nazareth, a man attested to you by God with mighty works and wonders and signs that God did through him in your midst, as you yourselves know—this Jesus, *delivered up according to the definite plan and foreknowledge of God,* you crucified and killed by the hands of lawless men. God raised him up, loosing the pangs of death, because it was not possible for him to be held by it."

And in Acts 4:27, Peter and John proclaimed in prayer to God, "for truly in this city there were gathered together against your holy servant Jesus, whom you anointed, both Herod and Pontius Pilate [the Roman officials who tried Jesus and ordered his execution], along with the Gentiles and the peoples of Israel to do whatever *your hand* and *your plan* had *predestined* to take place."

The answer to the question I raised above is clear. God was totally and sovereignly in control of every aspect of the death of His Son. And all of this was because of His love for His children. *Christ died so that those who believe in Him are able to obtain salvation, not through anything they can do, but through what Christ did on their behalf.* "For this is the will of my Father, that everyone who looks on the Son and believes in him should have eternal life, and I will raise him up on the last day" (John 6:40).

Would you like to hear the chilling truth? In that we are sinners in need of a Savior, *we* are also responsible for the death of Christ. He died so that we (His children) could live.

> *He* [Christ] *was delivered over to death* for our sins *and was raised to life* for our justification.
>
> ROMANS 4:25 NIV

THE SOVEREIGNTY OF GOD IN SALVATION

For he says to Moses, "I will have mercy on whom I have mercy, and I will have compassion on whom I have compassion." So then it depends not on human will or exertion, but on God, who has mercy.

ROMANS 9:15-16

AM I REALLY READY TO DIE?

Paula found him sitting in his leather recliner with his feet propped up, looking out the window. Sunshine streamed into the room, and outside birds chirped loudly. One of the hospice volunteers had made him a birdfeeder, and he was watching as the squirrels tried repeatedly to plunder it. A busy blue jay had captured his interest as it dive-bombed the squirrel again and again. Finally the squirrel, frustrated with his repeated failures, scampered away and ran up an old oak tree in the back of the yard.

Bachman was so intent that he didn't hear Paula come in. She observed him for a moment. He had grown so pale and thin. All those unsuccessful chemo treatments had left him bald and weak. In previous visits he'd joked that no one could resist rubbing his head. Paula always kissed him there when she came to visit. An ice-cold tumbler of Coke sat on the walnut table beside his chair, untouched and sweating with condensation.

Bachman looked pensive. Paula really didn't want to disturb him. She had come to love this man and his family and was beginning to feel just like one of the clan.

Suddenly he winced and pressed down on the seat of the chair with both hands and fragile wrists as he tried to reposition himself. It was becoming harder and harder to find a comfortable position. As he grunted with the effort, he looked up and spotted Paula.

"Good grief, girl!" he shouted in surprise and mock anger.

Paula laughed as she approached his chair. "I'm sorry I startled you, Bach. Penny called and told me she had to run to the grocery store and said to just come on in. She thought you were sleeping. I knocked, but I guess you didn't hear me."

He sighed heavily and looked back out the window. "No, I didn't hear you, but that's okay. Actually I'm glad you're here. It looks so cheery and bright outside, and it feels so gloomy in here."

"Well, let's go outside then." Paula got the wheelchair out of the hall closet and moved it into position at his side.

"Are you crazy? I can't go out there," he protested.

"Why, you can too. What's stopping you?"

"Can't you see I'm a sick, dying old man? Sick, dying old men can't go outside."

"This one can, I'll bet. Let's try it." She stood in front of him and braced his feet with hers. Then slipping her arms under his frail ones, she locked her hand onto her other wrist behind him as he clung weakly to her shoulders.

"One—two—THREE." On "three" she lifted, and he strained to stand. Once standing, she allowed him time to get his balance. Looking up into his eyes, she smiled mischievously and asked, "Shall we dance?"

"Yeah, right," was his retort. But he laughed anyway. Paula could always make him laugh.

She assisted him as he pivoted around to the wheelchair and half-sat, half-fell into the seat, breathing heavily. Then she covered him with the lap quilt volunteers had made and wheeled him out the French doors onto the deck, parking him at the table under the umbrella. Making sure he was safe and the wheelchair was in its locked position, she went to the kitchen, poured herself a Diet Coke, and brought his out with her when she came.

"Oh, I'll be right back. I need to go get my bag. I left it in there by your chair."

"Do you have to? Let's not do vital signs today, okay? Let's play hooky from vital signs. What do you say? Let's just talk."

"You're the boss. Okay with me, if that's what you want."

"Yeah, I'm just not in the mood."

"I noticed you were lost in thought when I came in. What's going on in that cute little bald head of yours?"

Bachman looked away from her and stared at the tulips he'd helped Penny plant two autumns ago. They were about four inches tall and poking their closed heads out enough that one could just see what color they would be. The grass and the leaves on the trees were starting to turn green again. The redwood deck was bordered on three sides by a thick growth of cheery yellow jonquils waving in the warm, light breeze and straining toward the sun. Though it was in the low 80s, Bachman pulled the quilt a little closer to his body.

"It's just so beautiful."

"Yes, I believe spring has sprung, hasn't it?" Paula responded. "It's lovely out here."

"I'm talking about life. Life is so beautiful and precious and fragile. I never appreciated that before." He took a sip from his Coke and carefully put it down on the glass and iron table next to him.

After another big sigh, he continued, "In a way it makes this dying thing much harder. All around us we see life. Flowers, leaves. Blue sky and sunshine. Birds and squirrels everywhere. The world is waking up from its sleep now, and it's showing off to get our attention."

"What a poet you are today. Are you okay, Bach?"

"Yeah. I'm okay. I never used to notice things like this. I've always been too busy. And I've been thinking a lot about dying—a lot about God too."

"Oh? What are you thinking about God?" Paula asked.

"I'm wondering if I'm . . . well, never mind."

"No, no, no. You can't do that to me. You've aroused my curiosity now. You're wondering what?"

"Well, I'm wondering if I'm really ready to die. I've been a Christian for over thirty years, Paula. But now that my time is coming soon, I'm just not totally sure I'm ready to go to heaven. What if I just *think* I'll go to heaven? What if I'm wrong? You know, I haven't always lived a godly life. I can be a stinker sometimes."

"We're all stinkers, Bach. Nobody lives a life good enough to *earn* their way to heaven."

"Hmm. I keep forgetting that. It doesn't even depend on us, does it? It depends on God."

"Yes, it does. It's actually a great deal. Since you're such a brilliant businessman, you've got to see the beauty in this deal. Christ came to the earth and lived a perfect life, never sinned even one time. He's the only one who can ever do that, you know—live a perfectly sinless life. Then He trades with us His perfect righteousness for our filthy, sinful, depraved lives. What a trade! So God the Father credits us with being good even though we fall far short. And when God looks at us, He sees only the perfect righteousness of His Son instead of our own sinfulness. So He welcomes us to Himself with open arms, loving us as He loves His own Son."

"I've never thought of it like that. He loves us like His real children. But not everyone will be His child. How can I know for sure that I am?"

"Do you remember that passage in Romans 10? It says that if we confess with our lips that Jesus is Lord and believe in our heart that God raised Him from the dead, *we will be saved*. You remember that?"

"Yeah, I do. I'd forgotten that too."

"Well, do you?"

"Do I what?"

"Do you confess with your lips that Jesus is Lord?"

"Of course I do. I know He is, and I've made Him Lord of my life."

"And do you believe in your heart that God raised Him from the dead?"

"Yes, I *know* in my heart He did."

"Then what's the promise? Do you remember?"

Bachman studied the flowers again, and his eyes filled with tears. "That we will be saved . . . that . . . *I* will be saved."

"That's exactly right. So you understand the promise, and you know we don't have to be good enough on our own to go to heaven. It doesn't depend on how good *we* are, but on how good *Christ* is. That's how you can be sure you're going to heaven."

A tear spilled down his face. He covered his eyes with a trembling hand and sobbed quietly. Paula got up and, standing behind him, held him in her arms. She placed her cheek lovingly on his head. After a moment or two, she handed him a napkin and sat back down. He wiped his face and nose and looked at her again. His bottom lip quivered as he croaked, "Thank you so much, Hon. I needed someone to remind me of all that."

"Any time I can be of service." The twinkle was back in her eyes now.

They looked up as Penny came out of the house.

"I've been looking all over for you guys. It's nice out here, isn't it?" she said, looking around.

Bachman took her hand in his and kissed it slowly. "It's even nicer now that you're here too." He looked up at the face he'd loved for so many years and smiled broadly at her as she took a seat beside him.

Paula left them sitting there, holding hands and talking quietly. Climbing into her car, she prayed a quick prayer of thanksgiving to God for allowing her the privilege of being there for Bach. She knew that God had used her that day to speak His truth. She felt humble but gratified that, at least for today, she had made a difference in someone's life through the grace of God.

Sometimes people who are dying feel guilty about questioning their own salvation, their readiness to enter the "hereafter." But this question is a normal response to dying. When it finally sinks in that you really are going to die, the next step is preparing for the event. Do you have your affairs in order? Have you said all the things you need to say to the people in your life? Do you *know* with certainty that your eternal life has been secured as well?

Would you do anything differently if you knew the exact date and manner of your death? Would you try to make amends for the mistakes you've made in life? To restore a relationship long gone sour? If so, when would you do it? Would you do it right now or wait until just a few days before your death? Unfortunately, our "deadline" is unknown. We simply don't have the luxury of procrastination since none of us knows when or how we will die. That's why it's so important to *be prepared*.

Bachman had all his business and legal affairs in order, but the one issue occupying his mind was his readiness for eternity. That issue should be uppermost in the minds of not only those who *know* they're dying, but of all people—because none of is guaranteed even one more hour on this earth.

We need to be prepared for eternity before we go there.

God's Authority over Salvation

LET'S TALK ABOUT THE BAD NEWS: CONDEMNATION

Now if God is the all-powerful, all-knowing, holy, almighty Lord over all things, from creation to life and death, He is certainly going to devise a way whereby His people (those He has loved since before the creation of the world) may find salvation and dwell with Him, glorifying Him forever and ever. And we are told in the Scriptures what that salvation entails and how to obtain it.

What do I mean by the term "salvation"? In general it means "preservation or deliverance from evil or difficulty."[1] In spiritual terms, though, the meaning becomes "the deliverance of man or his soul from the power or penalty of sin; redemption."[2] To simplify the dictionary's definition, salvation is the state of being rescued by God from the consequences of our sin—death and eternal hell and damnation. "For *the wages of sin is death*" (Romans 6:23b).

Theologian Millard Erickson defines salvation this way: "The divine act of delivering a believer from the power and curse of sin and then restoring that individual to the fellowship with God for which humans were originally intended."[3] It has been said that before we can hope to understand the good news of *salvation*, we must first understand the bad news of *condemnation*.

Society's thinking about the hereafter has mutated into something completely foreign to the truth of the Scriptures. I don't know exactly when or how this misconception came about, but let's look at the error of such thinking. Not everyone believes there will be a hereafter, for one thing. Those who do may imagine themselves very spiritual. Perhaps some are. But the common misconception I hear is that if we are treated fairly by God, we all *deserve* to go to heaven. Only those really bad people, "like Hitler," are going to hell. Others will join him there—murderers, child molesters, etc. You know—the scum of the earth. The rest of us will be in heaven, especially if we have "good hearts."

Well, to clear up the misconception, the "bad news" is that if we all got exactly what we deserved, we'd *all* be going to hell. "For the wages of sin is *death*" (Romans 6:23). All of us sin; therefore, all of us *deserve* our wage—death. So since we are all sinners, if we merit anything at all, we merit hell. We are, all of us, the scum of the earth apart from the grace of God.

Romans 3:10-12, 18 says, "*None* is righteous, *no, not one; no one* understands; *no one* seeks for God. *All* have turned aside; *together they* have become worthless; *no one* does good, *not even one*. . . . There is no fear of God before *their* eyes." The meaning of this passage is very clear. Paul didn't mince words. *All* are sinful and without personal righteousness. What an indictment. Can this possibly be construed as ambiguous? I think not. No one who has ever lived can be considered "good."

In a spiritual sense, the wickedness that dwells in our hearts and minds is hereditary. We get it from our father, Adam. In Romans 5:12, we read, "Therefore, just as sin came into the world through one man, and death through sin, and so death spread to all men because all sinned."

According to David Steele, "The central idea of the passage [5:12-19] is that men are saved in precisely the same manner in which they were lost—through the act of another. As Adam, by his one transgression, brought condemnation to all connected with him, so Christ, by His act of righteousness (His sinless life and substitutionary death) brought justification to all connected with Him."[4]

For those unfamiliar with this teaching, let me explain it this way. In the beginning of the world, God created Adam and his wife, Eve. He placed them in a lush and beautiful garden called Eden. Sin had not yet entered the world, and so they lived in perfect harmony with each other and with God.

There was only one restriction. There was a tree in the middle of the garden called the Tree of the Knowledge of Good and Evil. Adam and Eve were told not to eat the fruit from that tree, but they could eat the fruit from *any* of the other trees.

Then Satan appeared to Eve in the form of a serpent and spoke to her: "Did God actually say, 'You shall not eat of any tree in the garden?'" (Genesis 3:1b). See, he's misrepresenting what God said. But Eve corrected him in verses 2-3, saying, "We may eat of the fruit of the trees in the garden, but God said, 'You shall not eat of the fruit of the tree that is in the midst of the garden, neither shall you touch it, lest you die.'"

> *But the serpent said to the woman, "You will not surely die. For God knows that when you eat of it your eyes will be opened, and you will be like God, knowing good and evil." So when the woman saw that the tree was good for food, and that it was a delight to the eyes, and that the tree was to be desired to make one wise, she took of its fruit and ate, and she also gave some to her husband who was with her, and he ate. Then the eyes of both were opened, and they knew that they were naked. And they sewed fig leaves together and made themselves loincloths. (Genesis 3:4-7)*

(Read all of Genesis 3 for a complete record of the whole interaction.)

The serpent beguiled Eve by twisting God's words. He convinced her that the only reason God forbade them to eat the fruit was that He didn't want them to know as much as He did. In essence he said that if God told them they would die, He lied. So Eve was tempted to take the fruit (and we're never told what kind of fruit it was), and because it was pleasing to the eye and desirable for gaining wisdom, she took a bite.

She sinned.

Sin is breaking any command of God. I've heard seminary professor D. A. Carson say that Eve "followed her impressions instead of her instructions." The concept of sin was born. However, that's not where her sin ended. Adam, her husband, was with her. She convinced him also to take a bite, and he did.

He sinned.

Adam was held responsible for the sin they *both* committed against God. But the sin doesn't stop there either. We're told that they heard God as He was walking in the garden. Always before, they had met with God without shame. Now they realized their nakedness and covered themselves, and then when they heard God approaching, they hid.

We'll pick the story up in Genesis 3:9:

> But the LORD God called to the man and said to him, "Where are you?" And he said, "I heard the sound of you in the garden, and I was afraid, because I was naked, and I hid myself." He said, "Who told you that you were naked? Have you eaten of the tree of which I commanded you not to eat?" The man said, "The woman whom you gave to be with me, she gave me fruit of the tree, and I ate." Then the LORD God said to the woman, "What is this that you have done?" The woman said, "The serpent deceived me, and I ate." (vv. 3:9-13)

Interesting. When confronted with their disobedience, they started what has become one of the oldest tricks in the book—the blame game. Blame-shifting certainly comes naturally to us, doesn't it? As a result, God cursed the serpent (Satan). Then He turned His attention to Eve. Genesis 3:16-19 says:

> To the woman he said, "I will surely multiply your pain in child-bearing; in pain you shall bring forth children. Your desire shall be for your husband, and he shall rule over you." And to Adam he said, "Because you have listened to the voice of your wife and have

eaten of the tree of which I commanded you, 'You shall not eat of it,' cursed is the ground because of you; in pain you shall eat of it all the days of your life; thorns and thistles it shall bring forth for you; and you shall eat the plants of the field. By the sweat of your face you shall eat bread, till you return to the ground, for out of it you were taken; for you are dust, and to dust you shall return."

You might not think that a little thing like eating a piece of fruit was a very big deal, but it was disobedience to God, and disobedience is a *very big deal*. From that point on, everything changed. Until that time, there was no sin, no sickness, and no death. After that time, as a punishment for the sin, God caused women to suffer pains in childbirth and caused men to toil by the sweat of their brow for a living. No longer did they have dominion over the garden. They were cast out of it. Death was the result of the sin of Adam. Since God created Adam from the dust of the earth (Genesis 2:7: "then the LORD God formed the man of dust from the ground and breathed into his nostrils the breath of life, and the man became a living creature."), He determined that man would now return to the dust of the earth in death. This is the beginning of sin and the origin of death.

What is death? We're familiar with the concept of physical death—when we stop breathing, and our hearts beat no more. We're less acquainted with the meaning of spiritual death—that is, eternal separation from God and from His blessings.

Because of Adam's sin, an event commonly called the Fall, all the race of mankind is tainted with sin from birth. It doesn't take long for this sinful nature to manifest itself. Babies quickly learn to manipulate others to get what they want, and toddlers may throw fits to get their way. Early childhood is by definition a time where their every thought is directed toward themselves and the satisfying of their own needs and desires. They quickly exert their will over the household. Nobody teaches them this behavior. It comes naturally. When toddlers grow a little older and wiser, nobody needs to teach them to lie either. They instinctively understand how to do that.

Once, when my sons were little, we were playing in the yard. My oldest son, Scott, was about four years old. We had a little hibachi (remember those?), and he had been told to stay away from it. While I was playing with Paul, who was only about a year old, Scott came around the house covered with soot. His smiling face, complete with cherubic rosy cheeks framed with blond curls, was grimy with it. His chest and arms were black. His little hands were caked with charcoal.

I knelt down and looked squarely into his eyes. "Scott, were you playing in the charcoal?"

He looked right back at me and shook his head. "No," he said.

"Are you sure you didn't get into the charcoal?"

"I'm sure, Mommy. I promise."

Talk about being caught red-handed—or should I say, black-handed? My point is this: I didn't teach him to lie to me. He learned it completely on his own . . . and he suffered the consequences of his disobedience.

However, sin doesn't end with childhood. We are ruled by sin for our whole lives if we live outside of God's provision for us. We are slaves to sin until Christ makes us free. Without God's intervening grace on our behalf, we are condemned to die not only a physical death but a spiritual death as well. We will be eternally separated from God in hell. Death is the price, the wage, the consequence of our sinfulness before Him.

But God has provided a way of escape. Romans is perhaps the most helpful book in the Bible in setting forth God's salvation for His people and His condemnation of all others. It is like a textbook of Christian doctrine. The apostle Paul wrote this book (actually a letter) to the Christians in Rome.

The sinful state of mankind described above is called the doctrine of the total depravity of man. Romans 1 goes into detail about this state of being:

> *For the wrath of God is revealed from heaven against all ungodliness and unrighteousness of men, who by their unrighteousness suppress the truth. For what can be known about God is plain to them, because God has shown it to them. For his invisible attributes, namely, his eternal power and divine nature, have been clearly perceived, ever since the creation of the world, in the things*

that have been made. So they are without excuse. For although they knew God, they did not honor him as God or give thanks to him, but they became futile in their thinking, and their foolish hearts were darkened. Claiming to be wise, they became fools, and exchanged the glory of the immortal God for images resembling mortal man and birds and animals and reptiles. Therefore God gave them up in the lusts of their hearts to impurity, to the dishonoring of their bodies among themselves, because they exchanged the truth about God for a lie *and worshiped and served the creature rather than the Creator, who is blessed forever! Amen. (Romans 1:18-25)*

This chapter goes on to set forth a more graphic description of mankind's total depravity.

It occurs to me that people today also exchange the truth of God for lies. Sometimes the lie is that we will all go to heaven when we die. Sometimes the lie is that it doesn't matter what we believe as long as we're sincere. Sometimes the lie is that we can achieve a level of "goodness" that will earn us a place in heaven. Or sometimes the lie is that there really is no God at all, no heaven, and no hell.

Scripture clearly refutes these lies:

[B]ut for those who are self-seeking and do not obey the truth, but obey unrighteousness, there will be wrath and fury. (Romans 2:8)

Whoever believes in him [Christ] is not condemned, but whoever does not believe is condemned already, because he has not believed in the name of the only Son of God. (John 3:18)

Whoever believes in the Son [of God—Jesus Christ] has eternal life; whoever does not obey the Son shall not see life, but the wrath of God remains on him. (John 3:36)

Erwin Lutzer recounts a story of a woman who called in to a radio talk show he was doing. Her question was:

"My father, though religious, died without believing in Christ as his Savior. . . . Is there something I can do to get him out of where I think he probably went?"

I replied, "I have some good news and some bad news. First, the bad news: no, there is nothing you can do to change the eternal destiny of your father. The good news is that whatever God does will be just . . . not one single fact will be overlooked in judging your father's fate . . . there is no possibility that the information will be misinterpreted or the penalty unfairly administered.

"So far we have learned that death has two faces: *to the unbeliever the very thought of death is terrifying, or at least it should be.* But for those who have made their peace with God, death is a blessing. Death is a means of redemption, a doorway into a blissful eternity.

"When the curtain parts for us, nothing can keep us from answering the summons. *One minute after we die we will be either elated or terrified. And it will be too late to reroute our travel plans.*"[5]

LET'S TALK ABOUT THE GOOD NEWS: SALVATION

For by grace *you have been saved* through faith. *And this is* not your own doing; it is the gift of God, not a result of works, *so that no one may boast. For we are his workmanship,* created in Christ Jesus for good works, *which God prepared* beforehand, *that we should walk in them. (Ephesians 2:8-10)*

The riches of these short verses alone are enough to make my heart soar with gratitude to God. In three sentences Paul, through the inspiration of the Holy Spirit, describes salvation beautifully, thoroughly, and clearly.

What is salvation? I explained earlier that it is being rescued by God from the consequences of our sins—death and then eternal hell and damnation. Salvation is being in a right standing with God. We are considered *righteous* instead of *sinful* and *wicked.* Is this because we are basically good, and God can see that? Absolutely not. Romans 9:16 says, "So then *it depends not on human will or exertion, but on God, who has mercy.*"

Let's take a closer look at some of the truths taught in Ephesians

2:8-10. "For by grace you have been saved." It is God's sovereign grace that saves us. What is that exactly? "Grace" is a term that means "unmerited favor." It is a gift we do not earn or deserve. Grace is freely given simply because God wants to give it.

This concept was so wondrous to John Newton that he penned the words to what has become the theme song of Christianity: "Amazing grace, how sweet the sound, that saved a wretch like me." Another hymn writer wrote, "Amazing love! How can it be that Thou, my God shouldst die for me?" It has been said that nothing reflects the power of God more than the conversion of a sinner. Whether we recognize it or not, salvation is a miraculous event.

So what have we (if we belong to God) been saved from? An eternity in hell, separated from Him. Society today has twisted things around, and many people believe we will all go to heaven except the really, really bad people. Not true. "Hell is full of people who were humanly good."[6]

The truth is that because of the sin that *each* of us does, we *all* deserve hell. And without God's intervention that's where we *all* would go. But God, in His vast love, has chosen to shower His mercy on *some* of us. The ones He has chosen (in the Scriptures that group of people is called "the elect") are *saved* from what would be their future torment. Let me pose a question: If everybody were going to heaven, what would be so special about salvation?

The Ephesians passage goes on to say that we have been saved by grace "through faith." David Steele wrote in his book *Romans: An Interpretive Outline*, "Saving faith, like repentance, is a fruit of regeneration. *It's not our gift to God—but His gift to us.*"[7] Faith and regeneration occur *simultaneously* in response to the efficacious call of the Holy Spirit.

I marvel sometimes to think of the degree of faith we so often—and so easily—place in fallible human creatures. Every day people put their very lives in the hands of pilots who fly them around the world. Some people place a tremendous amount of faith in doctors. Past circumstances that have come to light demonstrate that even ministers and priests are fallible. Yet we sometimes put our faith in them.

When you think about it, you can't even put your faith in yourself. How many times I have let myself down? So what makes me think I can have such utter trust in others? But I can, with full assurance, place all my faith in an *infallible* God who loves me and gave His Son to pay the price for my sins.

What is faith? Hebrews 11:1 says, "Now faith is the assurance of things hoped for, the conviction of things not seen." Saving faith is an unshakable trust, a total confidence in, and reliance upon Jesus Christ as the Son of God and as our personal Savior. We know He is, though none of us living today has literally seen Him or touched Him or heard His voice. We believe the Scripture that teaches us who He is and what He did on our behalf. (My pastor, Lance Quinn, says the sweetest three little words in the world are "on our behalf.")

The Ephesians passage continues by explaining that this *faith* is "not your own doing; it is the gift of God." You see, even the faith that saves us does not come from within us but is given to us by God. He generates that faith in us. We are told in other passages also that it is a gift of God. We, as totally depraved, sinful people, do not have the *ability* to seek God or to generate such faith. So by God's grace, we are *given* this faith.

According to writer Loraine Boettner:

> [Death's] nature can be seen in part in the effects of sin which actually have fallen upon the human race. Its immediate and lasting effect was to cause *sin* rather than *holiness* to become man's natural element so that in his unregenerate state he seeks to avoid even the thought of God and holy things. The Scriptures declare him to be "dead" in "trespasses and sin," Eph 2:1, in which state he is as unable to understand and appreciate the offer of redemption through faith in Christ *as a physically dead man is to hear the sounds of this world.*[8]

I've heard the following illustration used to describe our basic *inability* to respond to the gospel message on our own initiative. In John 11, we're told about the time when Jesus was called to Bethany because His beloved friend Lazarus had died. Lazarus had been in the tomb for four days by the time Jesus arrived, and Jesus then performed one of His most spectacular miracles. He commanded Lazarus to rise and come out of the tomb. To the amazement of all present, the "man who had died came out, his hands and feet bound with linen strips, and his face wrapped with a cloth. Jesus said to them, 'Unbind him, and let him go'" (John 11:44).

David Steele wrote:

> Why did Lazarus (who was *dead*) hear and obey Jesus? What cause-effect relationship existed between Lazarus' obedience to Christ's command ("Come out.") and Christ's act of imparting life to him? Did the dead man's cooperation (his response, his obedience) enable Jesus to make him alive? Or did Christ's act of imparting life to the dead man enable Lazarus to hear, understand, and obey Jesus' command "Come out"? Was Lazarus active in his resurrection or was he passive (that is, was he acted upon from without)?
>
> In the case of resurrection from physical death the answer is obvious. A dead person cannot cooperate in his resurrection. Death by its very nature renders its subjects helpless. Death leaves its victim blind, deaf, unable to respond, unable to cooperate, unable to meet any condition, unable to obey any command. This is true of *spiritual death* no less than it is true of physical death.[9]

Spiritual birth is *God's* gift to us, not *our* gift to Him. We can do *nothing* on our own to earn the gift of salvation. God takes the initiative at every stage of salvation (justification, sanctification, and glorification). Peter's first letter begins by referring to "God's elect" who were "chosen according to the foreknowledge of God the Father" (1 Peter 1:1-2 NIV). John MacArthur expounds this passage in his book *Ashamed of the Gospel*:

> When Peter wrote that we are "chosen according to the foreknowledge of God the Father" (1 Pet. 1:1-2), he was not using the term "foreknowledge" to mean that God was aware beforehand who would believe and therefore chose them because of their foreseen faith. Rather, Peter meant that God determined before time began to know and love and save them; and He chose them with-

out regard to anything good or bad they might do. . . . He chose them solely because it pleased Him to do so.[10]

Again, in his letter to the Ephesians, Paul further explains faith as "the gift of God, not a result of works, so that no one may boast." You see, if salvation were based on works—that is, on our own "good-deed-doing"—we could take some or most of the credit for our own salvation. We could "boast" in our own goodness. But Paul (and the whole Bible, for that matter) emphasizes that we *cannot earn* our way to heaven by our good works. That's why God gets *full credit* for our salvation—because without His *gift of faith* we would never make it to heaven.

Jerry Bridges uses a wonderful example in his book *Transforming Grace*. He commented that many people believe that their own goodness can get them so far in their quest for heaven, and then God *makes up the difference*. Here's how he responds to such a theory:

> To say the grace of God makes up the difference of what God requires of us is like comparing two people's attempts to leap across the Grand Canyon. The canyon averages about nine miles in width from rim to rim. Suppose one person could leap out about thirty feet from the edge while another can leap only six feet. What difference does it make? Sure, one person can leap five times as far as the other, but relative to nine miles (47,520 feet), it makes no difference . . . both leaps are absolutely worthless for crossing the canyon. And when God built a bridge across the "Grand Canyon" of our sin, He didn't stop thirty feet or even six feet from our side. He built the bridge all the way.
>
> Even the comparison of trying to leap across the Grand Canyon fails to adequately represent our desperate condition. To use that illustration we have to assume people are *trying* to leap across the canyon; that is, most people are actually trying to earn their way to heaven. . . . Nothing could be further from the truth. Almost no one tries to earn his way to heaven. . . . Rather, almost everyone *assumes* that what he or she is *already* doing is sufficient to merit heaven.[11]

Therefore, we cannot boast of our own goodness. Instead, our boast is in the goodness of God. Salvation, though it rescues us, is actually designed for God's glory. *A correct view of salvation always glorifies God.* Too many people would like to take credit for their own salvation, thus glorifying themselves. Their attitude, in essence, is that "God is pretty fortunate to have me."

One of the reasons for this attitude is that we tend to judge ourselves in relation to each other—on a *horizontal* plane. That's why we're able sometimes to stick our thumbs in our lapels and say, "Hmm. I'm a good sight better than ol' what's-his-name over there."

However, God doesn't judge on that basis. He never has and never will grade on the curve. God judges us on a *vertical* plane. He looks at how we measure up to Him, to His holiness and perfection. So take your thumbs out of your lapels and think about how you measure up to *that* standard. We don't even have the right to lift our eyes to such a righteous and holy God. Yet He demonstrates His love for us with every beat of our heart. "A humble person is not just one who has seen how small he is but one who has also seen how great God is."[12]

The Ephesians 2 passage then explains that we are God's workmanship. He created us. He "knitted" us into being. We were "created in Christ Jesus for good works" (v. 10). "Hey," you might say, "I thought you said it was not by our good works that we are saved." That's right. We are not *saved* by our good works, but by the faith that the Holy Spirit produces in us. However, *after* we are saved (put in a right standing before God), we will begin to do good works. These are a *manifestation* of the salvation we have been given. If we are saved, we *will* do good deeds. There *will* be spiritual fruit in our lives. "But the fruit of the Spirit is love, joy, peace, patience, kindness, goodness, faithfulness, gentleness, self-control" (Galatians 5:22-23a). These should be the characteristics of each child of God. If this is not a description of you, I suggest you rethink your own standing with God.

James deals with this concept in James 2:17-18, 26: "So also faith by itself, if it does not have works, is dead. But someone will say, 'You have faith and I have works.' Show me your faith apart from your works, and I will show you my faith by my works. . . . For as the body apart from the spirit is dead, so also faith apart from works is dead."

You can look at it like this: We can't *see* faith. It is invisible and resides inside our hearts. It's like the wind. We can see *evidence* of the wind by what it produces—trees waving, leaves blown about. We can feel its coolness on our skin or see it blowing through our hair. Though we can't *see* faith, we can see *evidence* of faith by what it produces—*works*. So *works* is sort of what *faith* looks like.

Does this idea contradict the statement that we are saved by faith and not by works? By no means. It *supports* that statement. Faith happens *first,* and *because* of that faith, we are saved. *After* we're saved, we begin to change, to become more Christlike in our thinking, our natures, our attitudes, and our *actions.* The more Christlike we become, the more *works* we do. It is a proof of our life-changing salvation in Christ.

Think of it this way. Let's say a woman becomes pregnant. That event takes place in one moment of time. She may not *look* pregnant at first. She may not *act* pregnant. But the more time goes by, the more she will start looking and acting pregnant. Her body begins to show outwardly what is taking place inwardly. She is showing signs that are proof of her condition.

In this case, if all goes well, she gives birth to a baby. In a spiritual sense, our faith "gives birth" to works. The works are not the *cause* of our faith any more than a swollen belly is the *cause* of a woman's pregnancy.

The conclusion to the Ephesians passage is truly amazing to me. These works we will do are works "which God prepared *beforehand* that we should walk in them." First of all, the works we do were God's idea. The Holy Spirit places the opportunities to do those works in our pathway. But that's not all. These works were designed *beforehand* for us to do. So they are accomplished by the Spirit's enabling power. But *we* actually get the credit for those works. Now how wonderful is that?

In summary, the Ephesians passage says we are saved by God's grace, not by our works. But how did Christ's death on a cross save anyone from his or her sins? The answer is that Christ was a substitute. While He hung on the cross, all the sins of His people (the elect) were nailed there onto Him. He paid the penalty for *our* putrid sins.

In exchange, He gave us *His* perfect righteousness. "For our sake he made him [Christ] to be sin who knew no sin, *so that in him* we might become the righteousness of God" (2 Corinthians 5:21).

In the words of a beloved Christian hymn, Horatio Spafford wrote,

> *My sin—O the bliss of this glorious thought—*
> *My sin, not in part, but the whole,*
> *Is nailed to the cross, and I bear it no more:*
> *Praise the Lord, praise the Lord, O my soul!*

This sin would have caused us to be sentenced to death and hell. Instead, Christ paid that price for us. "For God so loved the world, that he gave his only Son, that whoever believes in him should not perish but have eternal life" (John 3:16). This was the ultimate act of love.

Romans 5:6-8 says, "For while we were still weak, at the right time Christ died for the ungodly. For one will scarcely die for a righteous person—though perhaps for a good person one would dare even to die—but God shows his love for us in that *while we were still sinners, Christ died for us.*"

I was in a Romans study group a long time ago, and I'll never forget the illustration my friend Kenny Sutton used when teaching about this passage. He and his wife had just had a baby boy whom they named Blake. Kenny created an imaginary character for us—a drunk living in the gutters, filthy, smelly, and evil. This man had beaten and raped sixteen women and killed three of them in the two and a half years he'd been living on the streets. He was grotesque in his appearance and disgusting in his habits and speech. Finally he was arrested and at his trial sat in the defendant's chair before the judge. The man stood for sentencing when the jury came back with a verdict of guilty. He deserved the death sentence they gave him.

Then Kenny posed this scenario. After hearing the sentence, what if Kenny had stood up before the judge and all gathered there, holding little Blake in his arms, his long-awaited and precious son. What if he had kissed the baby and held him out to the judge, saying, "Wait. Don't take this person's life. Here, take my son. Let him die in this man's place." Kenny looked at each of us with tears in his eyes. There was a hush. Then he quietly spoke these words: "That's what God did when He gave His Son to die on the cross for you."

In 1999 pastor and writer John MacArthur preached a sermon at our church as part of a conference we were hosting. In that sermon he summarized Christ's substitutionary death on the cross like this: "On the cross God treated *Christ* as though He was guilty of every sin of every believer even though He was guilty of *none* of them. God treated *us* as if we had lived Christ's life, when in fact we didn't."

Another illustration of this substitutionary act of Christ is given to us in the account of the Jewish Passover in the Old Testament. When the Israelites were slaves to the Egyptians, Moses was sent to bring them out of the land of Egypt and into their promised land. But Pharaoh refused to let the people go. So God, through Moses, brought certain plagues upon Egypt. However, Pharaoh still refused to let the people go. We'll pick the story up in Exodus 11:4-6:

> *So Moses said, "Thus says the LORD: About midnight I will go out in the midst of Egypt, and every firstborn in the land of Egypt shall die, from the firstborn of Pharaoh who sits on his throne, even to the firstborn of the slave girl who is behind the handmill, and all the firstborn of the cattle. There shall be a great cry throughout all the land of Egypt, such as there has never been, nor ever will be again."*

However, God made a provision for the Israelites. Each man was to select a lamb for his household and keep it until twilight of the day the plague would strike. Then they were to slaughter the lambs and mark the doorposts and lintels with the blood.

> *"For I will pass through the land of Egypt that night, and I will strike all the firstborn in the land of Egypt, both man and beast; and on all the gods of Egypt I will execute judgments: I am the LORD. The blood shall be a sign for you, on the houses where you are. And when I see the blood, I will pass over you, and no plague will befall you to destroy you, when I strike the land of Egypt."* (Exodus 12:12-13)

The Lord did exactly what He promised. At midnight all the first-born in Egypt died. "And Pharaoh rose up in the night, he and all his servants and all the Egyptians. And there was a great cry in Egypt, for there was not a house where someone was not dead" (Exodus 12:30). This tragedy finally persuaded Pharaoh to let the people go.

That event was a picture of what will actually take place on the day of judgment. The Passover shows why Jesus is sometimes referred to as the sacrificial Lamb or the Lamb of God slain for the sins of His people. His blood covers us, as the blood of the lamb covered the door-posts of the Israelites' homes. When God judges all people, He will only see the blood of Christ when He looks at us, and we will be saved from eternal death.

But when He looks at unbelievers, He sees nothing but their own sinfulness, and they will be condemned:

> . . . when the Lord Jesus is revealed from heaven with his mighty angels in flaming fire, inflicting vengeance on those who do not know God and on those who do not obey the gospel of our Lord Jesus. They will suffer the punishment of eternal destruction, away from the presence of the Lord and from the glory of his might, when he comes on that day to be glorified in his saints, and to be marveled at among all who have believed, because our testimony to you was believed. (2 Thessalonians 1:7b-10)

The Passover is an excellent illustration of the way Christ secures our safety and salvation at the judgment. Romans 3:21-25a says,

> But now the righteousness of God has been manifested apart from the law, although the Law and the Prophets bear witness to it—the righteousness of God through faith in Jesus Christ for all who believe. For there is no distinction: for all have sinned and fall short of the glory of God, and are justified by his grace as a gift, through the redemption that is in Christ Jesus, whom God put forward as a propitiation by his blood, to be received by faith.

A secular example I find helpful is from Star Trek. The Klingons' vessel had what they call a "cloaking device." Remember that? When they engage the cloaking device, their ship becomes completely invisible. It cannot be seen or detected. In the same way, Christ's blood, shed on that cross over 2,000 years ago, is our own "cloaking device." Its covering will protect us from condemnation and allow us to enter that heavenly kingdom where we'll dwell with Him for eternity.

Jesus died, nailed on a cross on a little hill outside the city of Jerusalem. His body was placed in a tomb, and the entrance was sealed with a gigantic stone. But His body didn't stay there. Three days after His burial, He miraculously rose from the dead.

He had predicted the Resurrection several times when teaching His disciples. They didn't understand it though until after it had come to pass. Henry Bast points out the significance of this event: "The Christian faith is that Jesus Christ conquered death in his resurrection. He brought life and immortality to light by his resurrection from the dead."[13]

The Resurrection is the most joyful part of the "good news" of salvation because it proclaims the triumph of Christ over the powers of death. Without the resurrection of Christ, there would be no Christianity. The apostle Paul responded to a group of people in the church in Corinth who said that Christ had not actually been resurrected:

> And if Christ has not been raised, then our preaching is in vain and your faith is in vain. We are even found to be misrepresenting God, because we testified about God that he raised Christ, whom he did not raise if it is true that the dead are not raised. . . . And if Christ has not been raised, your faith is futile and you are still in your sins. Then those also who have fallen asleep in Christ have perished. If in this life only we have hoped in Christ, we are of all people most to be pitied. But in fact Christ has been raised from the dead, *the firstfruits of those who have fallen asleep.* For as by a man [Adam] came death, by a man [Christ] has come also the resurrection of the dead. *(1 Corinthians 15:14-15, 17-21)*

What Paul is talking about in these verses is not only the resurrection of Christ, but the resurrection of all the dead as well. We will all be resurrected when Christ returns in glory—even unbelievers. But what happens after we're resurrected is another story. "[F]or a time is coming when all who are in their graves will hear his voice and come out—those who have done good will rise to live, and those who have done evil will rise to be condemned" (John 5:28-29 NIV).

So you see, all will rise, but not all will rise to live in heaven. Only those with saving faith in Christ will live in heaven with God. Those who do not believe in Christ are said to have "done evil." They will rise to be condemned to hell and eternal separation from God.

---

*The ultimate "good news" of salvation for believers is this:
Because of Christ's substitutionary death on the cross and His
resurrection from the dead, we are declared to be holy in the
sight of God and will inherit His eternal kingdom.*

Christ said:

All *that the Father gives me* will *come to me, and whoever comes
to me I will never cast out. For I have come down from heaven, not
to do my own will but the will of him who sent me. And this is the
will of him who sent me, that I should lose nothing of all that he
has given me, but raise it up on the last day. For this is the will of
my Father, that everyone who looks on the Son and believes in him
should have eternal life, and I will raise him up on the last day.*
(John 6:37-40)

HOW CAN I BE SAVED?

There's no hocus-pocus, abracadabra, or yabba-dabba-doo to being saved. There is nothing we can *do* to merit salvation. The only thing we bring to salvation is the sin that made it necessary.

Erwin Lutzer, pastor of Moody Church, writes:

How perfect do you have to be to enter into heaven? The answer,
quite simply: as perfect as God.
   . . . The question, of course, is: How can we as sinners be as
perfect as God? The answer: God is able to give us all of His per-
fections; His righteousness can be credited to our account so that

we can enter into heaven immediately at death without so much as an intermediate stop.

When Christ died on the cross, He made a sacrifice for sinners, which God accepted. Though Christ was perfect, God made Him legally guilty of all of our sins. In turn, we receive His righteousness. "He made Him who knew no sin (Christ) to be sin on our behalf, that we might become the righteousness of God in Him" (2 Cor. 5:21).[14]

We have already seen that God chose certain people from before the creation of the world to love and to save for eternal life in heaven: "[God] *chose us* in him *before the foundation of the world*, that we should be holy and blameless before him" (Ephesians 1:4).

How can you be saved? "If you confess with your mouth that Jesus is Lord and believe in your heart that God raised him from the dead, *you will be saved*. For with the heart one believes and is justified [put in right standing], and with the mouth one confesses and is saved. . . . For everyone who calls on the name of the Lord will be saved" (Romans 10:9-10, 13).

There is no formula for salvation. This gift is granted to those whom the Father has chosen. How do you know if He has chosen you? If it is the genuine desire of your heart for Him to save you, you know He has chosen you. He doesn't place that desire in the hearts of unbelievers. He *will* save you. He turns no one away who comes to Him in faith. "And those who know your name put their trust in you, for you, O LORD, have not forsaken those who seek you" (Psalm 9:10).

How does that truth reconcile with the fact that so many will remain lost and will follow the paths of destruction into the ultimate eternal torment of hell? It's simple really. *If you're not chosen by God as His child, you will never, ever desire that He save you.* That will never be a priority for you.

"For those whom he *foreknew* [fore-loved] he also *predestined* [before the creation of the world—Eph. 1:4] to be conformed to the image of his Son, in order that he might be the firstborn among many brothers. And those whom he predestined he also *called*, and those whom he called he also *justified*, and those whom he justified he also *glorified*" (Romans 8:29-30).

You see, if He did not choose you, He will not *call* you. And it is only by His calling that we are compelled to come to Him. "*No one* can come to me [Christ] unless the Father who sent me draws him" (John 6:44). He repeats this in John 6:65: "This is why I told you that no one can come to me unless it is granted him by the Father."

As our family was going home after church one Sunday, we were discussing the sermon. I posed what I thought would be a tough question for my children. "If God chose 100 people to be saved, and 101 really, really, really wanted to be, then how many would He actually save?"

My youngest son, Paul, who was about ten years old at the time, quickly said in an exasperated tone, "Mom, if God only chose 100 to save, then only 100 would really, really want to be saved." From the mouth of babes.

When I was first introduced to these truths at a Bible study, I bristled at the thought. I left that day sure that I would never return. However, one of the things I did was to write down all the Scripture passages we'd studied. For some reason, (now I realize that it was the promptings of the Holy Spirit) I couldn't get those passages out of my head.

One night, as I lay tossing and turning and trying *not* to think about these things, I reached the point that I had to confront them. I got up, turned on the lights, and read each one of them again, trying to find something to support *my* beliefs—that the choice depended on us. I couldn't. The passages said exactly what had been taught in that Bible study. I placed them all in context and studied the pronouns, and still the passages said something I had never seen before—that God, not man, determines whether or not he is to have saving faith.

Some of those life-changing passages we studied will be quoted below. I'm not telling you that you should change the way you think about salvation just based on what I'm saying. Don't believe *me* about a subject that important. What I am suggesting to you is that you read the passages below and *think* about what the *Scriptures* say. If you change the way you think about salvation, let it be God's Word (not mine) that changes your mind.

Jerry Bridges wrote, "We must allow the Bible to say what it says, not what we think it ought to say."[15] So prayerfully read the following passages and ask God to reveal the truths they teach. We can read passages like these all day long, but unless the Holy Spirit opens our eyes to the truth, we won't be able to understand or believe them. Here are just a few of the many passages that teach that God chooses His elect. We merely respond to His call.

All things have been handed over to me by my Father, and no one knows the Son except the Father, and no one knows the Father except the Son and anyone to whom the Son chooses to reveal him. (Matthew 11:27)

All that the Father gives me will come to me, *and whoever comes to me I will never cast out. For I have come down from heaven, not to do my own will but the will of him who sent me. And this is the will of him who sent me, that I should lose nothing of all that he has given me, but raise it up on the last day. For this is the will of my Father, that everyone who looks on the Son and believes in him should have eternal life, and I will raise him up on the last day.* (John 6:37-40)

"It is the Spirit who gives life; the flesh is of no avail. The words that I have spoken to you are spirit and life. But there are some of you who do not believe." (For Jesus knew from the beginning who those were who did not believe, and who it was who would betray him.) And he said, "This is why I told you that no one can come to me unless it is granted him by the Father." *(John 6:63-65)*

So the Jews gathered around [Christ] and said to him, "How long will you keep us in suspense? If you are the Christ, tell us plainly." Jesus answered them, "I told you, and you do not believe. The works that I do in my Father's name bear witness about me, but you do not believe because you are not part of my flock. My sheep hear my voice, and I know them, and they follow me. I give them eternal life, and they will never perish, and no one will snatch them out of my hand. My Father, who has given them to me, is greater than all, and no one is able to snatch them out of the Father's hand. I and the Father are one." (John 10:24-30)

She will bear a son, and you shall call his name Jesus, for he will save his people from their sins. (Matthew 1:21)

Notice that it doesn't say that He'll try really, really hard to save them if they'll only cooperate with Him. It says He *will* save His people.

John 17 records a beautiful prayer from Christ to His Father:

For I have given [the disciples] the words that you gave me, and they have received them and have come to know in truth that I came from you; and they have believed that you sent me. I am praying for them. I am not praying for the world but for those whom you have given me, for they are yours. . . . I have guarded them, and not one of them has been lost except the son of destruction [Judas], that the Scripture might be fulfilled. (John 17:8-9, 12b)

One of the most compelling passages I've read on this subject is in an introductory essay to John Owen's *The Death of Death in the Death of Christ.* Respected theologian J. I. Packer, author of the essay, wrote:

[God's saving purpose in the death of His Son was not] a mere ineffectual wish, depending for its fulfillment on man's *willingness* to believe, so that *for all God could do Christ might have died and none been saved at all.* He insists that the Bible sees the Cross as revealing *God's power to save,* not His impotence. *Christ did not win a hypothetical salvation for hypothetical believers, a mere possibility of salvation for any who might possibly believe, but a real salvation for His own chosen people.* His precious blood really does "save us all"; the intended effects of His self-offering do in fact follow, just because the Cross was what it was. Its saving power does not depend on *faith being added to it;* its saving power is such that *faith flows from it. The Cross secured the full salvation of all for whom Christ died.*[16]

Pastor Erwin Lutzer explains salvation like this: "What must we do to receive the gift of righteousness and a new nature within? The answer is to admit our helplessness, to acknowledge that we are dependent on God's mercy. Then we must transfer all of our trust to Christ as our sin-bearer; *we must believe in Him as the One who did all that we will ever need to stand in God's holy presence.* To believe in Christ means that as best we know, we trust Him for all that we need in this life and in the life to come."[17]

I believe it is beneficial to read how others describe salvation. But to summarize the way to salvation in my own words, I will say that you must first realize that you are a sinner—that there is nothing you can do to save yourself. You then recognize that because of this, you are in need of a Savior. You honestly face the reality of your own sins and ask God to forgive you. This entire process is made possible by God's grace to us. Only by this grace can we recognize our need of a Savior. If you then believe in Jesus Christ, the Son of God, and ask Him to save you, He will. It's as simple and yet as profound as that.

These steps are not a simple thing for unbelievers though. For them, there is nothing more impossible. They will not see themselves in need of a Savior. They will not trust Jesus Christ to save them. And they will die and be condemned to an eternity in hell. They will have to pay the penalty for their own sins. Their sins will not be redeemed (paid for) by the blood of Christ. But for those who believe, death is a happy event, a doorway to more bliss than could ever be imagined.

Perhaps you're not accustomed to praying. Perhaps you don't have any idea of what to say to God. Here is a prayer that may be used as a *pattern* for you. There is nothing magical in the words themselves. But when you actually *mean* the words you say, they are life changing. I offer the prayer for those who may need some guidance.

"Dear Lord Jesus, I know that I am a sinner and need Your forgiveness. I believe that You died for my sins, and I want to turn from them now. Please come into my heart and my life. I want to trust You as Savior and follow You as my Lord. Have mercy on me, Lord, and grant me Your salvation. Give me the faith to trust only in You. In Your sweet name, I pray. Amen."

&c &p

CASE STUDY

Jerry Faulkner lay in his bed in the nursing home with his eyes closed. His breathing had become more rapid and labored during the hour and a half I had been sitting with him. His wife watched him from a chair on the other side of the bed—that is, she watched him as much as her sleepy eyes would allow. She had been at his bedside since early that morning.

Barbara Faulkner's blonde hair was brushed back from her face and worn in one long, thick braid that fell down her back. Several rogue strands had escaped and hung in fragile wisps around her face. She looked at me with a tired smile and then allowed her eyes to close for several seconds.

"Mrs. Faulkner, you know that I'll be here with him all night. Why don't you go home and get some sleep?"

"I know I should, but I hate to leave. I keep thinking, What if something happens to him while I'm gone? I just want to be here at the end."

"I don't anticipate anything happening within the next few hours. I'll call you if I start to see any changes. He could be like this for days, and you're wearing yourself out. Besides, if God intends for you to be here, by doggies, you'll be here—no matter what."

She smiled again and looked down at her watch. It was 10:47 P.M. "Okay, I'll leave at 11:00. I'll just go take a shower and a nap and come back early in the morning. You're sure that's okay?"

I smiled reassuringly and nodded. "Most of the time," I told her, "we have advance warning before a death. Jerry's very close, but he's not showing any signs of dying within the next few hours. Sometimes things happen very quickly, and we don't have any warning. But in most cases, we can tell when the end is in sight. I'll be checking his vital signs every hour, like I've been doing. So I should be able to call you in time for you to get here. I can't guarantee that, but in my best judgment that's what I believe."

She watched as I picked up my Bible and opened it. Her head lifted slightly as she eyed the colorful pages that I'd color-coded while studying the passages. I got out my colored pencils and placed them beside the Bible, getting ready to study. But first, taking a sip of my Diet Coke, I gathered my nursing equipment and walked to his bedside again.

"Let me take his vital signs a little early this time so you'll know what they are before you leave, okay?"

"Good. Thanks. I appreciate that," she said.

I wrote the values down for temperature, blood pressure, pulse, and respirations and then checked the oxygen saturation level.

"No changes since last hour."

"Good. I guess I'll go then." But instead of getting up from her chair, she looked over at my Bible again.

"Is that your Bible?" she asked.

"Yes. I always bring it with me when I'm sitting with a patient. Between assessments I get some time to study and spend some quiet time with God."

"That's so good. I hadn't thought about reading my Bible up here. But it sure wouldn't hurt." She paused and then said, "Jerry's got a Bible at home somewhere. I'll try to find it and bring it with me when I come back."

"Is Jerry a Christian then?" I asked.

"Well, he said he was saved when he was a kid, but he's never been one for going to church or anything. Hated organized religion. But Jerry has such a big, generous heart that I can't imagine God turning him away. Jerry's always had a good heart."

"You know, that's exactly what his friend Bill said to me last time I was here," I told her.

"Well, anyone who knew him would tell you he'd do without to make sure someone else had what they needed. He was a good man. I'm sure he believed in God. We just never talked about it much."

She sighed, got up wearily, and stretched as she walked to his bedside and sat down beside him. She bent over him and kissed him on the cheek.

"I love you, baby. I'll be back soon."

No response. Jerry had slipped into a coma two days ago. His blood pressure had dropped, and his oxygen saturation levels were in the 80s instead of the normal 97-98 percent. Now as his heart rate and respirations increased, his skin was starting to feel cool and damp.

Earlier I had explained to his wife about the body's ability to compensate. When the blood pressure starts to drop, the heart and lungs take over to bring it back up. The heart starts pumping faster, and breathing speeds up in response to the heart. But I had told her that Jerry would be unable to compensate indefinitely, that it was only a matter of time before he took his last breath. That's why hospice was on the scene, watching, monitoring, and helping to ensure a peaceful and pain-free death. Hospice does nothing to hasten death. But it doesn't try to prolong life either.

Barbara sighed again and picked up her purse and keys. "Okay, then. I'll go home for a while. You don't know how much I appreciate you for staying. I'd never leave otherwise."

"I know. And you're welcome. We don't want him to be alone at the end either, you know."

She nodded, then slowly turned, and walked out the door.

I sat on the bed next to Jerry and took his hand in mine. He had been a vibrant man, full of life until three years ago when a massive stroke left him in a near-vegetative state. His wife was unable to take care of him at home; so she had placed him in a nursing home for round-the-clock care.

Until a couple of days ago he was able to open his eyes and look around. He couldn't communicate verbally, but his wife believed she could tell what he was thinking by the look on his face. Now there was nothing. He had sustained another stroke about two months ago. That's why he was admitted to hospice. She had decided not to prolong his suffering any longer. In the past he had voiced his wishes many times to her and to their friends that he never wanted to be kept alive artificially. So now we were just waiting and watching.

I looked from his face with its pale, sunken cheeks to the smiling image of a robust man I hardly recognized in a picture on his nightstand, taken before his first stroke. Hard to believe it was the same man. "He has such a good heart," I recalled them saying.

I leaned close to his face and told him, "Jerry, it takes more than a good heart to go to heaven." I'm not sure how much people can hear or comprehend when they are in a coma, but I'm told that the hearing is the last thing to go. I hoped that he could hear me.

"You remember learning about Jesus when you were a boy. Think about Jesus, Jerry. Remember Him. Ask Him to save you, Jerry, and He will. Just ask Him, Jerry. He'll forgive your sins. He'll take you to be with Him in heaven."

I didn't know what else to say. I didn't think he could understand a "sermon"; so I kept it as short and simple as I could.

I opened my Bible to a passage I love and read aloud:

> I love the LORD, because he has heard my voice and my pleas for mercy. Because he inclined his ear to me, therefore I will call on him as long as I live. The snares of death encompassed me; the pangs of Sheol laid hold on me; I suffered distress and anguish. Then I called on the name of the LORD: "O LORD, I pray, deliver my soul." Gracious is the LORD, and righteous; our God is merciful. The LORD preserves the simple; when I was brought low, he saved me. Return, O my soul, to your rest; for the LORD has dealt bountifully with you. For you have delivered my soul from death, my eyes from tears, my feet from stumbling; I will walk before the LORD in the land of the living. . . . Precious in the sight of the LORD is the death of his saints. . . . Praise the LORD. (Psalm 116:1-9, 15, 19)

"Ask Him, Jerry," I whispered to him. "Ask Him."

Please examine yourself as you read these words. Don't wait until you are helplessly lying in coma somewhere before you start thinking about your eternal soul. You may not even have *that* much time or opportunity. Life is so short. James 4:14b says, "What is your life? For *you are a mist that appears for a little time and then vanishes.*" The time to prepare for eternity is now. "Heaven is won or lost on earth; the possession is there, but the preparation is here."[18]

> Heal me, O LORD, and I shall be healed; save me, and I shall be saved, for you are my praise.
>
> JEREMIAH 17:14

6

THE PURPOSES OF SUFFERING

Through him we have also obtained access by faith into this grace in which we stand, and we rejoice in hope of the glory of God. More than that, we rejoice in our sufferings, knowing that suffering produces endurance, and endurance produces character, and character produces hope, and hope does not put us to shame, because God's love has been poured into our hearts through the Holy Spirit who has been given to us.

ROMANS 5:2-5

CAN WE UNDERSTAND OUR SUFFERINGS?

Penny answered the door and felt a surge of love as she saw Paula's impish smile.

"Paula!" She gave the nurse a big hug. "Bachman's really been looking forward to your coming. You know, your kidding around with him has done so much to improve his outlook and mood. You keep him from taking himself too seriously, and I'm deeply grateful."

"How is my buddy today?" Paula asked Penny, craning her neck to peek into the den.

"Oh, he's so much better since you put that pain patch on him. He hasn't complained of pain a single time since."

"That's great. Remember—if he should need a stronger dose, the patch comes in graduated strengths. We can make sure he has the one he really needs. I'm glad this one seems to be doing the trick though. I should warn you that with this much narcotic in his system, his bowels might slow down. You'll need to tell me if he goes more than three days without a bowel movement."

"Three days. Well, I don't think he's had one since Sunday or Monday."

"Hmm. That's five days. We'll probably need to get him started on a bowel regimen—you know, taking a laxative or stool softener every evening or every other evening. But if he hasn't gone in five days, I'm afraid we'll need to do something about it today. I'll check him for an impaction." Paula looked away from Penny and added softly, "I'm going to warn you in advance that if he has an impaction, this is going to be an unpleasant experience for him."

"What will you do?" Penny asked tentatively.

"I'll have to try to remove it manually, if you know what I mean."

"You've got to be kidding. He'd just hate that. You know how proud and modest he is."

"I know. And I hope I won't have to do anything. But this really does pertain to his overall comfort. I promise I'll do what I can to get him through this with his dignity intact."

"Okay." Penny looked miserable.

"He'll take his cues from us. If we act tentative, he'll pick up on it. We have to stay positive. I do appreciate your telling me about this. Every time I've asked him about bowel movements, he says he's not having any trouble."

"That's my husband, all right." Penny smiled.

Paula giggled as she and Penny walked into the den.

Bachman's whole face lit up when he saw them. "Hey. What are you two hens cackling about?" he bellowed in mock irritation.

"You, what else?" Paula responded.

She sat down by the bed and took Bachman's hand. "How's my boyfriend doing today?"

"Shhh, my wife will hear you."

"Oh, you guys haven't fooled me for a minute," Penny laughed. "I've suspected this all along."

They all laughed. This little routine was getting familiar.

"Penny tells me the patch seems to have taken care of your pain for the most part. What do you think?"

"Pain's better. Thanks."

Paula went to wash her hands, then came back and took her stethoscope and blood pressure cuff out of her bag. Stepping over to him, she warmed the end of the stethoscope in her hands as she talked.

"I'm so glad you finally let me have this hospital bed brought in for you. You look so much more comfortable today. Do you like it?"

"Yeah. I wish I'd had you get it in here sooner. It really has helped being able to raise the head of the bed up when I have trouble breathing. Seems like I can sleep better in it too."

"Good. You know how I love it when I'm right," she teased.

"Yeah, yeah." He waved her statement off.

"Now do me a favor and try not to talk while I listen to your chest," she instructed as she placed the stethoscope on him. "Of course, I know that's a real challenge for you."

He tried not to smile but did anyway.

She winked at him as she listened. She listened to his heart and lungs, checked his vital signs, and then examined his nail beds and his feet for any discoloration. After her examination, chatting all the while, she sat down next to him again. "You check out pretty good today. Got any complaints I need to know about?"

"Nope."

"How about the bowels? When was your last bowel movement?"

"You love talking about my bowels, don't you?"

"You know it. My favorite subject. Well, when was it?"

"Yesterday, I think." He looked away from her and studied a bird outside his window.

"Penny says she thinks it may have been more toward the first of the week, and this is Friday. I think I'd better check things out to see what's going on down there."

"Oh, boy," he snarled. "Don't you have anywhere else you need to be?"

"Nope. This is the highlight of my day. Now try to roll over onto your left side."

She and Penny helped him roll onto his side since he no longer had the strength to do it on his own. She lowered the head of the bed and put on her gloves, popping them loudly.

He looked over his shoulder and grumbled, "Watch out now."

She grinned at him. Then she said softly, "This is going to be a little uncomfortable, but I'll try to be as gentle as I can."

As she checked him for an impaction, she saw his whole body tense and his eyes squeeze shut.

"Sorry. Try to relax. You do have an impaction." She described the procedure to Bach and assured him she'd make it as quick and painless as possible. Then she turned to Penny. "Why don't you give him some of the liquid morphine you keep on hand for breakthrough pain while I get ready here." Then she went out to her car for supplies.

When Penny returned with the medicine, Bachman looked up at her. "Ain't this a deal? Did you ever think it would come to this?"

"I know, baby," Penny crooned to him, giving him half a dropper of the morphine. She stroked his shoulder and looked into his eyes, trying to be as comforting as possible.

Paula was back by then and putting gloves on again. She padded the bed to keep from soiling the linens.

"Okay, ready or not."

"Not," he retorted.

She spent about ten minutes evacuating as much as possible. She knew it was hurting him. He moaned once and, glowering over his shoulder, insisted that she stop.

"I'm so sorry, Bach. I'm almost finished, I think."

The enema was less painful, but the entire ordeal left him weak and pale. Paula and Penny cleaned him up and disposed of the soiled pads. Then they repositioned him in the bed. He was so tall he was forever sliding down until his feet were hanging off the end of the bed. When he was situated just right again, Paula raised the foot of the bed to keep him from sliding back down. Then she sat down beside him.

She took his hand and looked into his face. "I'm so sorry, Bach."

"That's okay. I know you had to do it. I actually feel some relief right now even though it wore me out."

She continued to look at him, her eyes betraying the pain of too much tenderness. "No, that's not what I mean. I *am* sorry you had to go through that. I can imagine how hard that must have been for you. But I am really just . . ." Her voice caught, and her lower lip trembled. "I'm just going to miss you so much."

She put her arm around his waist and, placing her head on his chest, began to sob. He looked down at her and, with considerable effort, placed his hand on her head. For several quiet seconds he stroked her hair—very gently.

"It'll be okay, Paula. I promise." His weak voice was soft and fatherly.

Penny watched them quietly with tears flowing down her face.

Paula raised herself and, wiping her face, tried to laugh as she asked, "Now what's wrong with this picture? The patient is comforting the hospice nurse instead of the other way around."

"Any time I can be of service." He smiled back.

"I'd better go now. I've done all the damage I can do for one day, I guess. I'll see you Monday, okay?"

"Leave your gloves at home."

"Hah."

She walked into the kitchen with Penny and gave her a long hug. Then she instructed her on which laxative to buy and when to give it. She also encouraged her to increase his fluid intake. He should have something to sip on all day long.

"Have you had any questions this week?" Paula asked.

Penny had started writing questions down, things she wanted to talk over with Paula. Those talks kept her from feeling helpless and desperate. She felt more in control since hospice had come on the scene.

"No, nothing more."

"Okay. Guess I'm ready to go."

On her way out, she turned back to Penny. "I'm sorry about breaking down like that. I really do love you guys, you know."

"Yeah, I know you do. That means a lot to us."

They both shed a few more tears safely out of Bachman's sight. Then Penny took Paula's hand in hers. "Don't worry about the tears, sweetie. Who would want someone cold and heartless taking care of him? Not me. I think it's a blessing that you care so much about him. You've helped us so much. *Both* of us."

"Thanks. I needed that." She left with her customary wave before getting into her car.

There's nothing glamorous about nursing, as you can see. And there's certainly nothing glamorous about dying. "Death with dignity" is a phrase we often hear, and we nod our heads as if we truly understand it. But we don't. We can work *toward* that goal, but we can never truly *achieve* it. As Pastor Erwin Lutzer has said, "Strictly speaking, no one 'dies with dignity.' Ever since sin entered into the world and brought death with it, death has always been the final humiliation, the one unalterable fact that confirms our mortality and reduces our bodies to ashes."[1]

First Corinthians 15 speaks volumes about death and resurrection, and one section says, "The body that is sown is perishable, it is raised imperishable; it is sown in dishonor, it is raised in glory; it is sown in weakness, it is raised in power; it is sown a natural body, it is raised a spiritual body" (vv. 42b-44 NIV).

Quite a list. Perishable. Dishonored. Weak. Natural. But on the other side of death, we are imperishable, glorified, powerful, and spiritual. Let me emphasize, though, that this is speaking of what happens to *Christians* when they die. This is not a promise given to unbelievers. *I say this not to offend or to hurt but because I do not want to be guilty of offering* false *hope to those who do not have a saving relationship with Jesus Christ.*

Suffering is all around us. We ask why with our eyes turned heavenward and our arms outstretched. However, we really shouldn't be shocked by the pain and trials that befall us. In fact, Jesus Christ assured us Himself that these *would* come. In one of my favorite verses, He says, "I have said these things to you, that *in me you may have peace.* In the world you *will* have tribulation [trouble]. But take heart; *I have overcome the world*" (John 16:33).

Yes, He tells us to expect trouble in this world. But He doesn't leave us there without hope. Instead, in the next sentence He gives us all the hope we need by telling us that the victory is already won. He has overcome (notice the past tense) the world. It hasn't happened yet and is yet to come, but it is already a "done deal" in the plan of God.

In a way it's like a basketball game that is hard-fought until the last six minutes. Then your favorite team gradually starts pulling together and scoring with every trip down the court. Now there are only 22.4 seconds on the clock, and your team is ahead 88-67. Though you can't *officially* say you've won, you know that in a matter of time, the victory is yours. You start the celebration before the game is even over. That's what we need to be doing. We can go ahead and start the celebration. As John MacArthur says, "I've read the end of the Book. We win."

But that doesn't mean the game is over. Though Christ has already won our victory, we still live in this world and must deal with the events of our lives, the bad as well as the good. "A Christian faces death with anticipation and faith, but he is not disinterested in this world. He is active in it."[2] Though our citizenship is in heaven, we must still focus on living here in a way pleasing to the One who bought us with His blood.

How can we do that when there is so much pain and suffering, misery and unhappiness in our lives? With a simple five-letter word: TRUST. Can you truly trust God when the going gets tough? If He's actually in control, then why did He allow your father to have cancer? How could He let such an event as the World Trade Center tragedy occur? Does God actually control all the circumstances in our lives?

Author Jerry Bridges writes, "I mistakenly thought I could not trust God unless I *felt* like trusting Him (which I almost never did in times of adversity). Now I am learning that *trusting God is first of all a matter of the will, and is not dependent on my feelings.* I choose to trust God and my feelings eventually follow."[3] Along the same lines, the psalmist encourages, "*When I am afraid, I put my trust in you. In God, whose word I praise, in God I trust; I shall not be afraid. What can flesh do to me?*" (Psalm 56:3-4).

Remember the promise: "And *we know* that *for those who love God all things* work together *for good,* for those who are called according to his purpose" (Romans 8:28). If we are Christians, we trust Him with our salvation. Therefore, we can also trust Him with our lives.

An Old Testament equivalent of this verse is found in the life of Joseph. Because of their jealousy, Joseph's brothers secretly sold him to the Egyptians, who took him back to Egypt as their slave. The brothers told their father that Joseph had been killed by wild animals. But Joseph, though he suffered significant hardship, never lost his faith in God.

Eventually God worked out the circumstances that led to Joseph's rise in authority in Egypt until he was second only to the king. Years later he and his brothers were reunited due to circumstances clearly brought about by God. The brothers were afraid that Joseph would have them killed in revenge. But Joseph didn't return evil for evil. He repaid them with love and provision, telling them, "As for you, *you meant evil against me, but God meant it for good*, to bring it about that many people should be kept alive, as they are today" (Genesis 50:20).

Theologian Wayne Grudem wrote, "God uses the experience of death to complete our sanctification . . . therefore, we should see all the hardship and suffering that comes to us in life as something that God brings to us to do us good, strengthening our trust in Him and our obedience and ultimately increasing our ability to glorify Him."[4]

If you remember anything at all about the purposes of suffering, let it be this: Everything that is brought into our lives comes because God either caused it or allowed it. And everything that comes into our lives does so for a reason designed by God for our best.

You might say to yourself, "Well, I just don't believe that." And that changes what? Nothing. *Truth* is just as true whether you believe it or not. However, I hope to show you—more, *to convince* you—that this is the truth according to the holy Word of God to His people.

Why should we believe the truth of Scripture? Because God has commanded it. In 2 Timothy 3:16-17, we read, "*All Scripture is breathed out by God* and profitable for teaching, for reproof, for correction, and for training in righteousness, that the man of God may be competent, equipped for every good work." The authors of the Bible wrote under the direct inspiration of the Holy Spirit. We believe that God, who has authority over all things, has preserved His Word for us to study and obey.

The worship pastor at our church, Todd Murray, wrote a song to help his children understand what the Bible is. He says in his text notes, "Written for my children . . . to help them understand that my fatherly love for them is at best a pale reflection of the perfect and infinite love of THE heavenly Father." Here are some of the words:

L O V E   N O T E

Daddy, help me. It's hard to understand
About the God you say who loves me
And who made me with His hand.
But God seems so big and heaven far away,
And yet you tell me that He hears me
When I bow my knees to pray.
But I can't see God. I can't touch Him.
I can't hold His hand.
I can't hear Him talking to me.
Daddy, I don't understand.
Refrain:
Just like Daddy leaves a love note on the kitchen table
Whenever he goes away
To remind you that I love you,
And that I'm coming back soon, and I want you to obey—
Well, just like me, your heavenly Father
Left a letter, and every word is true.
You'll find it written in the pages of the Holy Bible,
God the Father's love note just for you.

TODD MURRAY

The Bible is God's "love note" to His children, but also it's a strong warning for *all* mankind. Scripture, like God's love, becomes more beautiful the more you examine it. It is a treasure chest overflowing with the priceless jewels of *truth*.

THE PURPOSES OF SUFFERING AND DEATH

Although Jesus had *clearly* taught the disciples about His own resurrection, they just didn't "get it." They didn't understand (or perhaps they didn't even remember) what He'd told them until *after* it had happened.

Well, we can't be too hard on the disciples. After all, *we do the same thing* with the subject of affliction, suffering, and death. Statements about the purposes of affliction appear throughout the Bible. We are told to *expect* trials, suffering, death, resurrection, and ultimately eternal life. (All will have eternal existence, but only some will have eternal life, the rest eternal death.) But still we seem surprised when affliction and death actually intrude into our lives. We might ask, "Why is this happening to me?" or maybe, "What did I do to deserve this?" You see, we just don't "get it."

To better understand this difficult subject, let's look at the life of the apostle Paul. The Scriptures give no greater example of a man devoted and pleasing to Christ. Paul was keenly focused on living according to the commands of Jesus Christ and boldly proclaiming them to both Jews and Gentiles.

Since he was such a holy and wise man of God, he must have been exceedingly blessed by God, right? He must have had a pretty happy existence. God would just naturally keep anything bad from happening to him, wouldn't He? But if we look at Paul's life with our natural understanding, we might conclude that God did not like this man very much.

In 2 Corinthians 11:23b-28 NIV, Paul makes a point to the Corinthians, some of whom had cast suspicions on his motives and authority as an apostle. As part of the argument he says:

> *I have worked much harder,* been in prison *more frequently,* been flogged *more severely, and* been exposed to death *again and again.* Five times *I received from the Jews the* forty lashes minus one. Three times *I was* beaten with rods, *once I was* stoned, three times *I was* shipwrecked, *I* spent a night and a day in the open sea, *I have been constantly on the move. I have been in* danger from rivers, *in danger from* bandits, *in danger from* my own countrymen, *in dan-*

ger from Gentiles; *in danger* in the city, *in danger* in the country, *in danger* at sea; *and in danger from* false brothers. *I have* labored *and* toiled *and have often* gone without sleep; *I have known* hunger *and* thirst *and have often* gone without food; *I have been* cold *and* naked. *Besides everything else, I face daily the* pressure of my concern *for all the churches.*

Quite a life. Does it make you jealous? I think not. I sometimes complain if I break a fingernail or have to skip a meal. But this is the same Paul who said, "[F]or *I have learned to be content whatever the circumstances.* I know what it is to be in need, and I know what it is to have plenty. *I have learned the secret of being content in any and every situation,* whether well fed or hungry, whether living in plenty or in want. I can do everything through him who gives me strength" (Philippians 4:11-13 NIV).

Why did Paul have to suffer so? The world might say it was to make him tougher. That may have been one of the reasons. However, Paul gives another answer. He said that his afflictions made him rely on God instead of on himself (2 Corinthians 1:8-11).

In the Old Testament we're told about God's own people, the nation of Israel and the sufferings they encountered. We're told of David, who is called "a man after God's own heart," and the sufferings brought into his life. The many prophets and priests who belonged to God encountered grief and affliction, and sometimes death, at nearly every turn.

In the New Testament John the Baptist, most of Jesus' twelve beloved disciples, the apostle Paul, and some of Jesus' dear friends as well as some of His own family lived lives peppered with suffering. Through the New Testament and subsequent church history we find that most of these people were eventually put to death because of their allegiance to Christ.

Jesus Christ Himself lived a life of poverty and constantly had to deal with the schemes of the Jews, the betrayal by one of His disciples, isolation, and slander. He was mocked and beaten by soldiers, flogged, made to carry His own cross to Calvary, and then crucified by having His precious hands and feet nailed onto the cross with spikes. He was raised naked and bleeding in front of the masses of people gathered there, bearing intense agony as the cross was lowered with a thud into the ground. Then came the worst part of all—He had to accept the filthiness of the sins of His people, to take them upon Himself and to die at the hands of men He had created, suffering the agony of separation from His Father God. What a life! And He was *perfect*.

First Peter 4:12 says, "Beloved, do not be surprised at the fiery trial when it comes upon you to test you, as though something strange were happening to you." My point is this: If suffering and death were such a huge part of these sanctified lives, then why do we feel unfairly treated and betrayed when we don't get our way, when afflictions befall us, or when we lose loved ones to sickness and death? Shame on us.

WE JUST DON'T GET IT.

God, our heavenly Father, calls us to serve Him even when we are not in the mood, even when we're not where we want to be, and even when our lives are not easy. In fact, these are *especially* the times we should call out to Him for the grace to serve Him better.

It is with this understanding that we can then say, like the apostle Paul, "Not that I am speaking of being in need, for I have learned in whatever situation I am to be content" (Philippians 4:11). Once we begin to practice this important principle, despair and sadness give way to the quiet, calm assurance that all things rest within God's sovereign control. We can then demonstrate confidence and peace, knowing that God is working out all things in our lives for our best, whether we understand how or not. We are to simply trust Him even when we don't understand.

Jerry Bridges expands this thought:

> Trusting God is not a matter of my *feelings* but of my *will*. . . . Our *first priority* in times of adversity is to *honor* and *glorify* God *by trusting Him*. We tend to make our first priority the gaining of relief from our feelings of heartache or disappointment or frustration. . . . We honor God by choosing to trust Him when we don't understand what He is doing or why He has allowed some adverse circumstance to occur.

The first thing we have to do in order to trust God is determine if God is in control; if He is sovereign over the physical area of our lives. If He is not—if illness and afflictions "just happen"—then, of course, there is no basis for trusting God. But if God is sovereign in this area, then we can trust Him without understanding all the theological issues involved in the problem of pain.[5]

In the remainder of this chapter, let's look at some of the purposes of suffering. I hope that through this brief study, the Holy Spirit will bless our hearts with understanding, and we will indeed start to "get it."

Why Does Suffering Exist?

When God created the heavens and the earth, they were places of immeasurable beauty and peace. There was no suffering, sickness, pain, or sorrow. What happened to upset this utopia? Sin. As a result of mankind's disobedience in the Garden of Eden, sin entered creation, and we still see its consequences all around us.

Was God the author of sin? By no means! Yet God is, by His own nature, eternally omniscient. Though He is not the author of evil, He certainly knew that the Fall would produce evil and had already planned to use it for His own glory. For example, we are told that He chose the elect from before the foundation of the world (Ephesians 1:4). He fully comprehended that mankind would be eternally cursed and in need of a Savior. Otherwise there would have been no need to have chosen an elect. So while God did not cause Adam to sin, He planned for it from the beginning. Nothing happens that is not either caused or allowed by Him. What function does suffering have in God's plan? Ultimately God uses suffering to accomplish His purposes.

Though it is my desire to offer comfort through a better understanding of some of the *reasons* behind our own suffering and grief, *my ultimate goal is to glorify God's greatness in the workings of His perfect will.* His thoughts are above our thoughts. "For as the heavens are higher than the earth, so are my ways higher than your ways and my thoughts than your thoughts" (Isaiah 55:9). So no one will ever be able to thoroughly comprehend God's reasons for what He does. "Oh, the depth of the *riches* and *wisdom* and *knowledge* of God. How unsearchable are his judgments and how inscrutable his ways! 'For who has known the mind of the Lord, or who has been his counselor? Or who has given a gift to him that he might be repaid?' For *from* him and *through* him and *to* him are *all things. To him be glory forever*. Amen" (Romans 11:33-36).

With such a transcendent God as this, the ultimate reason for suffering is that He ordained it to be a consequence of sin. In other words, because God said so. Perhaps you remember when your parents used to say, "Because I said so." When I was young, I told myself I'd never give that answer to my children. I hated it when my parents said that to me. Imagine my surprise when I found myself telling my children, "Because I said so."

It wasn't until I had children that I realized that sometimes it is the *most* appropriate answer. That's when I realized how important the concept of authority is. Parents have a God-given authority over children. Children must recognize that authority and submit to it if order and discipline are to be maintained in the home. The family is a model—however imperfect—of our own submission to God. When a child questions your authority, there are times when you must remind him or her that obedience is required "because I said so."

There are other times when reasoning with children may be appropriate and, in fact, advisable. But "because I said so" demonstrates who is in control—not the child, but the parent, not the created, but the Creator.

God is under no obligation to us for anything. He is like the artist wielding the brush, like the potter shaping the clay, like the architect drawing the design. God is the ultimate sculptor of our very being—body and soul. He can do what He wants. He doesn't owe us any explanations. "[H]e does according to his will among the host of heaven and among the inhabitants of the earth; and none can stay his hand or say to him, 'What have you done?'" (Daniel 4:35).

"That's not fair," people might whine. So Paul addresses the "fairness" of the situation and anticipates the question readers might ask: "But who are you, O man, to answer back to God? Will *what is molded* say *to its molder*, 'Why have you made me like this?' Has the potter no right over the clay, to make out of the same lump one vessel for honored use and another for dishonorable use?" (Romans 9:20-21). It comes down to the fact that God is God. He can do whatever He wants to do. And He has the power and authority to back it up.

Jerry Bridges puts it this way:

> God's sovereignty involves *His absolute power* to do whatever pleases Him and *His absolute control* over the actions of all His creatures. But God's sovereignty also includes *His absolute right* to do as He pleases with us. That He has chosen to redeem us and to send His Son to die for us, instead of sending us to hell, is not due to any *obligation* toward us on His part. It is solely due to His *sovereign mercy and grace*. As He said to Moses, "I will have mercy on whom I will have mercy and I will have compassion on whom I will have compassion" (Exodus 33:19). By that statement God was saying, "I am under obligation to no one."[6]

The age-old problem people sometimes have in making sense out of suffering and pain is that some may think God is either totally good but not all-powerful, or God is all-powerful but not totally good. They have a tough time reconciling God's goodness and His power.

Fortunately we are not forced to choose between the sovereignty and the goodness of God. God is both. All-powerful *and* totally and completely good. His sovereignty and His goodness are both asserted in the Bible with equal emphasis. References to His goodness and lovingkindness, as well as His sovereignty, appear on almost every page.

Since the Fall brought suffering into the world, God integrates it into His plan for us. It should be enough for God to tell His poor, sinful children that suffering exists in this world in order to accomplish His purposes. But He is a merciful God who loves us enough to provide more specific answers. Here are some of them.

1. TO COMPLETE OUR SANCTIFICATION

After we become believers, our hearts and our minds become gradually transformed through what we learn about our Lord and our God from the Scriptures. We start to become more like Christ: "Do not be conformed to this world, but be *transformed* by the *renewal of your mind*, that by testing you may discern what is the will of God, what is good and acceptable and perfect" (Romans 12:2).

When we spend a great deal of time with someone, we naturally begin to take on some of his or her traits, picking up certain phrases, inflections in speech, attitudes, or characteristics. In the same way, when we spend more and more time with Christ, through prayer and Bible study, we begin to take on some of His characteristics. We become more Christlike.

Our minds, opened by the Holy Spirit to the truth, search out what we need to do to live lives pleasing to Christ. The more we understand the Word of God, the more we undergo that transformation in our minds and hearts. This ongoing transformation is called sanctification, or the process of becoming more like Christ. Sanctification means that we are being set apart for God.

Salvation, or justification, occurs in a moment of time—when you place your trust in Christ as your Savior and Lord. One is just as "saved" at that moment as he is thirty years down the road. It happens in an instant and remains constant forever. But sanctification is an ongoing process. It is gradual and progressive. We are to grow in Christlikeness for the rest of our lives, and we *never* attain that perfection this side of death. Christ's standard is the one we *strive* for but cannot achieve in this life.

What tools does God use to transform us into the people He wants us to be? He knows exactly what circumstances, both good and bad, are necessary to produce that result in us. He may use, in addition to our circumstances, all the gifts He gives us, all the people with whom we come into contact, and most of all the Scriptures. His tools are limitless.

Imagine for a moment that we are blocks of marble. God precisely "chisels" away everything around us until we are finally the image He wants us to be. The tools—the hammer and chisel—work through chipping, pummeling, scraping away, or pounding into shape. Sometimes that's what it feels like when trials and disappointments come our way. We can be so focused on the *feelings* of pain and discomfort that we don't recognize the good they are bringing forth.

God brings circumstances into our lives. That's true whether we're believers or unbelievers. But He's made a promise to believers. "And we know that *for those who love God all things* work together *for good*, for those who are called according to his purpose" (Romans 8:28).

What exactly is included in "all things?" Well, that would be . . . everything. Do adversity, suffering, grief, disappointment, sickness, and even death fall into that category? Absolutely. The point is this: Do we have to understand what God is doing and what His ultimate goal is for our life before we can trust in that promise? By no means.

Todd Murray, worship pastor at the Bible Church of Little Rock, has composed many incredible Christian songs. One of my favorites is "I Am Not Alone." In one verse he wrote:

> *I will not resist You,* when You move Your hand to mold me.
> *I will not* insist *You show me all Your plans today.*
> I will not despise the tools You're using now to shape me.
> *I will not require* understanding *to* obey.

His tools, you see, sometimes chip away, change us, and mold our thinking, behavior, attitudes, and even our lifestyles. God uses these tools to make us better—that is, to make us more like Him. Sometimes the tools are suffering and adversity.

"There is no question that adversity is difficult. It usually takes us by surprise and seems to strike where we are most vulnerable. To us it often appears completely senseless and irrational, but to God none of it is either senseless or irrational. He has a purpose in every pain He brings or allows in our lives. We can be sure that in some way He intends it for our profit and His glory."[7] Jeremiah 29:11 says, "For I know the plans I have for you, declares the LORD, plans for *wholeness* and *not for evil, to give you a future and a hope.*"

In years past I've wondered how certain circumstances in my life could *possibly* work to my good. For example, there was the time when I was a single mom with two little boys to support. Finances were almost impossibly tight, and we really had to struggle just to get by. Looking back, I can see multiple benefits from being so poor and working so hard to make ends meet. I'll share a few.

• Looking back, I realize that those days were some of the best I've ever had. The closeness of the relationship with my boys was something I'll treasure forever. We didn't have money to do fancy things or to go to expensive places. I had to think creatively about finding *free* opportunities to experience joy and togetherness. We spent a lot of time in parks and museums, having little picnics, finding a sandy place where they could build castles, or looking up at the stars at night. I taught them to play tennis and throw a football, to catch and hit a baseball. We had races and invented competitions. We visited with friends and family. We went for walks or had sword fights with empty wrapping paper tubes. At the time I felt sorry for them, wishing I could give them more. But remembering those times, I am so thankful for them. My boys didn't miss all the extras. They had what some kids never get—wonderful family times and memories of being loved.

• Being poor gave me a frame of reference and an appreciation I wouldn't have had otherwise. Sometimes when things are a little tight financially, my husband tends to worry. He's never had the "blessing" of poverty. My experience has given me the opportunity to encourage and minister to him, providing a perspective he sometimes lacks.

• Because of my own poverty, I've been better able to empathize with others. I can never look down on those less fortunate. I know firsthand what some of these people are going through. What a blessing that has become.

• Frequently I was reminded of God's providence and mercy to me, and His utter goodness and grace to provide for His children. On paper it didn't look like I'd be able to make all my payments every month. Yet I did. Something always happened to make it possible. For instance, he placed people in my life who helped make it possible—the sweet old man who owned the grocery store, my mother who taught me how to budget, my friends, my pastor, and a few of my neighbors. They knew how tough things were for me. I know those people were placed in my life by a loving God. He was not *punishing* me by making me poor. He was *blessing* me. It just didn't seem like it at the time.

But eventually I came to appreciate it as such. After a while, I started to remember it *during* a crisis. Now I know *in advance* that *whatever* He brings into my life will ultimately be for my good and will make me better in the process. He has delivered me so many times. He *never* fails in His purposes. The trials He's brought into my life have only served to strengthen my trust and faith in Him. I know I am the person I am today because of the lifetime of experiences He has given me. And it's not over yet. He's still blessing me and changing me. I'm a work in progress . . . and so are you.

As we grow in maturity, we seek to become more like Christ. Galatians 2:20 says, "I have been crucified with Christ. It is no longer I who live, but Christ who lives in me." Can you say that? Only God can bring us to that point in Christian maturity. Doug Reed, pastor at Thorncrown Chapel in Eureka Springs, Arkansas, commented on this verse: "Two of the great tools God uses to bring us to this realization are our sufferings and our failures . . . so, let us press on to maturity knowing full well its definition: *more* of Christ and *less* of us."[8]

Therefore, don't despise the tools God uses to make you better. It has been said that He never puts too much of the "salt" of adversity into the recipe of our lives. His blend of adversity and blessing is always exactly right.

Romans 5:3-5 says, "[W]e rejoice in our sufferings, knowing that suffering produces *endurance,* and endurance produces *character,* and character produces *hope,* and hope does not put us to shame, because God's love has been poured into our hearts through the Holy Spirit who has been given to us." Rejoice in our sufferings? Hah. Only a masochist would do that, you might say: "Ouch. That hurts and I love it." That's not what the Bible is talking about in this passage. We rejoice for the *benefit* sufferings bring us—and also because we realize sufferings are the *gift* of God for our lives, whether we understand them or not.

He does not ask us to rejoice because a loved one has been stricken with cancer, because we have lost our job, or because we have constant pain. But we *can* rejoice because He has assured us that He is in control of all our circumstances, and we know they will ultimately work for our good.

"Count it all joy, my brothers, when you meet trials of various kinds, for you know that the *testing of your faith produces steadfastness* [perseverance]. And let steadfastness have its full effect, that you may be *perfect and complete, lacking in nothing*" (James 1:2-4). In other words, we cannot be completely mature without perseverance, and we can't obtain perseverance without facing trials. *That kind of spiritual maturity will get us through every trial, every adversity without despair—knowing that our loving Lord holds us safely in the palm of His hand.*

Think of the hours of training, the conditioning, the investment in time and energy, the struggle of sweat and tears athletes must go through to achieve excellence in their sport. Why do they do it? Because they love it. The end result is worth all the pain involved in getting there. The phrase "no pain, no gain" applies to our spiritual lives as well. If we are to endure to the end, we have to build endurance, and the *only way to build endurance is to endure.*

The Cecropia moth is a good example of how suffering increases growth and maturity. Jerry Bridges tells its story in *Trusting God*:

> One of the many fascinating events in nature is the emergence of the Cecropia moth from its cocoon—an event that occurs only with much struggle on the part of the moth to free itself. The story is frequently told of someone who watched a moth go through this struggle. In an effort to help—and not realizing the necessity of the struggle—the viewer snipped the shell of the cocoon. Soon the moth came out with its wings all crimped and shriveled. But as the person watched, the wings remained weak. The moth, which in a few moments would have stretched those wings to fly, was now doomed to crawling out its brief life in frustration of ever being the beautiful creature God created it to be.
>
> What the person in the story did not realize was that the struggle to emerge from the cocoon was an essential part of developing the muscle system of the moth's body and pushing the body fluids out into the wings to expand them. By unwisely seeking to cut short the moth's struggle, the watcher had actually crippled the moth and doomed its existence.
>
> The adversities of life are much like the cocoon of the

Cecropia moth. God uses them to develop the spiritual "muscle system" of our lives. . . . We can be sure that the development of a beautiful Christlike character will not occur in our lives without adversity.[9]

When my oldest son started walking, I used to take him outside every day to play. At one place where the sidewalk met the grass he would always fall down. I started helping him from one surface to the other so he wouldn't fall. But soon I realized that unless I allowed him to figure this out himself, he would continue to need my help every time. So I stood back and let him fall a few times. The fall into the grass didn't hurt him, and after a couple of falls, he began to adjust to the different surfaces and could easily go from one to the other without my assistance.

What I am saying is that when God takes us through difficulties, He makes us better, stronger, smarter than we would be without them. We should learn to respect our adversities in advance for the good God is bringing through them.

2. TO DRIVE US TO GOD

One of the by-products of adversity is that we sense our utter helplessness and inability to change the events of our lives. We begin to realize that something more powerful than we are controls life's circumstances. For unbelievers, that *thing* in control is chance. Fate. Luck. Their lives are subject to a toss of the dice or the flip of a coin. Unfortunately, some believers who don't understand how God works in their lives may substitute chance for divine providence.

We don't use the term "providence" much today. What does it mean? God's providence is His tireless attendance to our needs. Everything we have comes from Him. He provides for us, cares for us, and lovingly rules over us for His own glory and the good of His people.

Christian believers should not believe that fate, chance, or anything else apart from God controls our lives. We must *know* that God is in control. Often we lose sight of that. It's easy to start believing that *we* are in control, especially when things are going our way. We see *ourselves* as masters of our own fate, so to speak. We can carelessly glide through life that way until when? Until we are brought face to face with a situation *definitely, obviously, and completely* out of our control. "Our tendency to self-sufficiency can only be overcome when our situation is beyond our sufficiency."[10]

It is then that we should fall to our knees in prayer, begging God to help us and to forgive our arrogance. And ironically it is then that we are our strongest, because we acknowledge God as our only true source of strength. And there is *no* strength mightier than God's.

Pastor Doug Reed reiterates this idea in his thesis on spiritual maturity:

> Those, like [the apostle] Paul, who have been through many trials soon begin to realize that tribulation has a much greater purpose than to make us stronger. On the contrary, the Lord at times allows us to be "burdened beyond our strength" that we might find Him as our strength. *Suffering does not make us good. It leads us to the place where we find Christ as our good.* It brings us to the end of ourselves that we might reach the beginning of God. Often, it is in the midst of our greatest weakness that we learn to be strong in the Lord and in our greatest failure that we find the Lord as our good.[11]

Over a hundred years ago, J. C. Ryle wrote in one of his commentaries on the Gospels:

> There is nothing which shows our ignorance so much as our impatience under trouble. We forget that every cross is a message from God, and intended to do us good in the end. *Trials are intended to make us think—to wean us from the world—to send us to the Bible—to drive us to our knees. Health is a good thing but sickness is far better if it leads us to God. Prosperity is a great mercy; but adversity is a greater one if it brings us to Christ.* Anything, anything is better than living in carelessness and dying in sin.[12]

CASE STUDY

Abe Caldwell was a mere shell of the man he once was. As a trainer at the racetrack, he was well known to the fans there. He'd trained a handful of top-quality horses over the years. Many people respected his experience and his heart. But that was before the big stroke he suffered a couple of years ago.

Now he lay comatose in a nursing home. He couldn't move, was badly contracted, and had shrunk to nothing but skin and bones despite a feeding tube. He couldn't speak or acknowledge in any way that he understood what people said to him. The family worked on the assumption that he could understand them—he just couldn't respond.

For the past few days he had seemed to be hovering near death. Most of his friends and family had stopped visiting. His wife was even uncomfortable there now. It hurt too much to see him that way. But they had a young friend, more like a daughter, who came faithfully. Often Ruth would comb his hair, speaking softly to him, telling him all the news from the track. She chattered away until she'd told him everything; then she'd pull the chair up to the bedside and just sit with him, occasionally reaching over to stroke his cheek or kiss his gnarled claw of a hand.

One night we were both there with him. Her eyes hardly left his face as she explained in hushed tones how he and his wife had taken her under their wings early in her life. She was more or less raised in their home. When she was old enough and skilled enough, he paved the way for her to be a "pony-girl," one who escorts racehorses from the paddock to the starting gate. She loved the life. She owed it all to Abe, and she loved him for it.

After a pause in our conversation, she looked at me and quietly asked, "Why is this happening to someone as nice as Abe? Why does he have to suffer like this? Why doesn't God just take him on to be with Him?"

"I don't know, Ruth," I answered. "But I'm absolutely convinced that there are reasons. We're told in the Bible that all the days of our lives are numbered before even one of them comes to be. The bottom line is that he's still here because it's not his time yet."

"Well, for the first time in my life, I've actually been reading my Bible. I've been trying to find something in there that will help me understand why this is happening. I pray all the time that God will just take him. I can't stand to see him like this."

"This is the first time you've prayed or read your Bible?"

"Well, I've prayed before. I was raised Catholic; so I never really had to read the Bible. But I'm certainly getting a lot out of it now. I've never felt closer to God. But I don't understand why He's leaving Abe here like this."

I smiled at her. "Could one of the reasons be that this is what it took to draw you closer to God and to encourage you to start reading His Word and praying? You say you've never felt this close to God before. Could it be that you wouldn't have this new closeness with Him if all this hadn't happened?"

She opened her mouth in shock. "Oh, my! You're probably right. But if that's the case, I'm so sorry Abe had to go through all this for my sake."

"He didn't, Ruth. There are likely many reasons why this is happening. That may just be one of them. You know, God uses whatever He wants to draw His children to Him. Don't waste this experience, Ruth. Even after this is over, I suggest you continue reading and praying. And know that nothing you've ever done or ever will do will make you good enough to go to heaven."

"Then what does?"

"Christ. Just Christ. You have to trust in His righteousness, not your own. If you are one of His children, you will believe He is your Lord, and you'll ask Him to forgive your sins and save you from hell. And He will."

Tears were rolling down her cheeks now. Her bottom lip quivered as she whispered, "I do believe that."

We prayed together, and then I gave her a hug. She smiled. "Even though I still don't know all the answers, I do feel better now. I know that there's a purpose to all of this. It really is all in God's hands, isn't it?"

"Yes, Ruth. It really is."

Abe died early the next morning.

3. TO TEACH US GOD'S LAW

Here is the correct response to affliction: "It is good for me that I was afflicted, that I might learn your statutes. The law of your mouth is better to me than thousands of gold and silver pieces" (Psalm 119:71-72). The writer of this psalm certainly had a love for God's Word, for His commands, decrees, and laws. As much as I love the Word of God, I confess I fall desperately short of this depth of passion. The psalmist is an excellent example for us.

But don't lose sight of the point—that adversity sometimes serves to teach us the decrees of God, our Father. Our circumstances can bring us to a place where we hungrily turn to the Word of God for answers to the questions raised by our sorrow. Since God teaches us through adversity, it is our responsibility to learn from it. How do we do that?

We can submit to God's will. Our submission should not be reluctant—as the defeated general submits to his conqueror. We submit to God's will in the same way a patient on the operating table submits to the surgeon's skilled hands.

We can bring the Word of God to bear on the situation. We must pray that God will reveal passages in the Scriptures to us that will illumine our situation. As the Holy Spirit applies these passages to our hearts, we receive the grace to trust God through any adversity. The Scriptures help us to better understand adversity, and in turn, adversity helps us to better understand the Scriptures.

The Scriptures have an unusual quality about them. I can read and even study a passage of Scripture and gain an understanding of what the passage teaches. As the situations in my life change and my experience expands, I can read that same passage, and it's as though I've never read it before. I suddenly find some truth I've missed. I frequently find myself saying, "How could I have missed that?"

Knowledge of the Scriptures deepens with repetition. In some ways it's a little like my favorite Greek pastry, *baklava*—its delights exist in layers of delicious sweetness. God's Word contains *layers* of understanding. The first time through, you understand the first layer. In subsequent meditations on a passage you discover another layer, then another. No one can say he or she knows everything there is to know about the Bible. If someone says that, don't believe him.

We must remember our adversities in order to profit from the lessons we learn from them. God won't remove the adversity until we have received the intended benefit or developed in the way He had in mind. That's what wisdom is. You take the lessons you've learned from the experiences God has given you and *apply* that knowledge to the next situation. Adversity makes you wiser *only* if you can make that application.

One way to look at this is to think of a doorway with a very low opening. The first time you walk under it, you might bump your head. The next time you'd remember the bump and duck down. People who cannot apply lessons learned simply keep bumping their heads. I hope none of us are like that. Let's pray that God gives us the grace to apply the lessons He's teaching us.

4. TO TEACH US TO TRUST GOD'S PROMISES

You might remember a time when as a child you were standing on the side of a swimming pool or on a dock over the water. Your father was in the water, holding his arms out to you, urging you, "Jump. I'll catch you." You were probably terrified the first time you did it. Would he really catch you? Would you sink to the bottom and drown? Would you get water up your nose? But you finally mustered all the courage your little heart possessed, and you leaped out over the water into the waiting arms of your father.

Mission accomplished. When you got out of the water and back onto the side of the pool, you were less frightened about jumping into your father's expectant arms. You knew he caught you before, and he could do it again. So you jumped again. He caught you again. You shrieked with laughter as you climbed out of the water to do it again and again. Before long, there was no fear at all—only the trust and assurance that your dad would catch you. What once caused fear became an activity more enjoyable than anything else you could imagine.

That's a mere *shadow* of the kind of trust we can have in God, our heavenly Father. The first time we take a leap of faith into His arms, we may be terrified. Will He really be there for us? The next time, you *know* He'll keep you from falling because He did it before, because He says He will, and because He does not lie. After several such leaps you begin to recognize the utter reliability of God. Though adversity makes it necessary for you to jump, your heart can rejoice in the faithfulness and lovingkindness of our Father who is waiting there to catch you. "Cast your burden on the LORD, and *he will sustain you*; he will *never permit the righteous to be moved [fall]*" (Psalm 55:22).

A relationship of trust and faith develops in this way. God tells us in the Scriptures that we can place our trust in Him. He tenderly cares for us. As it is written in Isaiah 40:11, "[God] will tend his flock like a shepherd; he will gather the lambs in his arms; he will carry them in his bosom, and gently lead those that are with young." We are His lambs if we have chosen to follow Christ, the Great Shepherd.

When we're facing death or the death of a loved one, can we still trust in the promises of God? Absolutely. The more hurtful the trial, the *more* we can rely on His faithfulness to us. In *Dying Thoughts*, Richard Baxter, when facing his own impending death, wrote, "Never did God break his promise with me. Never did he fail me, or forsake me. And shall I now distrust him at last?"[13] His answer was that in *everything* we can trust our God.

"It is often in the very midst of our adversities that we experience the most delightful manifestations of His love,"[14] advises Jerry Bridges. One of my dear friends had aortic valve replacement surgery. At one point the doctors didn't hold out much hope for him to live. It was certainly not a pleasant experience for him to be that close to death, but he had told many of his friends and family that he was relying totally on the sovereignty of God for his life. If God chose to take him, he was ready, and if God chose to leave him here with us for a time, he was appreciative of that as well. My friend demonstrated a tender faith and trust in our almighty Father. As it turned out, it pleased God to make the surgery successful.

But along with the discomfort, the suffering, and the apprehension of this experience, my friend experienced firsthand numerous gestures of love and support from his friends, family, our church body, and the pastoral staff. He was amazed by all this attention. He knew he had many, many friends, but it took this experience to demonstrate to him the depth of our caring. In the midst of this adversity he experienced some delightful manifestations of God's love for him.

So, you see, adversity drives us to God and to His Word. And along with the blessing of learning to lean on both comes some surprising bonuses—the strengthening of our faith and the comfort of resting in Him. Consider the words of David in Psalm 145:13b-21:

> *The LORD is faithful in all his words and kind in all his works.*
> *The LORD upholds all who are falling and*
> *raises up all who are bowed down.*
> *The eyes of all look to you, and*
> *you give them their food in due season.*
> *You open your hand;*
> *you satisfy the desire of every living thing.*
> *The LORD is righteous in all his ways and*
> *kind in all his works.*
> *The LORD is near to all who call on him,*
> *to all who call on him in truth.*
> *He fulfills the desire of those who fear him;*
> *he also hears their cry and saves them.*
> *The LORD preserves all who love him,*
> *but all the wicked he will destroy.*
> *My mouth will speak the praise of the LORD,*
> *and let all flesh bless his holy name forever and ever.*

5. TO DEMONSTRATE GOD'S LOVE

Suffering and death occur to demonstrate God's love? It sure doesn't *seem* like it, does it? It *seems* as if God has something against us. But that's not the case at all.

We do not have a God who is subject to the moods that sway our own attitudes and behaviors. He never gets up on the "wrong side of the bed." In James 1:17 NIV, we read, "Every good and perfect gift is from above, coming down from the Father of the heavenly lights, *who does not change like shifting shadows.*" In one of his sermons, Dr. D. A. Carson said, "God does not have bad days. He doesn't get up one morning and say, 'Boy, do I feel grumpy today.' He is *invariably* good and can be nothing *but* good."

Jerry Bridges assures us that "God does not exercise His sovereignty capriciously, but only in such a way as His infinite love deems best for us."[15] God is *faithful* to keep His promises, and He has promised to work everything for our *good* (see Romans 8:28). As we're reminded in Romans 8:29, it is all for the purpose of conforming us to the image of His Son: "For those whom he foreknew he also predestined to be conformed to the image of his Son, in order that he might be the firstborn among many brothers." So even the affliction we encounter is a demonstration of His kindness toward us. The *result* will be for our good. Affliction is the tool He uses to accomplish the result.

We don't have to worry about God changing His mind about us from day to day. His love for us is constant. We may think that when we are "good," He loves us more than when we are "bad." Not so. Our standing with Him is not that precarious. Doug Reed explains:

> We may think our standing with God is based on who we are and what we have done. If this is our opinion, we will feel like our favor with the Lord changes from day to day or even from hour to hour. If we measure up, God will bless us; if we don't, He seems far from us. . . . *Because of Who* [Christ] *is and what He has done, He has become the measure of our favor with God.* . . . Therefore, *God's kindness towards us never changes*, because the power of the blood of the Lamb never changes. *Jesus is the measure of our standing with God when we do well and even when we fail.*[16]

6. TO DISCIPLINE HIS WAYWARD CHILDREN

Another point worth mentioning here is that because He loves us, often He will bring adversity into our lives to discipline us when we are disobedient. This chastening is also intended for our good as it serves to increase our spiritual maturity and to make us who He wants us to be. "My son, *do not despise the LORD's discipline or be weary* of his reproof, for the LORD reproves him whom he loves, as a father the son in whom he delights" (Proverbs 3:11-12).

One of the best-known passages about discipline is found in the book of Hebrews:

> It is for discipline that you have to endure. *God is treating you as sons. For what son is there whom his father does not discipline? If you are left without discipline, in which all have participated, then you are illegitimate children and not sons. Besides this, we have had earthly fathers who disciplined us and we respected them. Shall we not much more be subject to the Father of spirits and live? For they disciplined us for a short time as it seemed best to them,* but he disciplines us for our good, that we may share his holiness. *For the moment* all discipline seems painful rather than pleasant, *but* later it yields the peaceful fruit of righteousness to those who have been trained by it. *(Hebrews 12:7-11)*

We should appreciate discipline for the same reason that we can rejoice in our sufferings—because of its resulting benefit. God's discipline will always be for our good and not a harsh punishment. We can't make that statement for unbelievers. (This idea will be expanded later in this chapter.)

7. TO EQUIP US TO COMFORT OTHERS

So far, as we've covered the purposes of suffering and death, we've examined the benefits they bring to us and the glory they bring to God. But we haven't discussed how they prepare us to benefit others. And that is an important purpose.

God's blessings to us are generous and gracious, so much more than we deserve. But those blessings extend also to those with whom we come in contact. Later in this book, I devote an entire chapter to the subject of the comfort we get from God and from His Word—the Bible.

In this chapter, I'll discuss the comfort we can obtain from others and bestow on others because of the sufferings in our own lives. One of the reasons we go through trials is to equip us to comfort others. We are not given comfort from others so we can merely be *comfortable*. We are given comfort so that we can, in turn, become *comforters*.

Indeed, the Scriptures teach this principle. In 2 Corinthians 1:3-5 Paul wrote, "Blessed be the God and Father of our Lord Jesus Christ, the Father of mercies and *God of all comfort, who comforts us in* all *our affliction, so that we may be able to comfort those who are in any affliction, with the comfort with which we ourselves are comforted by God.* For as we share abundantly in Christ's sufferings, so through Christ we share abundantly in comfort too."

Susan Hunt addresses this verse:

> The God of *all* comfort comforts us in *all* our troubles. Nothing is outside the range of His ability to comfort us. This comfort is so compelling that it not only gives us relief, it also equips us to comfort others. So our pain has a purpose. Without pain we would not experience God's comfort. Without experiencing God's comfort we are not equipped to comfort others. Now of course this makes no sense to the self-centered approach to life which has no concern about comforting others. However, it makes perfect sense to the servant whose life-purpose is God's glory. It makes perfect sense to the follower and imitator of the One who suffered in our place.[17]

I've heard it said, "Don't waste the pain. Use it for good." God does not bless us and intend for the blessing to stop with us. That blessing has the capacity to keep going and going and going. Because He has blessed us with His comfort, we can pass that blessing on to others who can, in turn, pass it on to still others. What a beautiful concept.

I hear people say they don't know what to say to comfort others. I tell them not to worry about it. Sometimes you don't have to say a word. Sometimes all the words in the world don't have the impact that one long, silent hug can have on a person newly grieving—a hug that says, "I'm trying to understand how you feel, and I'm so sorry, and I do so want to help."

Someone sent me a little story over the Internet (author unknown):

Author and lecturer Leo Buscaglia once talked about a contest he was asked to judge. The purpose of the contest was to find the most caring child. The winner was a four-year-old child whose next-door neighbor was an elderly gentleman who had recently lost his wife. Upon seeing the man cry, the little boy went into the old gentleman's yard, climbed onto his lap, and just sat there. When his mother asked him what he had said to the neighbor, the little boy said, "Nothing. I just helped him cry."

There are also words that hurt. In our effort to comfort, sometimes we can come off as being superior or insincere. Sometimes we offer platitudes. Susan Hunt provides this helpful perspective:

As long as my message is, "I did it; you can too," I will be a great discomfort to a hurting person. When I have been under pressure beyond my internal resources to handle and have learned how to rely on God, then I have a message of comfort. . . . Hurting people require an enormous energy just to survive. We can be a further drain on their energies through insensitive remarks or neglect, or we can provide an atmosphere of love that makes it easier for them to experience God's comfort.[18]

Regardless of which *method* we use to comfort others—whether through words or acts or cards—we are told to do so. We are not to hold on to our blessings of comfort. We are to freely give to others what we have received from God. That continuity of comfort makes a big difference to a hurting world.

8. TO PREPARE US FOR COMING GLORY

The Scriptures repeatedly juxtapose suffering and glory. These opposing concepts are yet intricately interwoven. Suffering and glory are so linked that sometimes it's difficult to see one without the other. We must live with eternity's values in view. We're told that a beautiful reward awaits those who remain steadfast under trial—the crown of

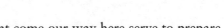

life (James 1:12). The trials that come our way here serve to prepare us for heaven.

In a sermon at the Bible Church of Little Rock in 1999, Dr. D. A. Carson reminded us: "If you look at trial through God's perspective, you can rejoice through your tears because you know God is building perseverance in your life, and you cannot possibly be Christianly mature apart from such perseverance. And in the midst of your tears you can rejoice."

He also said that our ultimate reward is the consummation of our relationship with God in heaven. It is the culmination of our work. We must walk with Christ here, and we'll walk with Him there. We must know God here, and we'll know Him better there. We must work for God here, and we'll work for God better there.

The apostle Paul wrote, "For I consider that the sufferings of this present time are not worth comparing with the glory that is to be revealed to us" (Romans 8:18). None of us has had to suffer to the degree Paul did, and yet he was able to make such a statement. Our sufferings last for such a little while compared to the glories of heaven.

Jesus Christ is the model of suffering followed by glory. He was mocked, beaten, abused, arrested, tried, falsely accused, and crucified. He completed what He was placed here on the earth to do. He came to the earth to live a sinless life, to suffer, die, and rise from the dead, and to ascend to the glory from which He came. In doing all this, He secured the salvation of all of His children.

You see, after His suffering He was glorified, and He will be glorified in a greater way when He comes back to earth as the King of Kings and Lord of Lords. Paul describes our Savior's glorious return: "For the grace of God has appeared, bringing salvation for all people, training us to renounce ungodliness and worldly passions, and to live self-controlled, upright, and godly lives in the present age, waiting for *our blessed hope, the appearing of the glory of our great God and Savior Jesus Christ, who gave himself for us* to redeem us from all lawlessness and to purify for himself a people for his own possession who are zealous for good works" (Titus 2:11-14). Christ Himself spoke of His return in glory in Mark 13:26: "And then they will see the Son of Man coming in clouds with great power and glory."

If *Christ* first suffered and then was glorified, why are we surprised when *we* are called to suffer in preparation for future glory? My pastor, Lance Quinn, once preached, "There *will be* trials, tests, suffering, pain, and persecution in this life. *Through the midst* of that pain, *because* of that pain, *as a learning tool* for us, we will ultimately, *through* that pain, reach *glory*."

When we suffer, we can be encouraged, comforted by the knowledge that through our suffering we are being prepared for ultimate glory with Christ. We do not rejoice in the suffering itself, but in the *result* of the suffering.

Why don't we look at our trials through God's perspective? I believe it's because many times we are so focused on our own suffering that we don't look around the corner at the glory awaiting us. We become so locked in to our own pain that we can't see anything else.

Pastor Quinn made another good point in his sermon. He gave several examples of how glory ultimately followed suffering in the Scriptures. Then he gave examples of how the same pattern occurs in our lives. He continued, "Do we say, 'I want the *suffering* but not the *glory*?' Of course not. But how many of us would say, 'I want the *glory* without the *suffering*?' That's different, isn't it? We *do* want the glory without the suffering."

I've heard Christians—sometimes jokingly and sometimes not—admonish others that they should *never* pray for patience. This quality is not just zapped into our character. Patience is the result of perseverance through trials of many kinds. So they are admonishing others not to pray for patience unless they want to be tested and tried by the fires of adversity.

However, if we are truly serious about developing the spiritual fruit of patience or perseverance, adversity should not be avoided but rather experienced. And we should give thanks for the ultimate outcome—spiritual maturity.

Don't get me wrong. I am not there yet. I personally do not pray that God will send me problems and trials. But I do pray that God will give me the grace to embrace the adversities He brings into my life with my eyes focused on the good it will produce in me and in those around me. I *try* to view the problems as a *gift* presented to me to make me better and stronger and closer to Him. I have fallen short time and again of mastering this quality, but, by God's grace, I *am* moving *closer toward* that goal. Pastor Quinn's conclusion was: "If you are headed for glory, you *will* suffer."

9. TO GIVE US OPPORTUNITIES TO WITNESS

Sometimes we speak more loudly by our actions than by our words. Sometimes we have greater opportunities to show Christ in our lives through adversity than through obvious blessing. The courage and devotion of the men and women of the Bible demonstrate that truth. Even now their attitudes and their responses to hardship and suffering teach us, encourage us, and even inspire us to develop those same qualities.

I once had the blessing of being seated next to Dr. Joseph Tson at an event held in his honor at our church. Dr. Tson is a well-known and beloved man of God who faithfully ministers in Romania. He has lived through persecution and received threats to his life on many occasions. He has had his home invaded and his library destroyed. The Communist party dealt him many blows, but every time he faced them with courage and spoke to them of the blessedness of Christ.

He told us of one time when a Communist soldier held him at gunpoint. He stood up to the soldier and essentially said, "Go ahead and kill me. For the moment you do, my words will take flight and spread to all the world. My tapes and my books will flourish. You will make my words more powerful by killing me than they could ever be if you don't."

As a result, not only was he spared, but a proclamation was issued that under no circumstances was he to be harmed. Suddenly the Communist party began looking out for him and protecting him. They didn't want to create a martyr.

I asked him if he had thought about what he was going to say ahead of time, because I didn't think I could come up with such words if I'd been in that situation. He told me not to worry—that at such a time the Holy Spirit would give me the words and the courage I would need. I am further encouraged by the words of Billy Graham: "He has taken away the fear of death for those who trust in Him. We do not need to be ashamed of our fear, but we can rest assured that He will give us strength when we have none of our own, courage when we are cowardly, and comfort when we are hurting."[19]

The way Dr. Tson handled adversity in his life truly inspired me to want to respond in the same way to hardships. But if he had not undergone such trials, I probably would never have heard of him. His life would not have been such an example to me and to thousands upon thousands of others. His adversity gave him an opportunity to witness for Christ.

The same principle applies to you and me. We have the opportunity, through the way we handle suffering and pain and death, to speak loudly and clearly to those around us. They can sense our devastation and despair, or they can see our quiet, accepting submission to God's will.

Hear the challenging words of the great preacher Charles Spurgeon:

> If Jesus loves you, and you are sick, let all the world see how you glorify God in your sickness. Let friends and nurses see how the beloved of the Lord are cheered and comforted by him. Let your holy resignation astonish them, and set them admiring your Beloved, who is so gracious to you that he makes you happy in pain, and joyful at the gates of the grave. If your religion is worth anything it ought to support you now, and it will compel unbelievers to see that he whom the Lord loveth is in better case when he is sick than the ungodly when full of health and vigour.[20]

The New Testament encourages us to view our own death not with fear but with joy if we are believers in Christ. The apostle Paul says in 2 Corinthians 5:8, "Yes, we are of good courage, and we would rather be away from the body and at home with the Lord." He also wrote, "For to me to live is Christ, and to die is gain. If I am to live in the flesh, that means fruitful labor for me. Yet which I shall choose I cannot tell. I am hard pressed between the two. *My desire is to depart and be with Christ, for that is far better.* But *to remain in the flesh is more necessary on your account"* (Philippians 1:21-24).

Do you think this is an unrealistic attitude? Well, though Paul is exemplary, the attitude he demonstrates here *is* attainable by the grace of God. The more we grow in the understanding of who He is, and the closer our relationship with Him becomes, the more we can embrace these same thoughts. Suffering and adversity teach us God's utter reliability and faithfulness to His promises. When we are that trusting, we can't help but reflect His light to the world around us.

10. TO MAKE US MORE GRATEFUL AND APPRECIATIVE

You've heard the stories again and again. Someone is diagnosed with a terminal disease, and suddenly the person gains a new appreciation for life. Even the little things seem so precious. Priorities change with this new perspective, and the person sees the world around him with new eyes.

In my Bachman story, Bachman was a better person toward the end. He finally learned to stop and smell the roses, to look around at all the beauty in his world. He also learned to really appreciate the people who loved him.

I've seen this scenario so many times. Even the air we breathe seems fresher. Colors are more vibrant. The world is more beautiful. The touch of a hand is dearer, sweeter somehow. People stop taking for granted things scarcely noticed in the past.

One of my ongoing campaigns with my children, my husband, my parents, and my friends has been to encourage them to notice those precious things. Stop and smell the roses now. Don't wait until something tragic occurs before you decide to stop your busyness long enough to notice the beauty and the wonder and the sweetness of the world.

I learned not to take things for granted a long time ago. When I was young, I overheard someone crying at a funeral, "Oh, if only he knew how much he meant to me. There are so many things I wish I had told him." That statement shook me. I decided I would *never* have the need to say that. The people I love would *know* how much they mean to me *all* the time, not just on their deathbed.

That's one reason I encourage the family members I work with to talk to their loved ones who are dying. I tell them to say the things they want their loved ones to know while they can still understand and respond. I am giving you the same advice. Tell them you love them and tell them good-bye before it's too late. My grandmother used to say, "Don't send me flowers after I'm gone. Send them to me now so I can enjoy them." And I did.

If there was no suffering, how would we even recognize the good times, the blessed times, when we are so completely happy? If we didn't feel bad every now and then, why would we ever thank God for the times when we are pain-free and feeling great? We would just take the good times for granted, wouldn't we? Suffering gives us the contrast we need to become grateful for what we have.

11. TO WEAN US FROM THIS WORLD

Would you like to live your life completely free from pain, problems, suffering, and death? Of course. Well, guess what. Those of us who have a faith relationship with Christ will get to live that existence—it's called *heaven*. Ask yourself a question: If you *were* living in a pain-free, problem-free, suffering-free world, how anxious would you be for heaven? Therefore, one of the purposes of suffering and death is to make us long for heaven. If we were always youthful, slim, great-looking, healthy, wealthy, and wise, how much would we actually look forward to God taking us home?

Yet for the Christian, the more spiritually mature we become, the more beautiful heaven is to us. Those who know God the best are those who long to be with Him the most. The apostle Paul speaks of our heavenly dwelling with longing and eager anticipation: "For we know that if the tent, which is our earthly home, is destroyed, we have a building from God, a house not made with hands, eternal in the heavens. For in this tent we groan, *longing to put on our heavenly dwelling*" (2 Corinthians 5:1-2).

I confess that I cannot say I *long* to be clothed with my heavenly dwelling. I do not pray, "Lord, take me now." However, if He does, I'm ready to go. But I also will tell you that the more I find out about that incredible and amazing place, the *more* I *want* to be there. As with so many other things, it's something I'm working toward. I've known many, though, who *have* reached that place in their lives. And what has impelled them to that place? The burdens of this world.

Suffering takes many forms. For some, the ultimate suffering is physical. For others, the ultimate suffering is emotional, and for a few, the ultimate suffering is spiritual, continuing to live in this sinful body apart from the God who saved them. Whatever your idea of suffering may be, it is often that very suffering that may bring you to the place in your life where you can say, "Take me, Lord. I long to be with You at last."

12. TO CREATE ULTIMATE GLORY AND REWARD IN THE LIFE TO COME

Significant rewards await us in heaven. Our rewards are things we want to think about and to anticipate if we are heirs with Christ. We wouldn't have been told about them if that were not so. No, I don't think rewards should be our *primary* motivation for obedience or our *total* focus in desiring heaven. If that were the case, we'd be looking toward heaven to fulfill *ourselves*, for our own selfish gain. No, that won't happen. Greed does not exist in heaven. However, it might heighten our desire for heaven if we understood more about the rewards awaiting us there. Here are just a few:

> He who overcomes [those who have been saved by faith in Christ alone] will inherit all this, and I will be his God and he will be my son. (Revelation 21:7 NIV)

We won't be servants in heaven, although if that were all we were, it would still be much more than we deserve. Actually, we will be *heirs* of the kingdom—"heirs of God and fellow heirs with Christ" (Romans 8:17). John MacArthur wrote, "heaven will be our home, and we will dwell there not as mere guests, but with all the privileges of family members—children of the master of the house."[21]

Henceforth there is laid up for me [Paul] the crown of righteous-ness, which the Lord, the righteous judge, will award to me on that Day, and not only to me but also to all who have loved his appear-ing. (2 Timothy 4:8)

Blessed is the man who remains steadfast under trial, for when he has stood the test he will receive the crown of life, *which God has promised to those who love him. (James 1:12)*

And when the chief Shepherd [Christ] appears, you will receive the unfading crown of glory. *(1 Peter 5:4)*

Rejoice and be glad, for your reward is great in heaven. *(Matthew 5:12)*

To the one who conquers [overcomes] I will grant to eat of the tree of life, *which is in the paradise of God [in heaven].* *(Revelation 2:7b)*

To the one who conquers, I will grant him to sit with me on my throne, *as I also conquered and sat down with my Father on his throne. (Revelation 3:21)*

There are many more rewards awaiting us in heaven, but we will explore this topic further in a later chapter. Be assured that the suffer-ings we undergo here on earth, if we are believers in Christ, will not be for nothing. They are not only for our good while here on earth, but God will also work them for our good through an eternity in heaven.

13. TO LOOSEN OUR GRIP ON THE PEOPLE AND EARTHLY THINGS WE LOVE

One of the observations I've made as a hospice nurse is that early in a person's illness, the focus of the patient, as well as that of the family, is on making the person well. When it becomes apparent that the patient is not going to get well and is admitted to the hospice program, the patient and their families begin the process of letting go.

Many people confuse letting go with "giving up," which is a different thing altogether. The change in the family's mind-set is gradual and subtle. The goal changes from making the patient well, an unrealistic and unattainable goal, to keeping the patient comfortable, both realistic and attainable.

I have come to believe that another change also takes place. As the disease progresses and the family witnesses the loved one becoming more and more distant, they discover that it gradually becomes easier to let go.

One of the purposes of the suffering of others is for our benefit.
It enables us to finally let go.

Eventually we get to a point where we can honestly say that we would rather our loved one pass away than to stay in his or her present state.

Perhaps the patient is in a vegetative state and has been that way for days, weeks, or even months. Perhaps the dying person has to take larger and larger doses of narcotics to manage the pain. Perhaps the patient's breathing is such a struggle that the family is finally ready for the battle to end. Whatever the situation, witnessing the suffering of those who have no hope of improvement makes us wrestle with our affections until we start to truly seek what would be best for the patients. Saying good-bye is always difficult, but it becomes more doable after we've watched them drift further and further away from us.

Their suffering becomes a blessing to us when we are finally able to entrust them over to death. It helps when the family knows that their loved ones are going to a better place, one where they will never suffer again. But, sadly, many do not have that eternal hope.

Suffering—the gift of God. Who would have thought it?

14. TO REVEAL SIN IN US

In an earlier chapter I quoted David in Psalm 139 saying, "Search me, O God, and know my heart! Try me and know my thoughts! And see if there be any grievous way in me, and lead me in the way everlasting!" He needed God to show him his sin so that he might repent of it. One of the ways God reveals sin in us is by sending us through trials and suffering.

How we go through adversity says a lot about our inner character. Do we fret and wring our hands as if there were no God at all? Do we get angry and throw things and lash out at everyone around us? Do we feel sorry for ourselves to the point of despair and hopelessness? Do we blame God and accuse Him of not loving us? These are all symptoms of sinful thinking. These symptoms can help identify what's wrong with us so we can repent and obtain God's help to change.

Notice I'm wording this as if I were talking about a physical ailment because that's exactly the way it works. If I were to tell a doctor I had a runny nose, watery eyes, a nonproductive cough, sneezing, and had been outside rolling in the grass with my kids earlier, she might say I was suffering from allergies. She would tell me to take an antihistamine. But the most effective way of staying healthy would be to stop rolling in the grass—remove the irritant to my system.

The same process works with sin. The way we act, or *react*, the way we think, the expressions on our face, the words we say, our tone of voice—all of these can point to a "diagnosis" of sorts. The sin diagnosis might be faithlessness, selfishness, pride, pettiness, arrogance, laziness, jealousy, or many, many other sins. The best way to "fix it" is to repent, to turn away from such sin, and to remove the irritating trigger mechanism for our sinful thinking. *Stay away from things that tempt you to sin.* That sounds easy enough, but often it is surprisingly difficult. However, we are commanded to overcome sin, and we can only do that with the help of Christ, the sinless One, who lives in us. We can work *toward* the goal of being sin-free, although we will never *achieve* that particular goal this side of heaven. The blessing is in the progressive holiness we experience.

God blesses us by revealing sin in us. Many times we are suffering under the burden of sin without even realizing it. It is easy to overlook our own faults, weaknesses, and sins. If we are to clean up our lives (and/or our thinking), we *need* our sins exposed. Then we can deal with them with the Holy Spirit's enablement and move on toward greater maturity. Other times we may not see ourselves clearly enough, or—even seeing ourselves clearly—we may be unable to deal with the sin ourselves. That's when it's time to "call the doctor."

Bible-based spiritual counseling is important. Go to someone you view as a man or woman of God, whether in a position of leadership in a church or simply someone spiritually mature. Be honest with the person. Then *listen* and weigh what he or she tells you. Don't be afraid to ask where the advice can be found in the Scriptures. If it doesn't come from God, it can be dangerous, or at best unreliable. Pray that God will give you the grace, strength, and wisdom to fight the sin you're facing and to truly repent or *turn away* from it. True repentance brings real change in your thoughts and actions. But realize that though it is your responsibility to repent, it is God who grants such repentance. "And the Lord's servant must not be quarrelsome but kind to everyone, able to teach, patiently enduring evil, correcting his opponents with gentleness. *God may perhaps grant them repentance* leading to a knowledge of the truth" (2 Timothy 2:24-25).

Just as physical signs and symptoms can point to a diagnosis and cure, so also spiritual signs and symptoms brought on by suffering and adversity can point to a diagnosis of sin that can be addressed and alleviated through the Word of God.

15. TO PUNISH THE WICKED

I have saved this purpose for suffering and death until the last for a reason. All the other reasons relate primarily to *believers* (though some can also be a blessing to unbelievers). Jerry Bridges wrote in *Trusting God*, "But this which should distinguish the suffering of believers from unbelievers is the confidence that *our* suffering is under the control of an all-powerful and all-loving God; *our* suffering has meaning and purpose in God's eternal plan, and He brings or allows to come into our lives *only* that which is *for His glory and our good.*"[22]

However, God is a God of wrath for those who do not believe in His Son. John MacArthur writes, "God's wrath is almost entirely missing from modern presentations of the gospel. It is not fashionable to speak of God's wrath against sin or to tell people they should fear God."[23] It's just not *nice*. Well, guess what. Sometimes you need to talk about things that are not *nice* for the sake of those who need to hear it.

We are all eternal creatures. After suffering a physical death here on earth, each of us will enter into an eternal existence on the other side of death. Some will immediately be in the presence of God in a blissful state that will last forever. Others will immediately be separated from God and will live forever in torment and darkness. There is One who stands as a dividing instrument for each life—Jesus Christ. How each of us responds to Him in this life determines where we'll spend the next.

> . . . inflicting vengeance on those who do not know God and on those who do not obey the gospel of our Lord Jesus. They will suffer the punishment of eternal destruction, away from the presence of the Lord and from the glory of his might. (2 Thessalonians 1:8-9)

> *Now I want to remind you, although you once fully knew it, that Jesus, who saved a people out of the land of Egypt, afterward* destroyed those who did not believe. . . . *just as Sodom and Gomorrah and the surrounding cities, which likewise indulged in sexual immorality and pursued unnatural desire, serve as an example* by undergoing a punishment of eternal fire. *(Jude 5, 7)*

This is the ultimate punishment of hell. Even in *this life*, though, God may use suffering to punish disobedience and wickedness. Here are a few examples:

"Some sat in darkness and in the shadow of death, prisoners in affliction and in irons, for they had rebelled against the words of God, and spurned the counsel of the Most High. So he *bowed their hearts down with hard labor*; they fell down, with none to help" (Psalm 107:10-12). There is a happy ending though because in the next two verses it says, "Then they cried to the LORD in their trouble, and he delivered them from their distress. He brought them out of darkness and the shadow of death, and burst their bonds apart."

In the book of Daniel, we are told that King Nebuchadnezzar ruled over Babylon. Daniel 4:29-32 recounts the story of his punishment by God:

> *At the end of twelve months he was walking on the roof of the royal palace of Babylon, and the king answered and said, "Is not this great Babylon, which I have built by my mighty power as a royal residence and for the glory of my majesty?" While the words were still in the king's mouth, there fell a voice from heaven, "O King Nebuchadnezzar, to you it is spoken: The kingdom has departed from you, and you shall be driven from among men, and your dwelling shall be with the beasts of the field. And you shall be made to eat grass like an ox, and seven periods of time [seven years] shall pass over you, until you know that the Most High rules the kingdom of men and gives it to whom he will."*

God punished the king because he was taking all the credit and glorifying himself instead of God. You might find it interesting that the result of this punishment was that after seven years of grazing in the fields with the cattle like a madman, the king lifted his eyes heavenward in repentance, and his sanity was restored. Then he praised God and honored and glorified Him, and his kingdom was given back to him. The moral? King Nebuchadnezzar says it himself in verse 37: "Now I, Nebuchadnezzar, praise and extol and honor the King of heaven, for all his works are right and his ways are just; and *those who walk in pride he is able to humble.*" I'll say.

There are many, many other examples we could examine, but I think you get the point. God punishes the wicked in this life, and without repentance they are ultimately doomed to a Christless eternity. Christians, however, need not dread that judgment. "There is therefore now *no condemnation for those who are in Christ Jesus*" (Romans 8:1).

What Is the Bottom Line?

Don't think God is oblivious to our tears and pain. Charles Spurgeon once wrote, "When a tear is wept by you, think not your Father does not behold, for, 'Like as a father pitieth his children, so the Lord pitieth them that fear him.' Your sigh is able to move the heart of Jehovah, your whisper can incline His ear to you, your prayer can stay His hands, your faith can move His arm. Oh, think not that God sits on high in an eternal slumber, taking no account of you."[24]

The bottom line is that regardless of the specific reason for suffering and death in our lives, God is the author and designer of all things that happen to us. God's overarching purpose for all believers is to conform us to the likeness of His Son, Jesus Christ. He also has a unique, tailor-made plan for our individual lives that serves a specific purpose.

The truth of the matter is that suffering and death are powerful tools at His disposal. However, Christians can rest assured that He wields the tools carefully, precisely, lovingly, and always for our good and for His glory.

The Lord will fulfill his purpose for me; your steadfast love, O Lord, endures forever. Do not forsake the work of your hands.

PSALM 138:8

PREPARING FOR APPROACHING DEATH

It is important that when we come to die we have nothing to do but to die.

DR. CHARLES HODGE

WHAT SHOULD WE EXPECT?

"He's just not acting right."

Paula looked into Penny's troubled eyes, waiting for her to continue.

"He won't even *try* to eat anymore. And he's sleeping almost all the time. Even when he's awake, I don't think he's always aware that I'm in the room with him." Penny leaned closer to Paula and whispered, "Sometimes he talks out of his head, and I don't know what to say when he's like that. It's like my husband has vanished, and I don't even know this man."

"I'm so sorry, Penny." Paula placed her hand over Penny's. "These are all things we can expect from here on, and it will more than likely keep getting worse."

"But he's got to eat something, doesn't he? I tried to make him eat a bowl of chicken noodle soup yesterday. He clamped his mouth shut and wouldn't even take a bite. Then he knocked the bowl out of my hand. That's just not Bach."

"When people are dying, they sometimes go through some pretty dramatic changes in their personalities, Penny. The thing for you to remember is that this is not something Bach can control. At this point, he may not even know what he's doing. We really can't hold him responsible for anything he may say or do from now on. You know, when a person has cancer, it seems like you say good-bye to them in stages. What you're feeling now is grief because whether you realize it or not, you've already said good-bye to the Bach you've always known."

Penny reached for a tissue and held it over her eyes with clenched fists. Paula gave her time to cry. When Penny took the tissue away, she sat straight up in her chair and took a deep breath. "You're right. In a way he's already gone. Tell me what I should do now."

"First of all, he's not gone completely. There will probably be times when you can see glimpses of the old Bach. My advice to you is to just hold on to those times and enjoy them. They won't last long. Let's go over the literature I gave you when I admitted him to hospice. We looked at it briefly then, but it's time now to review it thoroughly. It describes what we can expect from here on, and I firmly believe that the more you understand, the better you'll be able to handle it."

Wordlessly, Penny got up from the kitchen table and opened a drawer in the china cabinet. She removed a folder, leafed through it quickly, and brought it back to the table. Paula meanwhile had retrieved the coffeepot and poured them both another cup.

"You can do this, Penny. We'll go over the changes, and I'll teach you what to do in each case. You're not going through this alone."

Penny nodded and smiled slightly as she dabbed at her eyes. Then she turned her full attention to Paula so she could learn how best to help her husband as he looked into the face of death.

Once I heard a tape by Alistair Begg on the topic of death and dying. He made a statement that really stuck in my mind: "In the home or in the hospital, painfully or peacefully, quickly or slowly, by disease or by violence, with or without warning, one day somebody, some-where will pronounce me dead." Unless Christ comes first, that will be true for each and every one of us.

Death is inevitable. There is nothing we can do about it. "[F]or death is the destiny of every man; the living should take this to heart"

(Ecclesiastes 7:2 NIV). "Nothing is more certain about life than the fact of death. It may be long-delayed, but it will surely come."[1]

Since this is the case, it is imperative that we prepare for this inevitability. "It has been said that someone found St. Francis working in his garden and asked him, 'What would you do if you knew that you would die in ten minutes?' St. Francis replied, 'I'd try to finish this row.'"[2] Now *that's* being prepared, isn't it? Let's look at several ways to prepare.

• There is a physical element. It will help us to understand the changes that take place in the body before death occurs. We learn what to do in response to these changes.

• There is also a legal element. It is important that we make our last wishes known before we die. Usually this is done in the form of estate planning, the writing of a will, and/or the signing of a living will, if that is your choice. It's also helpful to let our families know if we wish to become organ donors and put those wishes in writing. It would be wise to sign advanced directives regarding the use of heroics at the end of life. A DNR (Do Not Resuscitate) order takes the burden off your family by stating your own desires in this regard—to allow nature to take its course by refusing the use of heroic measures (ventilator support, CPR, dialysis, etc.).

• Lastly, there is a spiritual element to our preparedness. This is, by far, the *most* important aspect.

In this chapter, we'll begin by discussing the physical aspects. These are the things Paula taught Penny that day, sitting at the kitchen table, to prepare her to deal with the progression of Bachman's illness—and ultimately his death.

WHAT TO EXPECT

There are four things my patients seem to fear most about dying. They fear pain. They fear the progression of their deterioration and disability, and they fear the loss of control over personal decisions. But what they fear most is the act of dying. Most patients tell me that they are not afraid of death itself. I reassure them that I will do all I can to prevent suffering or discomfort at the end. That seems to alleviate some of their apprehension. To the families, however, I explain things in greater detail, for they will be witnessing the events.

Early Physical Signs and Symptoms (within days or weeks of dying)

Not all these symptoms will occur with every person; nor will they always occur in this particular sequence. But it has been my experience that most people exhibit some of these symptoms. So, for the purposes of the book, I will deal with them as generalities.

SLEEPING

One of the most common changes in the course of nearly every terminal illness is that the patient will start *sleeping more* and *eating less*. This is one of the earliest signals the body gives that the end is near, usually taking place from a couple of days to a month before death. The reason for this dramatic change is usually an alteration in body chemistry. It causes periods of sleep to increase until the patient actually spends more time asleep than awake.

He may be uncommunicative or unresponsive, and at times difficult to arouse. My recommendation: Let him sleep. Sounds simple, doesn't it? However, you'd be amazed at the number of family members I've seen trying to stimulate their loved one in order to keep him awake—sometimes even shaking or yelling at him. Many times they do this in the misguided belief that if they keep him alert, the patient will get better. That's simply not true for someone in the dying process. Instead, just try sitting with him, holding his hand. Don't talk about him in his presence as if he's not there. Many times the patient will not have the energy to open his eyes. He may be listening to everything and responding to nothing. So be careful and be sensitive about your conversations in his presence. When you speak to him, talk to him directly as you normally would, even though there may be no response. The sense of hearing is the last sense we lose.

"Some talk as if a comatose patient were already dead in their presence. One nurse told how she talked quietly and encouragingly to her patient all the time she was caring for his needs, even though the doctors said he didn't know anything that was happening. He miraculously came out of his coma and upon hearing the voice of this nurse said, 'Oh, you're the one who talked to me.'"[3] Therefore, don't say anything that you don't want the dying person to hear. Always assume he can hear you and alert all visitors to that fact.

FOOD AND FLUID DECREASE

There is much misunderstanding about this symptom, even on the part of medical personnel who do not routinely deal with dying people. As the patient progresses toward death, the organ systems gradually shut down. One of the first seems to be the digestive system. The person may want little or no food or fluid. The body will naturally begin to conserve energy. Once the digestive system starts shutting down, it will no longer be able to digest food effectively. If the patient does eat, a number of gastro-intestinal problems can occur as a result: bloating, cramping, vomiting, indigestion, excessive gas production, diarrhea, or constipation (depending on the individual). Do not try to force food or fluids into the person or use guilt to manipulate her into eating or drinking. This only makes her more uncomfortable. Most family members have the notion that if the patient would only start eating again, she would get better. Not true. In fact, it could be a cruelty to force food into a gut that has stopped working properly. Instead, you might try offering food but honor the patient's wishes about whether to eat it. If she is able to swallow, fluids may be given in small amounts. Most patients can tolerate soft, cool foods better than hot, spicy, or solid foods. For instance, you might try pudding, Popsicles, mashed potatoes, applesauce, gelatin, or ice cream. Small chips of ice, frozen Gatorade, or juice may be refreshing in the person's mouth.

CASE STUDY

I sat at the kitchen table facing six family members gathered to discuss hospice for the husband and father who was dying. The youngest daughter, Mary, sat glowering at me while I was talking about the cruelty of force-feeding a patient who had stopped eating. I could sense her smoldering anger although she had not said a word.

Suddenly she stood up, scooting her chair behind her with a loud scrape. "You mean you want us to sit by and watch him starve to death?" she asked incredulously.

I looked her right in the eyes with as much calm and compassion as I could muster and said firmly, "Yes, if it comes to that."

She stood looking at me for a moment longer, then burst into tears, and ran toward the back of the house. "Let me explain," I said to the rest of the family. "It probably will not come to that. It takes a long time for someone to starve to death. Actually I've seen people live for over a month without a bite of food. Although, without water, it's usually more like a week to ten days."

I looked at each of them before I continued. I explained about the digestive system shutting down and what was happening inside his body. "He most likely will not die of starvation. I really don't think he'll be with us long enough for that. But we have to think about what is most comfortable for him right now, and forcing food down him would not be."

Mary came back into the room. She had been listening from the hallway. Taking her seat again, she said, "But won't it be uncomfortable for him to be so hungry?"

"No," I answered as gently as I could. "He's not experiencing hunger like you or I would. Mary, I'm not saying to withhold food from a man who is starving for it. I'm saying, go ahead and prepare him something, offer it to him, encourage him if you want, but don't force him to eat if he doesn't want to. You know, sometimes it makes us feel better when we can get him to eat. We think he'll get better if only he would eat something, but that's just not true. Even if it makes us feel better, it makes him feel worse."

We discussed the subject for a few more minutes. Then Mary said, "I'm sorry. I'm just so worried about him. I'm not ready to let go of him yet. But what you're saying makes sense. I didn't realize all that before."

This family became like my own during the weeks before Mr. Scott *died. Mary and I were advocates together for her father. She took the lead in taking care of him and was invaluable to me. Mrs. Scott and I became close friends and still write and visit to this day. They did beautifully through the whole experience. Like most families in crisis, they just needed a little guidance and encouragement. Their love and support for each other and for the Lord saw them through their painful loss. It was an honor to get to know and love them.*

Many of you will have to deal with the question of artificial hydration and nutrition for the terminally ill. I hope what I say here will help you make this difficult and sometimes controversial decision. As the person begins to die, the need for food and fluid decreases. There is evidence that a person's body knows when nutrition is no longer needed.

Many people, including medical personnel, worry about dehydration. They push for IV hydration or tube feeding. This may sound harsh, but dehydration is a dying person's friend. It is one of the most peaceful ways to exit this world. Many times in the hospital, IV hydration is begun, but that can create fluid overload and bloating, adding to the patient's discomfort. If the circulatory system is compromised, it may not be able to handle additional fluids. In most cases, the extra fluid goes to the lungs, and what follows is an unpleasant "respiratory" death. The patient sounds as if he is drowning in the fluid filling his lungs. In contrast, when a person dies in a state of dehydration, he just becomes weaker and weaker until he goes to sleep and peacefully drifts away. Of the two deaths, I'd prefer the latter. Wouldn't you?

This statement from a hospice brochure is helpful:

There is widespread agreement, including opinions of the American Medical Association, the American Nurses' Association and the National Hospice Organization, that nutrition and hydration may be withdrawn or withheld when it is futile, when it provides no benefit to the patient, or when its benefits are out-weighed by its burden (such as prolonged suffering or loss of dignity). When the person will die no matter what is done, further hydration may well increase the suffering and provide no benefit. When a person is permanently unconscious there can be no benefit from hydration or nutritional support. . . . The hospice concept promotes patient comfort without the prolongation of life. Consistent with that philosophy the Arkansas State Hospice Association Ethics Committee opposes the use of hydration or nutrition for the sole purpose of extending life.[4]

Whenever possible, it is a great comfort and benefit to know what the patient wants to do about these life-prolonging options before the time comes to make these difficult decisions. When families have to make such decisions without knowing the patient's preference, they sometimes substitute quantity of life for quality of life.

DISORIENTATION

The patient may become confused about time and place and the identities of people, including those close and familiar. This confusion can be due in part to metabolic changes. Identify yourself by name before you speak rather than expecting the patient to guess who you are. Speak softly, clearly, and truthfully. Try not to let the patient's memory lapses hurt your feelings.

INCONTINENCE

Don't be surprised if your loved one begins to have "accidents." Try to take it in stride, and do what you can to preserve the patient's dignity as you assist in cleaning her up. Make sure her private parts are covered whenever possible, asking other people to leave the room while you're working with her and never, never shaming her. Try not to make faces showing revulsion. (If the smell bothers you, here's a trick I use. Open an alcohol swab and wipe it under your nose. All you'll be able to smell for a few minutes will be the alcohol.) Many times the patient is already unresponsive at this time or incapable of understanding what she has done. But if she is aware that she has made a mess, it will cause her pain and grief and be a tremendous blow to her already-suffering ego. Your hospice nurse can offer helpful suggestions for protecting the bed and for keeping your loved one clean and comfortable. When appropriate, a catheter may be used to enhance her comfort and care.

RESTLESSNESS

The patient may make restless and repetitive motions such as pulling or picking at linen or clothing. Restlessness can be caused by decreased oxygenation, pain, metabolic changes, or as a side effect of certain medications. Try repositioning the person first. If that doesn't help, offer a medication for pain or anxiety. If he is not already on oxygen therapy, you might try adding it. That may resolve the restlessness. However, if the behavior continues, it may be due to just . . . restlessness!

People may become restless when they've been in the same position too long or if they're becoming bored with their surroundings. Regardless of the cause, don't interfere or try to restrict their movements unless they are likely to hurt themselves. Some interventions we use to calm restless patients are decreasing external stimuli (TV, loud conversations, babies crying, bright lights, visitors, etc.); speaking in quiet, calm, soothing tones; stroking the hair; massaging them lightly; reading to them; or playing or singing soothing music.

One effective tool we use for restlessness, especially with women, is to provide them with a baby doll. I've seen them calm down instantly upon holding their "baby." Something about that experience somehow gets through the fog of confusion or medication, perhaps awakening a long-lost memory of a time when life was more pleasant. This doesn't work every time, but if your loved one can't seem to get settled, it's worth a try. Pet therapy or offering a stuffed animal may also help.

URINE DECREASE

The volume of urine output will normally decrease and may become dark in color—referred to as "concentrated" urine. This is due to a decrease in fluid intake and a decrease in circulation through the kidneys. If possible, increase the patient's oral fluid intake. Consult your hospice nurse to determine whether she needs to insert a catheter.

Early Emotional Signs and Symptoms
(within days or weeks of dying)

WITHDRAWAL

She may seem gradually less responsive, more withdrawn, or in a comatose-like state. This is part of the process of letting go of this world and preparing to go to the next.

RESTLESSNESS

The person may perform repetitive, agitated, or restless tasks. I've seen patients go through the motions of sewing, driving a big rig, folding, or exhibiting "picking" behaviors. Physical indications of restlessness were covered in the last section, but sometimes the cause for such behaviors can be emotional. As patients get closer to death, they begin the process of letting go. If they have unresolved issues, they may be restless until they find resolution. For instance, many times a patient will feel the need to see a family member with whom there may be some unresolved conflict. Once that family member visits and assures the patient of his or her love, the patient can relax and find the peace to truly let go. Of course, all of this is in harmony with God's timing. Patients will not die one moment before or after they're supposed to.

DECREASED SOCIALIZATION

Don't be surprised if the number of visitors diminishes. Early in the illness, the patients' energy level permits them to visit with a lot of people. But as the illness progresses, they just don't have the strength. They conserve their energy for a gradually narrowing group. Sometimes they want only one person at their side. Sometimes they withdraw from everyone. If you are part of the final circle of support, the patient will need your assurance, love, and encouragement. If you

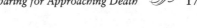

are not, it does not mean you are not loved or are unimportant to the patient. It just means you have already fulfilled your task. It may be time for you to say good-bye.

Signs and Symptoms of Imminent Death (within days or hours)

After witnessing so many deaths, hospice nurses can identify certain signs and symptoms that occur close to the time of death. With the start of these signs, we begin to prepare the family for what is to come. At this time many hospices will change the status of care for the patient to "Watch" or to "Continuous Care."

A Watch status alerts everyone that death is imminent but still some days or hours away. At this level of care, we call to check on the patient every two to four hours. We are waiting for other signs to occur before moving the patient to a Continuous Care status. Some hospices don't utilize this Watch status.

Many times the family is perfectly capable and willing to handle the last hours leading up to death on their own—especially if they have been previously taught what to expect and how to respond. They may not want the intrusion of hospice personnel. In those cases, we wait for a call from the family to notify us of the death, and it is at that point that we go to the home to help with the details.

To those families who would feel more comfortable with hospice support on hand during those last hours, we offer Continuous Care. That status is usually called when we suspect the death is actually very close—within hours. Continuous Care means that hospice personnel will monitor the patient continuously, twenty-four hours a day until the patient either improves or dies. Different hospice organizations may have differing criteria for when to change the status to Continuous Care. In my experience, it is done when the patient begins to show some of the later signs of the dying process.

Below are some of the signs we look for. I usually teach these signs to the families I work with. This instruction enables them to understand what is happening with their loved one and gives them a greater sense of control. They can determine for themselves how far the patient has progressed in the process of dying without having to rely on a nurse to confirm it. If they know what to expect, they will be able to handle these things with more composure.

CHANGE IN PATTERN OF BREATHING

When I am sitting with a patient, I more or less "lock in" on the normal breathing pattern of that patient. I may be doing other things, such as talking to the family, reading my Bible, doing paperwork, or studying, but the entire time I'm *fixed* on the person's breathing. When I detect a change in the pattern, it definitely gets my attention. Elevating the head of the bed can greatly help the patient to breathe. Hold her hand. Speak to her gently. Sometimes giving an anti-anxiety medication can help her respiratory effort. When she relaxes, she can pull more air into her lungs with less effort.

A word of caution: Many times I have instructed a caregiver (over the telephone) to make sure the patient's head is elevated. Upon my arrival, I often find the patient lying completely flat with her head cranked up at a ninety-degree angle to her body! Instead of enhancing her breathing effort, that position can actually cut off her airway. The goal is to elevate the entire torso and maintain its proper alignment—a straight line from head to hips.

If she is in a hospital bed, position her toward the head of the bed until her bottom rests at the bend of the bed. That way, when the head of the bed is raised, the patient's airway is intact as her whole chest and head are elevated.

If she is in a regular bed, raise her to a sitting position and place pillows from her back to the head of the bed so that when you lower her to the pillows, her upper body is in good alignment and elevated.

The use of oxygen may also be helpful at this time. Oxygen is considered more of a comfort measure than a life-prolonging therapy. Oxygen will not *make* patients breathe. It just gives them more oxygen with every breath they do take. And to clear up another misconception—some people think a patient must breathe through his nose to get the oxygen. Not true. Even if the patient is breathing through his mouth, and the oxygen is going into his nose, he is still getting oxygen. The tubing forces oxygen to accumulate in the back of the throat. When a patient pulls air through the mouth into the lungs, it takes that oxygen with it.

You may notice three specific types of breathing patterns with your loved one:

- *Apnea* is characterized by pauses in the patient's breathing. It literally means "without breathing." People who snore sometimes experience this cessation of breathing. So do people in the process of dying. The part of the brain that controls breathing becomes compromised by the metabolic changes occurring inside the body. Such changes cause occasional interruptions in the normal breathing pattern. These interruptions may last only a few seconds at first and happen only occasionally. However, during the dying process, the interruptions occur more frequently and increase in duration as well—sometimes lasting twenty to sixty seconds.

- *Cheyne-Stokes Breathing* is an irregular pattern. The patient may be panting at forty-eight to sixty breaths per minute, then experience apnea, followed by two or three long, slow, deep breaths. Then the pattern may repeat itself.

- *Agonal Breathing* is usually the last pattern. "Agonal" is merely a descriptive term for this particular pattern, referring to the struggle that may precede death. It does not mean the patient is in agony; in fact, she is typically comatose by this time. Medical professionals sometimes refer to this as "fish breathing" because that is what it resembles. The patient opens her mouth when she inhales and closes it when she exhales. Usually the respiratory rate slows to fewer than ten breaths per minute, and each breath requires more physical effort. Eventually, she merely goes through the motions of taking a breath. Very little air exchange is actually occurring. This may go on for an hour or so, but normally when she is no longer able to move air in and out of her lungs, she will die within a few minutes. When I notice a patient lapse into agonal breathing, I call the family to the bedside.

MOTTLING AND INCREASED COLDNESS OF THE EXTREMITIES

This symptom occurs as the body compensates. In order to distribute more blood to the vital organs (kidneys, liver, heart, brain, lungs, etc.), the body restricts blood flow to the extremities (arms, nose, and legs). As a result, those areas begin to cool. With such cooling, they may become discolored. Mottling is a splotchy or speckled discoloration of the skin, usually purple or blue. It generally starts in the toes and works its way up the legs. However, some never show this mottling at all.

INCREASED CONGESTION

Some people begin to have an accumulation of fluid in the lungs. They may lose the ability to swallow their own saliva. Whatever the reason, many make a "gurgling" sound with every breath they take. It sounds like they are breathing through water, and in essence they are. The sound indicates the passage of air through fluid. In most cases, the patient is not conscious by the time this occurs; so I believe it can be harder on the ones listening to it than on the patient. Suction usually increases the secretions and causes sharp discomfort to the patient. Elevating the head of the bed is the most helpful intervention. You also might try gently turning the head to the side to allow gravity to drain the secretions. We sometimes use a medication in the form of a patch placed behind the ear to help to dry up these secretions. In most cases it is effective.

VISION-LIKE EXPERIENCES

The person may speak or claim to have spoken to people who have already died or to see places not presently accessible or visible to you. He may talk about seeing an angel or angels at his bedside. Don't assume such claims are always hallucinations or drug reactions. "Reports of seeing Christ or relatives long dead might have some validity. We should not expect such experiences, but they could happen."[5] Do not contradict, explain away, belittle, or argue about what the person claims to have seen or heard. Just because you cannot see or hear these things does not mean they are not real to your loved one. Affirm the experiences. They are not uncommon. If they frighten your loved one, explain that these experiences are a normal part of the process. However, usually these experiences seem to comfort or soothe. Fear is rarely experienced.

SIGNIFICANT CHANGES IN VITAL SIGNS

Many times the vital signs (blood pressure, heart rate, respiratory rate, and temperature) are the last changes to occur. But in most cases, the vital signs give us hints about what's going on internally. When the blood pressure begins to drop, the heart and lungs pick up the pace in an attempt to maintain the blood pressure. This is the body's attempt to compensate. Since this compensation mechanism can't last indefinitely, the heart eventually begins to fail. As the heart rate declines, the blood pressure drops until it can no longer sustain life. At that point, the other vital signs begin to plummet. The patient stops breathing, and eventually his heart stops beating.

We have learned to interpret all these signs in such a way that we can *generally* predict when a patient is dying. But we can never be completely accurate in that prediction. God alone determines the *exact* moment of our death, and in Him alone can we place our trust. The important thing is this: "If you are a Christian, trusting Christ alone for your salvation, Scripture promises that the moment you leave this life you go to heaven."[6]

HOW TO KNOW WHEN DEATH HAS OCCURRED

Although you may be prepared for the dying process, you may not be ready for the actual moment of death. Sometimes it is a confusing time. It helps to know what it looks like. The signs of death include no breathing, no heartbeat, no response, skin color changes, eyelids slightly open, pupils enlarging, jaws relaxing, and mouth open.

If your loved one is not in a hospice program, call 911. The local police or sheriff's office is required to file a report on every death occurring at home. But if you're with hospice, nothing needs to be done immediately except to call the hospice nurse (if she is not already in attendance). The hospice nurse will come as soon as she can get there. She will, most likely, be the one who will pronounce death and notify the police, coroner, funeral home, and the physician. She will guide you through this experience.

SAYING GOOD-BYE

There are two difficult but necessary actions I encourage family members to take when the end is obviously approaching. The first we call giving permission. Usually a dying person will work hard to hold on even though it brings prolonged discomfort. Some suspect he or she may be waiting for reassurance that those who are left behind will be all right. Therefore, your ability to release the dying person from this particular concern and give this needed assurance is a lovely gift for your loved one.

You might say something like, "It's okay. If you need to go, you go. We'll be okay. I promise. We love you." Often you can see the person visibly relax. Giving permission not only reassures the patient, but it frees us to find the peace and acceptance we need in order to let go. The wonder is that somehow this all works in conjunction and complete harmony with God's plan and perfect timing.

The second difficult task is saying good-bye—our final gift of love. It may be a simple "Good-bye. I love you." It may include recounting favorite memories or talking about the places and activities you have shared. It may mean saying, "I'm sorry for . . ." It may also include, "Thank you for . . ."

Tears are a normal and natural part of saying good-bye. They do not need to be hidden from your loved one or apologized for. Tears express your love and sorrow at being parted. And never be ashamed of tears around a hospice worker. In many cases, we shed them right along with you.

IT'S OKAY TO GRIEVE

Grief is a perfectly natural and healthy response to losing someone we love. If our heart breaks to see a friend move away to another part of the country, how much more will it break to lose a loved one to death? In both cases, we may not be able to see them again for a long, long time.

I believe I have a healthy and biblical perspective about death and dying. I have complete confidence in God's perfect will, eternal plan, and total sovereignty over all things. That doesn't mean it doesn't hurt to say good-bye to those I love.

Recently my parents' dog died. Starsky was almost fifteen years old and was suffering from severe arthritis and heart failure. To us, he was a member of the family. When he died, I sobbed along with my parents and my brother. He had been such a good companion. We remembered when he was a frisky, little white ball of fluff bounding all over the house, and we cried to think he wouldn't be there with us anymore.

And he was a dog! What makes us think it is inappropriate, weak, or even wrong to grieve over a *person* we have loved? Even Christ wept over the death of His friend Lazarus. There's no disgrace or dishonor in weeping for those we've lost. In fact, it is essential. Unexpressed grief can affect us in unhealthy ways, sometimes many years later.

Loraine Boettner writes, "We sorrow for the loss of our friends. . . . But we rejoice that they have gone to the heavenly home. The loss is ours, not theirs."[7] Of course, that is true only if our friends were believers in Christ. If they were not, then we really have reason to grieve for them. But with the death of Christian friends and family we feel a mix of sorrow and joy—sorrow for those of us who will miss them, but joy for those who have departed.

Boettner dealt with the issue of losing our loved ones to death in the book titled *Immortality*:

[I] have found the following illustration quite helpful in class work to show what our attitude should be toward the departure of loved ones [who are believers]. Suppose a relative or friend is given a trip around the world with all expenses paid, all hotel accommodations and sight-seeing tours arranged, and in association with a very desirable group of friends. . . . Such a trip would be considered a great privilege. It would mean temporary separation, but we would be happy that our friend should have such a privilege, and we would look forward to seeing him after the trip was over. The experience of death is somewhat like that—the breaking of personal ties, temporary separation, then permanent reunion in that better land. Even in this world when friends come together after years of separation, the intervening time seems to fade away as if there had been no separation at all.[8]

First Thessalonians 4:13 says: "But we do not want you to be uninformed, brothers, about those who are asleep, that you may not grieve as others do who have no hope." We do have the hope (a confident expectation), if we are believers, that we *will* see them again in eternity.

However, there is no mix of joy and sorrow for those who die unbelieving. As theologian Wayne Grudem states, "[I]t would be wrong to give any indication to others that we think that person has gone to heaven. This would simply be to give misleading information and false assurance and to diminish the urgency of the need for those who are still alive to trust in Christ."[9]

I used to wonder how to comfort family members when an unbeliever died. I couldn't very well say, "Well, at least they're not suffering anymore" or "They're in a better place." That would be giving false hope to those who are still living. I have learned that I can still be supportive to the families by directing my words of comfort to their own grief. I console them that their ordeal is over now, and the new task of recovery is beginning. When appropriate, I say a prayer with them, asking God to be merciful to the family and to draw them closer to Himself. If they want to talk to me further about Christianity, I make myself available.

Let me insert a word here about what to tell children concerning the death of a loved one. I urge you to be honest with them. Saying, "She's only sleeping," or "He went to sleep and didn't wake up," can cause terror in children. I've heard of more than one story of a child unwilling to go to sleep for fear of not waking up. In the same way saying that someone "has taken a trip" can cause fear of abandonment. Remember, you don't have to go into great detail, but make it clear that the person died because he or she couldn't get well.

SPIRITUAL PREPARATION FOR APPROACHING DEATH

It is of vital importance that we prepare spiritually *before* we get sick, *before* we are in a car wreck or an explosion that takes our life, *before* we pass through that door that leads to eternity—either an eternity in hell or in heaven.

Pastor Erwin Lutzer says, "We will meet Him there, because we have met Him here. The tomb is not an entrance to death, but to life."[10] The day of death will be most joyous for those who have saving faith in Christ. But those without that faith will face an eternal torment like nothing they can imagine.

> *. . . when the Lord Jesus is revealed from heaven with his mighty angels in flaming fire, inflicting vengeance on those who do not know God and on those who do not obey the gospel of our Lord Jesus. They will suffer the punishment of eternal destruction, away from the presence of the Lord and from the glory of his might, when he comes on that day to be glorified in his saints, and to be marveled at among all who have believed, because our testimony to you was believed. (2 Thessalonians 1:7b-10)*

The preparation for that day must be done *now*. None of us is guaranteed another hour upon this earth. "*No man* knows when his hour [of death] will come" (Ecclesiastes 9:12 NIV).

John MacArthur, in his wonderful book *The Glory of Heaven*, wrote, "So while we do not yet live physically in heaven, we do have our spiritual citizenship in the heavenly realm. Therefore we should be preoccupied with heavenly things."[11] He goes on to say that the very purpose of his book is to direct readers' thoughts, imaginations, and yearnings toward heaven and all the glories therein. But he was writing this statement to Christians. It does not apply to unbelievers.

What applies to all of us—Christians or not—is the last statement he made above: "Therefore we should be preoccupied with heavenly things." One thing that seems to happen with imminent death is a

renewed interest in the hereafter. People generally become more receptive to talking about this subject when they realize that the issue is now
relevant to them. Of course, we know death has *always* been relevant
to each of us, but some don't acknowledge that fact.

Some people would say, "Sorry, I just don't believe that." But that
doesn't change the *truth*, does it? The other day I was working in one
of my flowerbeds, and my husband was outside talking to me. I heard
the phone ringing in the house and said to him, "Honey, the phone's
ringing."

"No, it's not."

"It is. I hear it. That's the third ring." (I couldn't go answer it
because my hands were encrusted with mud and dirt and sweat.)

But because he never heard the phone, he didn't believe me.

That little episode made me think about the truth of Scripture.
There are those who say the Bible is not true, that it is all just fairy
tales and nonsense, that they believe something else, and that we who
believe the Bible are foolish and pathetic. One extremely wealthy
celebrity even stated that Christianity is a religion for losers. But, folks,
just because some can't hear the phone ringing, that doesn't mean it
isn't ringing. Truth is truth whether we believe it or not.

The Scriptures teach us that those who cannot see the truth are
blind. Those who cannot hear the truth are deaf. Romans 11:7-8 says,

> *What then? Israel failed to obtain what it was seeking.* The elect
> *[those God chose to be His children] obtained it, but the rest [those
> who were not His children] were hardened, as it is written,* "God
> gave them a spirit of stupor, eyes that would not see and ears that
> would not hear, *down to this very day.*"

In John 8:47 Jesus told the Pharisees, "Whoever is of God hears
the words of God. The reason why you do not hear them is that *you
are not of God.*" Strong language, to be sure. By that time, He had
been telling them the *truth* for three years, but they still did not believe
Him. That fact does not diminish the truth. The phone was ringing,
but they couldn't hear it.

So what is to be done if God is the One who chooses His children?

What should be our response? We should throw ourselves on His mercy and humbly ask Him to forgive our sins and deliver us into His heavenly kingdom. First John 1:9 states, "If we confess our sins, he is faithful and just to forgive us our sins and to cleanse us from all unrighteousness." This sounds like a promise to me.

As our day of death draws closer (and it does for all of us, not just those who *know* they are dying), let us be ever more mindful of heavenly things. This spiritual preparation is the most crucial part of our entire lives on this earth. Don't take it lightly.

Those of us who are believers in Christ have nothing to fear from death. He's made us a very special promise that we hang onto, breathless with anticipation: "Let not your hearts be troubled. Believe in God; believe also in me. In my Father's house are many rooms. If it were not so, would I have told you that I go to prepare a place for you? And if I go and prepare a place for you, I will come again and will take you to myself, that where I am you may be also" (John 14:1-3).

God has warned that the wages of sin is death. Sin *will be* punished. If our sins are not forgiven by God through the death and resurrection of His Son, Jesus Christ, we will be punished for them eternally in hell. Think about it. Jesus said, "And do not fear those who kill the body but cannot kill the soul. Rather fear [God] who can destroy both soul and body in hell" (Matthew 10:28).

If we are to become more preoccupied with our hereafter, it is important that we develop a biblical understanding of the subjects at hand. The next chapters will deal in greater detail with what God says in His Word about the subjects of angels, demons, death, heaven, and hell.

The porter God chooses to summon us will come our way, knock on our door, and it will be time to leave.
ERWIN LUTZER

8

THE TRUTH ABOUT ANGELS AND THINGS THAT GO "BUMP" IN THE NIGHT

I, John, am the one who heard and saw these things. And when I heard and saw them, I fell down to worship at the feet of the angel who showed them to me, but he said to me, "You must not do that! I am a fellow servant with you and your brothers the prophets, and with those who keep the words of this book. Worship God."

REVELATION 22:8-9

A FOOT ON EACH SIDE OF THE CURTAIN

Bachman seemed more alert today. It was a joyous occasion. His oldest daughter, Sarah, had just announced her engagement over lunch. To make it even more of a celebration, the whole family was together for the first time since Easter. Sarah and her fiance, John, were here from college. In the fall they would both enter their senior year at John Brown University, a Christian college in Siloam Springs, Arkansas. Since they both worked there during the summer, they didn't get to come home often. They had decided to get married after graduation.

Laura, the youngest daughter, was home now for the summer. She wanted to stay at home with her dad, but both he and Penny had insisted that she take a summer job. So she was working full time at a local cinema selling tickets and helping in the concession stand. It wasn't a very exciting job, but two of her old friends from high school also worked there. As a perk, she received discounts to all the theaters in town. Watching movies had always been one of her favorite activities. Lately movies took her mind off her dad's condition, even if it was only for a couple of hours.

But today they were all together. John and the girls were laughing and teasing each other in the den, trying to draw Bachman into the fun. Penny was in the kitchen cleaning up after dinner since the girls had surprised her by cooking the entire meal.

Bachman was awake but had a vacant, preoccupied look. Occasionally he'd respond to something that was said. But mostly he just stared at a point somewhere between the fireplace and the big leather chair he used to sit in. The head of the hospital bed was elevated so he could breathe more easily and better participate in the family get-together.

"Of course, you'll want me to be your maid of honor, won't you?" Laura asked. She knelt down in front of Sarah, folded her hands in mock supplication, and whined, "Please. Please."

"Oh, quit it. Who else would I want to be maid of honor?"

"What are your colors going to be? I look marvelous in any color except Pepto-Bismol pink."

"You know, I'm not at all concerned about whether *you* look marvelous or not. And actually I *was* leaning toward Pepto-Bismol pink," Sarah teased.

"Daddy, tell her to choose a color I'll look good in, okay?" Laura sat on the bed next to Bachman and covered his hand with hers.

He looked over at her and seemed to start to say something. Then he reached up weakly and touched her nose, like he used to do before he got sick. Laura's eyes filled with tears, cherishing the gesture. Looking away from her again, Bachman said weakly, "What do you want?"

"What, Daddy?"

"Okay. But what did Mama say? Is she going too?"

With wide eyes Laura looked back over her shoulder at Sarah and John, who were sitting in stunned silence, watching Bachman. Laura shrugged and softly spoke to Bachman again. "Daddy, what are you talking about?"

"I wasn't talking to you," he said curtly.

"Then who were you talking to?"

"To him." He nodded his head toward the space between the fireplace and the leather chair, pointing one thin finger. They all looked but saw nothing.

"You were talking to whom, Daddy? John?" Laura strained her ears to hear his muffled reply.

"To . . . the angel," he managed to explain.

Laura got up from the bed and stood looking down incredulously at her father. "Daddy, there aren't any angels in here."

Bachman was silent, staring. The light in the room cast shadows under his prominent cheekbones, only too visible now.

Sarah got up and walked to the kitchen to tell her mother.

Laura plopped down on the sofa. John looked from Bachman to Laura and back. Then Sarah came into the room with Penny, who was drying her hands on a dishtowel. Sitting down in a chair next to Bachman's bed, Penny slowly stroked his arm and hand, cooing to him quietly. But Bachman said nothing. He just lay there staring, his lips pressed together tightly.

"Well, that just gave me the willies," said Laura with a shudder. "Do you think he's hallucinating or something?"

"Sometimes he does talk out of his head," Penny whispered back to her. "But I've never heard him talk about angels. However, Paula, our hospice nurse, told me it wouldn't be unusual for him to start doing that."

Bachman closed his eyes and seemed to drift off to sleep.

"That was just too weird," Laura replied, opening her eyes wide and looking from one face to the other.

"I don't know," John said. "Before my mom died two years ago, she started talking to her mother just like Grandma was really there. We tried to convince her that she wasn't, but Mom insisted she was. One time she even pointed at the chair by her bed and said, 'Don't you see her? She's sitting right there.'"

Sarah spoke up. "Well, we actually don't know what happens at the end. The Bible talks about Lazarus and the rich man. It says the rich man went to hell, but the angels came and took Lazarus to heaven, to be 'in the bosom of Abraham.' Maybe angels do come for us when we die."

"Shhhh," Laura scolded. "Don't talk like that around Daddy. He might hear you."

"Do you think he doesn't know he's dying?" Sarah glared at Laura before continuing. "We've already talked about it. He knows. He told me he's ready to go. He's tired of being sick."

"Really! Do we have to talk about this?" Laura crossed her arms and sank against the coolness of the leather.

Penny spoke up. "Why not? Why shouldn't we talk about it?"

John asked, "What did the hospice nurse say about it?"

Penny, still holding her husband's hand, turned to the kids. "She said lots of times people think they see loved ones who have already died, or angels, or even Jesus when they're getting close to the end. She said she used to argue with them about that, but she doesn't anymore, because whether they really see them or not, they *think* they see them, and it is usually a soothing experience. They're very *real* to the patient. So why argue? We're supposed to let him believe what he wants about who's here and who's not."

She looked over at Bachman, lovingly touching his sunken cheek with the back of her fingers. "Sometimes I think he's more aware of the spiritual world than he is of ours. Sometimes I think we're losing him more and more each day."

"Mother," cried Laura, "I really don't want to talk about this."

"Well, just don't let it frighten you when he talks like that. Just be glad he's giving you a glimpse into his world right now. Pretty soon he won't be able to do that."

"I think it's pretty cool," ventured John.

Sarah placed her hand in John's hand, and he gave it a squeeze. "What's pretty cool, sweetie?"

"I think it's pretty cool that there might be an angel here in the room with us right now, and we just can't see him," replied John.

"Well, I think it's totally spooky." Laura sat thoughtfully for a moment. "You think he's got wings and stuff?"

"Laura, grow up. It's time for you to face things head-on." Sarah's gentle rebuke only made Laura more argumentative.

"Well, what do *you* know, Sarah? None of us really knows anything about it. Nobody's an authority on angels. Daddy's probably just gorked out of his head on all those drugs he's getting. But I notice that you're totally untouched by all of this. I've never seen you even shed a tear over him. Maybe you just don't love him like I do."

"Girls, that's enough." Penny looked from one to the other and pointed her finger at Laura. "You need to remember that your father may be hearing everything you're saying. We need to be strong for him right now, not weaklings. If he can face this as graciously as he has, then we can too. Do you hear me?"

Sarah scowled at her little sister. "Don't you ever accuse me of that again. We all handle things differently, that's all. Just because you haven't seen any tears doesn't mean there haven't been any. Believe me, there have been plenty of those. John can attest to that. But I realize that when I'm crying, I'm mostly crying because I'm sad for *me*, not for Daddy. Daddy's troubles will be over soon. He'll be in the presence of God and happier than he's ever been in his life. Why should I want him to stay here like this?"

She gestured toward Bachman. "This isn't *living*. This is *existing*. So if he's seeing angels, his mama, or anyone else, we shouldn't think he's nuts or hallucinating. Just because we can't see them doesn't mean they aren't there. There's a whole spiritual world right here existing with ours. Don't you know that?"

"Who says?" Laura asked defiantly, lifting her head and crossing her arms in front of her again.

John joined Sarah in the discussion. "I remember that story in the Old Testament about some prophet, either Elijah or Elisha, I can never remember which, who prayed that God would open his servant's eyes and let him see the spiritual world. The servant was scared to death that they were outnumbered by their enemies. God opened the servant's eyes, and when he looked around, there were armies of angels all around them, waiting to fight for them."

"I remember that too." Sarah smiled at John appreciatively. "You are so wise . . . and smart . . . and wonderful." Leaning over closer to him, she gave him a quick kiss between every word.

John grinned from ear to ear, only slightly embarrassed. "Well, I ought to remember it. We covered that in Old Testament Survey in my sophomore year."

"You're still wonderful." She kissed him again, and his eyes twinkled as he smiled back at her.

"Oh, brother." Laura rolled her eyes.

Penny just smiled. When they looked at Bachman, he was smiling too. But about what, they couldn't be sure.

ANGELMANIA: SOCIETY'S RECURRING EPIDEMIC

There is so much about angels we just don't understand. The subject is fascinating to explore, but we need a proper perspective. The Scriptures do not focus on angels. *That should be an indication in itself of the relative importance of this topic.* The emphasis of Scripture is directed toward God the Father, the Son, and the Holy Spirit. Angels are treated as peripheral, usually taking a secondary place to the action of the passages that mention them.

There are many myths about angels. These are not new but have existed in many different cultures and societies throughout history. However, in today's world of mass merchandising and television and film consumption, and even in the world of art and literature we see more and more propaganda directed toward the phenomena of angels. In light of these popular myths, we need to discuss what the *Bible* says on the subject.

This fascination with angels is not trivial, a harmless act of spiritual worship. John MacArthur gives a stern warning in his book *The Glory of Heaven*: "'Angelmania' turns out to be sheer occultism, with all its horrible effects. Many people have been drawn into serious demonic bondage by these practices and *Christians should be strongly warned against them.*"[1]

What practices is he talking about? Angel worship. If there is only one fact you remember from this section, let it be this: *Angels are not designed to be worshiped.* They are merely beings created by God to serve His purposes on earth and in heaven. They are very different from human beings, but that does not mean we should give them more honor or more attention than they deserve.

Dr. MacArthur concurs: "[I]*t is God who should be the focus of our praise and gratitude, not the angelic beings. . . .* The whole fixation [on angels] is of questionable value, and undoubtedly it is causing far more spiritual harm than good."[2]

You might say, "Hey, I don't worship angels." Perhaps you don't, but I hear more and more people (and not always Christians) refer to angels, pray to angels, collect angels, read about angels, try to communicate with angels, and even think they hear or see angels. Whether you consider yourself to be worshiping angels or not, perhaps you should ask yourself if you give more attention and adoration to angels than you do to Jesus Christ. If so, beware.

"What's the harm?" you might ask. The harm is that *anything* you place above God and His Son is an idol in your mind and in your heart. It has been said that the human heart is a factory for idols. And we're told that God is a jealous God. It does not please Him when we worship what He has created instead of worshiping Him, the Creator.

> *You shall have no other gods before me. You shall not make for yourself an* idol *in the form of anything in heaven above or on the earth beneath or in the waters below. You shall not bow down to them or worship them; for I, the* LORD *your God, am a jealous God, punishing the children for the sin of the fathers to the third and fourth generation of those who hate me, but showing love to a thousand generations of those who love me and keep my commandments." (Exodus 20:3-6 NIV)*

God deserves *all* our praise, worship, and adoration. He doesn't intend to share His glory with anyone or anything else. This passage states clearly that there will be severe punishment to those who hate Him (who *do not* keep His commandments), and a lovely, blessed reward for those who love Him (who *do* keep His commandments). And the generosity of His blessing far exceeds the extent of His wrath.

But what of these creatures who so easily capture our imaginations and our hearts?

THE TRUTH REGARDING ANGELS

Theologian Wayne Grudem defines angels in this way: "Angels are created, spiritual beings with moral judgment and high intelligence, but without physical bodies."[3] Let's discuss some of the biblical attributes and characteristics of angels.

Created by God

"Praise him, *all his angels*; praise him, *all his hosts*! Praise him, sun and moon, praise him, all you shining stars! Praise him, you highest heavens, and you waters above the heavens. Let them praise the name of the LORD! *For he commanded and they were created*" (Psalm 148:2-5).

The apostle Paul in Colossians 1:16 says, "For by him *all things* were created, *in heaven* and on earth, visible and *invisible . . . all things* were created through him and for him." So you see, not only were the angels created *by* God, but they were created *for* Him as well.

In *The Glory of Heaven*, John MacArthur writes about angels as created beings: "And since there is no procreation among angels (Matt. 22:30), they must have all been created at once—in a sweeping creative act. God instantly commanded, and untold numbers of creatures came into existence, each one independently unique. They do not reproduce, so there can never be any increase in the number. They do not die, so there's no decrease."[4]

Notice that the Bible does not teach that when we die, we become angels. I've heard so many of my patients' family members voice this belief. "Mama's going to be an angel soon. She's going to watch over us forever and ever." Not true. We are transformed, but not into angels.

I'd like to make a distinction here. The Bible never says that angels were created in the image of God. But there are several passages declaring that mankind was made in God's image. Grudem wrote,

"Since being in the image of God means to be like God, it seems fair to conclude that we are more like God even than the angels are."[5]

God's Messengers

Multiple passages in both the Old and New Testaments describe angels as heralds, or messengers, spreading the news or delivering messages from God. For example, when Christ was born, a multitude of angels delivered the joyful news to shepherds watching over their sheep by night. Luke 2:9-14 describes the scene in this way:

> *And an angel of the Lord appeared to them, and the glory of the Lord shone around them, and they were filled with fear. And the angel said to them, "Fear not, for behold, I bring you good news of a great joy that will be for all the people. For unto you is born this day in the city of David a Savior, who is Christ the Lord. And this will be a sign for you: you will find a baby wrapped in swaddling cloths and lying in a manger." And suddenly there was with the angel a multitude of the heavenly host praising God and saying, "Glory to God in the highest, and on earth peace among those with whom he is pleased!"*

In fact, it was an angel who told Mary that she had been chosen to be the mother of Jesus, the Son of God:

> *[T]he angel Gabriel was sent from God to a city of Galilee named Nazareth, to a virgin betrothed to a man whose name was Joseph, of the house of David. And the virgin's name was Mary. And he came to her and said, "Greetings, O favored one, the Lord is with you! . . . Do not be afraid, Mary, for you have found favor with God. And behold, you will conceive in your womb and bear a son, and you shall call his name Jesus." (Luke 1:26-31)*

Throughout the book of Revelation, we are shown the important role angels have in carrying out the will of God. Revelation 1:1-2 starts out by saying, "The revelation of Jesus Christ, which God gave him to show to his servants the things that must soon take place. He made it known by sending his angel to his servant John, who bore witness to the word of God and to the testimony of Jesus Christ, even to all that he saw."

In Matthew 28:5-7 we read, "But the angel said to the women, 'Do not be afraid, for I know that you seek Jesus who was crucified. He is not here, for he has risen, as he said. Come, see the place where he lay. Then go quickly and tell his disciples that he has risen from the dead, and behold, he is going before you to Galilee; there you will see him. See, I have told you.'"

WHAT DO ANGELS LOOK LIKE?

This might be a good place to stop for a moment to notice a startling point about angels. In the passages above, you will see something in common. Angels frequently opened their messages by saying, "Do not be afraid" or "Fear not." In nearly every passage where angels deliver messages, the recipient was described as visibly frightened by their appearance.

This fact would seem to contradict the idea that angels are cute little pudgy children with wings, harps, and blond ringlets of curls framing their cherubic faces and rosy cheeks. They obviously do not appear to be beautiful, willowy-thin women either, with long, thick, curling hair, beautiful gossamer wings, and long, flowing robes. Neither of these images would be especially frightening.

However, in all the angelmania merchandise that's how we most commonly see them portrayed. Here's a shocker. We're not even told in the Bible that angels have wings. Isaiah 6:2 says that the *seraphs* (specialty angels, so to speak) have wings, six of them. They use two wings for flight, two to cover their faces, and two to cover their feet. In Revelation 4:8, we read that the living creatures (another type of the heavenly host) also have six wings. In addition they are covered all over with eyeballs, even under their wings. I've never seen *that* depicted on a calendar or on gift-wrapping paper!

However they look to people, angels must appear terrifying and powerful. In fact, in each passage where angels are mentioned, they are male. There is not *one* female angel in the Bible.

Usually angels are invisible to us. They have only occasionally appeared to people and then always on a mission from God. John MacArthur says, "Heb. 1:14 specifically calls the angels 'spirits,' which implies that they do not have material bodies. Nonetheless, they may appear in visible form when God chooses to let them be manifest."[6]

To quote from Dr. Wayne Grudem's book:

> Since angels are spirits (Heb. 1:14) or spiritual creatures, they do not ordinarily have physical bodies (Luke 24:39). Therefore they cannot usually be seen by us unless God gives us a special ability to see them (Num. 22:31, 2 Kings 6:17, Luke 2:13). In their ordinary activities of guarding and protecting us (Ps. 34:7, 91:11, Heb. 1:14), and joining us in worship to God (Heb. 12:22), they are invisible. However, from time to time angels took on a bodily form to appear to various people in Scripture (Matt. 28:5, Heb. 13:2).[7]

Many in this day and age deny the reality of anything they cannot see. But biblical teaching on the existence of angels reminds us that there is an unseen world that is very real.

In Bachman's story at the beginning of this chapter, Sarah's fiancé, John, recounted an event from the life of the prophet Elisha:

> *When the servant of [Elisha] rose early in the morning and went out, behold, an army with horses and chariots was all around the city. And the servant said, "Alas, my master. What shall we do?" He said, "Do not be afraid, for those who are with us are more than those who are with them." Then Elisha prayed and said, "O LORD, please open his eyes that he may see." So the LORD opened the eyes of the young man, and he saw, and behold, the mountain was full of horses and chariots of fire all around Elisha. (2 Kings 6:15-17)*

The Bible goes on to tell how the Lord delivered them from their enemies.

We find another example in the book of Numbers: "Then the LORD opened the eyes of Balaam, and he saw the angel of the LORD standing in the way, with his drawn sword in his hand. And he bowed down and fell on his face" (22:31).

Did you know that whenever we come together to worship, we gather with innumerable angels that we cannot see? Dr. Grudem finds a strong indication in Hebrews 12:22 that this is what happens. Just knowing angels are present should fill us with both awe and joy.

We cannot see the spiritual plane that exists with and beyond our physical one. We do not know what or when or how many spiritual beings are with us at any given time. *And it's not important that we know.* If it were, we would be instructed on the subject. Suffice it to say that we must trust God *in everything*—including what He chooses to do with His angels.

DO ANGELS APPEAR TO PEOPLE TODAY?

Many people would say no. However, a passage in Hebrews 13:2, urging us to be hospitable to people, says, "Do not neglect to show hospitality to strangers, for thereby some have entertained angels unawares." Some say with certainty that this only happened in the past, that when the Scriptures were complete, such phenomena ceased to occur. That may be true, but I don't rule out the possibility of angels appearing today in bodily form by God's decree and for a specific purpose in accordance with His will. We're not *definitely* told one way or the other.

When Christ ascended into heaven, the disciples were looking up after Him, watching until they couldn't see Him any longer. "They were looking intently up into the sky as he was going, when *suddenly two men dressed in white* stood beside them. 'Men of Galilee,' they said, 'why do you stand here looking into the sky? This same Jesus, who has been taken from you into heaven, will come back in the same way you have seen him go into heaven'" (Acts 1:10-11 NIV).

These guys knew too much about the whole situation to be just two blokes walking along at the time. No, they weren't ordinary men. We are not *specifically* told they were angels, but angels were frequently dressed in white, and the fact that they *suddenly* appeared beside the disciples also lends support to the conclusion that these, most likely, were angels. However, they appeared as men in this passage, unlike those who appeared in other forms (more frightening, as discussed earlier). So if angels appeared in human form then, possibly they also do it now.

One rule of thumb about Bible study is that if the Scriptures are silent on a subject, there is no way we can know the validity of that subject *with any certainty*. All anyone can do is to speculate or deduce, from what we *are* told in the Scriptures, conclusions consistent with other biblical teaching. Ultimately, all I can say about whether angels appear to us today is that I just don't know.

Dr. Grudem offers a word of caution, and I fervently agree. He says if anyone believes he has seen an angel, and that angel said something to him that would *contradict* what we're *clearly* taught in the Scriptures, *we should not believe this to be an angel of God*. True angels, who are singularly devoted to God and to the truth, would *never* contradict His Word. It is, therefore, of the utmost importance that we make sure we have a proper and thorough understanding of the Scriptures. It is only by that standard that we can judge discerningly.

However, remember that Satan and his angels masquerade as angels of light (2 Corinthians 11:14-15). Satan's goal is to confuse, to confound, and to draw people away from the truth so he might destroy them.

In light of this, *beware*. Don't believe everything you hear. Compare it with the teaching of Scripture. And remember that those who may believe such things may be very sincere. You may tend to take their word because of the affection or trust you have for them. Whatever their intentions, they can knowingly or unknowingly mislead you because they can be knowingly or unknowingly misled. There is such a thing as being sincerely wrong.

OTHER PROPERTIES OF ANGELS

"Angels are persons. That is, they are beings with all the attributes of personality: intellect, feelings, and volition. They have personalities,"[8] wrote John MacArthur. Though we, as members of the human race, are created in the image of God, we have also been given individual personalities, characteristics, and weaknesses. We are not *clones* of one another. There are similarities in our appearance, but our features and bodies are all different and unique. In the same way, angels, who are also created by God, seem to have unique, individual qualities (though there is no way we can be certain of that until we get to heaven).

One difference between humans and angels is that angels can see the face of God now, and we can't. Their whole existence is devoted to serving God. We can't say that about the human race. That's something we can *strive toward* but can never truly attain this side of death. I'm afraid we cannot get past looking out for number one—and usually our number one is . . . ourselves, not God. When the angels of our Lord look out for number One, you can bet their number One is God, without a thought for themselves.

(It disturbs me to see movies about angels caught in terrific internal struggles, trying to decide whether to stay an angel in God's service or to become human so they might enjoy the love of a woman. That is utter fantasy. Holy angels have no such struggles. There's no way this could happen, in view of their intense devotion to God as the Scriptures describe. They have a front-row seat in heaven with all its joys. It's *ridiculous* to imagine they'd ever choose to become mortal for the love of a woman or for any other reason. Of course, that's just the movies, right? The problem is that many impressionable people are actually lulled into believing such things—based on a movie—not caring if it's supported by the Word of God. This is all part of Satan's strategy of deception.)

In Dr. MacArthur's statement above, he says that angels are *intelligent* beings. The Scriptures show us that angels *knew* certain things: "But the angel said to the women, 'Do not be afraid, *for I know* that you seek Jesus who was crucified'" (Matthew 28:5). The angel also told the women what to do next and when and where the disciples would next meet with Jesus.

In many other passages we are told of angels appearing to people to declare what was and is and is to be. In this context they serve as God's messengers. In fact, that's primarily what angel means—"messenger," from the Greek word *angelos*.

Yes, they are obviously highly intelligent creatures. But we needn't believe that they share God's attribute of omniscience. They know only what God gives them to know. First Peter 1:12b NIV states, *"Even angels long to look into these things,"* referring to certain truths contained in the gospel.

Angels are *emotional* beings. They rejoice. In Luke 15 Jesus tells a series of parables regarding rejoicing over finding something that was once lost. At the conclusion of one parable, He said, "Just so, I tell you, *there will be more joy in heaven* over one sinner who repents than over ninety-nine righteous persons who need no repentance" (Luke 15:7). (He is being tongue-in-cheek about saying "righteous persons." In this context, He means people who *perceive* themselves as being righteous and not in need of repentance.) Likewise, at the conclusion of another parable, He says, "Just so, I tell you, *there is joy before the angels of God* over one sinner who repents" (Luke 15:10).

So angels *share* in the joy of God the Father. It is doubtful that meaningful worship can truly take place apart from emotion. John MacArthur says, "Of course, sheer blind emotion does not equate to real worship, but 'worship . . . in spirit and in truth'—the kind of worship God seeks (John 4:23)—is not possible apart from authentic feelings. *The purest worship involves rejoicing in the truth* (cf. 1 Cor. 13:6). And the fact that angels are often seen worshiping around the throne of God indicates that they do have emotions."[9]

WHAT POSITION DO ANGELS HAVE IN RELATION TO MAN?

That is a question with a two-part answer. What position do they have *now*? What position will they have in the future kingdom of God?

We know that human beings were made a little lower than the angels (Hebrews 2:7). Also we're told, ". . . angels, *though greater in might and power*, do not pronounce a blasphemous judgment against [sinners] before the Lord" (2 Peter 2:11). No one can dispute that angels can do things we simply cannot do.

However, when we come into the kingdom of God, we will sit in judgment over the angels (1 Corinthians 6:3). In having authority over angels, saved mankind could be said to have a position elevated above the angels.

Our place in heaven and in God's heart is also demonstrated by a passage in Hebrews 1:13-14: "And to which of the angels has he ever said, 'Sit at my right hand until I make your enemies a footstool for your feet?' Are they not all ministering spirits *sent out to serve for the sake of those who are to inherit salvation?*"

So though the angels serve God by serving us now, it would seem that someday in the kingdom of God, we will certainly judge the angels and may even rule over them.

ANGELS ARE NOT TO BE WORSHIPED

The Scriptures are very clear on this point: "Let no one disqualify you, insisting on asceticism and *worship of angels*, going on in detail about visions, puffed up without reason by his sensuous mind" (Colossians 2:18).

And in Revelation 19:10 we read, "Then I fell down at his feet to *worship* [*the angel*], but he said to me, 'You must not do that! I am a fellow servant with you and your brothers who hold to the testimony of Jesus. *Worship God.*'"

Revelation 19:10 is one of the verses John MacArthur had in mind when he wrote: "It also suggests that angels—like all other intelligent creatures—were designed to render worship to God, not to receive worship themselves. In fact, in every case in Scripture, whenever angels are offered any form of worship, they always rebuke the worshiper and redirect all worship to God alone (cf. Rev. 19:10, 22:8-9)."[10]

I have found in my experience that this tendency to glorify angels (sometimes even more than people glorify Christ) is generally embraced by non-Christians, new or "baby" Christians, or by those Christians ignorant of the Bible's teaching on the subject. More mature believers, who have studied the Bible and gained spiritual wisdom, know that the *object* of our worship, adoration, praise, and attention should *only* be God the Father, Son, and Holy Spirit.

Professor Wayne Grudem cautioned about over-attention to angels: "They are not to be worshiped, prayed to or sought by us."[11] We do not need anyone or anything to intercede for us. According to 1 Timothy 2:5-6a, Christ is the only mediator needed between God and man: "For there is one God, and there is *one mediator between*

God and men, the man Christ Jesus, who gave himself as a ransom for all."

The popularity and novelty of angelmania is a growing problem. It is my desire, not in an attitude of arrogance but one of deep conviction, to urge you to offer to God your obedience by worshiping *Him,* and Him alone. I'm not saying that we can't be fascinated by angels or that we shouldn't have a healthy respect for them and for their work, or that we shouldn't look forward to seeing them someday. What I am saying is that God should hold for us the greatest fascination, and we should strive to learn more and more about *Him.*

ANGELS CONTINUOUSLY WORSHIP GOD

In fact, this is their primary function. In Revelation 5:11-12, we find: "Then I looked, and I heard around the throne and the living creatures and the elders the voice of many angels, numbering myriads of myriads and thousands of thousands, saying with a loud voice, 'Worthy is the Lamb who was slain, to receive power and wealth and wisdom and might and honor and glory and blessing!'"

And again in Revelation 7:11-12, "And all the angels were standing around the throne and around the elders and the four living creatures, and they fell on their faces before the throne and worshiped God, saying, 'Amen! Blessing and glory and wisdom and thanksgiving and honor and power and might be to our God forever and ever! Amen.'"

Let me encourage you to follow the example of the angels. As they find it their greatest joy to *praise God continuously,* shouldn't we also delight each day to praise God and count this as the highest and most worthy use of our time? Praising Him should bring us our greatest joy.

ANGELS ARE MINISTERING SPIRITS TO THE ELECT

"Are [angels] not all *ministering spirits* sent out to serve for the sake of *those who are to inherit salvation [the elect]?*" (Hebrews 1:14). John MacArthur writes, "*As ministering spirits who minister to the elect,* angels are no doubt active in human affairs, though usually unseen. Undoubtedly they do many things on our behalf, but *nowhere does Scripture encourage us to look further into how this occurs. We are never encouraged to try to discern the unseen work of angels in our lives."*[12]

Another passage in the Bible that teaches that the angels minister to God's people is Psalm 34:7: "The angel of the LORD encamps around those who fear [God], and delivers them."

Therefore, God uses His angels to serve us. They watch over us and protect us. But they are serving God by serving us. Our gratitude belongs to *Him* for providing them for us.

DO WE EACH HAVE A GUARDIAN ANGEL?

In Matthew 18:10, Jesus says, "See that you do not despise one of these [children]. For I tell you that in heaven their angels always see the face of my Father who is in heaven." What are we to make of this? It does seem to support the idea of guardian angels, even though we are not given a clear teaching of their existence.

Dr. Grudem offers a wonderful illustration: "[O]ur Lord may simply be saying that angels who are assigned the task of protecting little children have ready access to God's presence. (To use an athletic analogy, the angels may be playing 'zone' rather than 'man-to-man' defense). . . . There seems to be, therefore, no convincing support for the idea of individual 'guardian angels' in the text of Scripture."[13] This illustration says to me that there may be certain angels whose job description is watching out for people *in general*. We do not know if there are guardian angels assigned to each of us individually or not. We are just told that angels do watch over us.

ANGELS MAY BE OUR ESCORTS TO HEAVEN

"What can we expect one minute after we die? While relatives sorrow on earth, you will find yourself in new surroundings which just now are beyond our imagination. Most probably, you will have seen angels who have been assigned the responsibility of escorting you to your destination, just as the angels carried Lazarus into 'Abraham's bosom.'"[14]

Many people very close to death report seeing angels. One woman we took care of saw an angel on the left side of her bed. He would wake her sometimes, she said, by tapping her on the arm three times. She would turn her head and look at him. He never said anything. They would just look at each other. She reported this occurrence every day for several days before she died.

This is not an isolated incident. It happens fairly frequently. I'm not saying absolutely that an angel is there. I'm just saying that's what people sometimes report.

What do the Scriptures teach about this? Well, if you think there is a verse somewhere that says, "And the angels of the Lord visit those who are dying and take those who belong to God into heaven," you can forget it. However, in Luke 16:22 Jesus told a parable about Lazarus and the rich man: "The poor man [Lazarus] died and was carried *by the angels to Abraham's side [in heaven]*." So in this case, the angels *did* serve as an escort to heaven. Can we say then that angels take all of us who died believing in Christ to heaven? No, but it does seem to be a reasonable possibility.

I am reminded of the story of Jim Elliott, a missionary to the Auca Indians. Pastor Erwin Lutzer tells the story this way: "Back in January of 1956, five young missionaries were speared to death in the jungles of Ecuador. The offenders have now become Christians and have told Steve Saint, the son of one of the martyrs, that they heard and saw what they now believe to be angels while the killings were taking place. A woman hiding at a distance also saw these beings above the trees and didn't know what kind of music [they were singing] until she heard a Christian choir on records."[15]

ANGELS ARE GOD'S AGENTS OF DESTRUCTION

This is probably the least known function of angels. Popular angel mythology shows them as airy, benign beings of good will to all men. Not necessarily. One of their functions—throughout history, at present, and especially in the future—is to carry out God's will regarding the destruction of mankind as well as of the very earth we inhabit.

Shocking? Perhaps, but true. Here are a few passages supporting this claim:

And the angel of the LORD went out and struck [down put to death] a hundred and eighty-five thousand in the camp of the Assyrians. (Isaiah 37:36).

So it will be at the close of the age. The angels will come out and separate the evil from the righteous and throw them into the fiery furnace. In that place there will be weeping and gnashing of teeth. (Matthew 13:49-50)

The fourth angel blew his trumpet, and a third of the sun was struck, and a third of the moon, and a third of the stars, so that a third of their light might be darkened, and a third of the day might be kept from shining, and likewise a third of the night. (Revelation 8:12)

The third angel poured out his bowl into the rivers and the springs of water, and they became blood. (Revelation 16:4)

Angels are powerful creatures when on their missions from God.

ANGELS ARE GOD'S AGENTS OF DELIVERANCE

Just as they can be instruments of destruction, angels can also be instruments of deliverance for mankind. God determines their purpose, and they do His will. Here are a few examples from the Bible:

Behold, I send an angel before you to guard you on the way and to bring you to the place that I have prepared. Pay careful attention to him and obey his voice; do not rebel against him, for he will not pardon your transgression, for my name is in him. But if you carefully obey his voice and do all that I say, then I will be an enemy to your enemies and an adversary to your adversaries. (Exodus 23:20-22)

In all their affliction he was afflicted, and the angel of his presence saved them. (Isaiah 63:9)

Here is a famous escape narrative from the book of Acts:

Now when Herod was about to bring him out, on that very night, Peter was sleeping between two soldiers, bound with two chains, and sentries before the door were guarding the prison. And behold, an angel of the Lord stood next to him, and a light shone in the cell. He struck Peter on the side and woke him, saying, "Get up quickly." And the chains fell off his hands. And the angel said to him, "Dress yourself and put on your sandals." And he did so. And he said to him, "Wrap your cloak around you and follow me." And he went out and followed him. He did not know that what was being done by the angel was real, but thought he was seeing a vision. When they had passed the first and the second guard, they came to the iron gate leading into the city. It opened for them of its own accord, and they went out and went along one street, and immediately the angel left him. When Peter came to himself, he said, "Now I am sure that the Lord has sent his angel and rescued me from the hand of Herod and from all that the Jewish people were expecting." (Acts 12:6-11)

According to John MacArthur, "The life and the world of angels is as involved and as active and as complex as ours is. They dwell in another dimension, but our worlds intersect often, and at least some of their business is related to the affairs of this world."[16]

In conclusion, let me urge you to appreciate angels for what they are—servants and tools of the Almighty. They only do His bidding. They are not gods themselves to be worshiped. Instead, give praise and worship and glory to God, who deserves all praise.

Worthy are you, our Lord and God, to receive glory and honor and power, for you created all things, and by your will they existed and were created. (Revelation 4:11)

WHAT ABOUT GHOSTS AND GHOULS?

Ghost stories. They've probably existed throughout history. I remember Girl Scout camps and sleepovers during my youth. We would sit around and tell the scariest stories we'd ever heard. Some people were better than others at this kind of storytelling.

I've told my share of them, to be sure. I used to love to watch my fellow campers' eyes get bigger and bigger, see them biting their nails, and watch as they covered their ears so they couldn't hear any more. Then came the punch line at the end when they all screamed little-girl screams, and we'd fall over backwards, laughing. Great fun. Right?

Supernatural events. Do they really happen? Perhaps. Some reports appear to have some authenticity. I do not, however, believe that these supernatural events are of a *godly* nature. No—in fact, I believe their nature is *occult*. Why should we put it past Satan and his demons to manifest themselves occasionally in spooky, frightening, confusing ways?

However, I believe Satan is much more dangerous when he appears as an angel of light. That's *really* spooky because then he is able to work against the church, the body of believers, confusing them—causing them to stumble, to doubt, and even to sin.

As long as he appears to us in monstrous form, there is little danger that we'll follow him. In fact, most would run like crazy from him. But if he's beautiful, successful, and rich, has a charming personality and speaks words from the Bible, then he does become dangerous. That's why we're told to be on our guard, to watch out for the deceiver. That's why we're warned there will be wolves in sheep's clothing within Christ's flock who will rise up and seek to devour whoever they can.

> *Be sober-minded; be watchful.* Your adversary the devil prowls around like a roaring lion, seeking someone to devour. *Resist him, firm in your faith. (1 Peter 5:8-9a)*

> *Beware of false prophets,* who come to you in sheep's clothing but inwardly are ravenous wolves. *You will recognize them by their fruits. (Matthew 7:15-16a)*

> *You are of your father the devil, and your will is to do your father's desires. He was a murderer from the beginning, and* has nothing to do with the truth, because there is no truth in him. When he lies, he speaks out of his own character, for he is a liar and the father of lies. *(John 8:44)*

We need to heed these warnings to be on our guard against the craftiness of Satan. Why would the Bible repeatedly warn us if he were not a very real danger? How are we to fight against him? By knowing the *truth*. If we know what God's Word teaches, we have a standard to go by. Whenever we hear something that departs from that standard, our ears should perk up, the red flags should be raised, and the alarms should go off.

Take the alphabet, for instance. We have a thorough knowledge of its precise order. If someone, even someone we respect, tells us that "d" doesn't really follow "c" anymore, but instead we are to place a "q" there, we would instantly recognize that this person is in error. The same goes for someone who *knows* the Word of God. Once we understand it, we can better recognize error when we hear it. In this way we are to "test" (or question) the content of what we hear. "Beloved, *do not believe every spirit*, but *test the spirits to see whether they are from God*, for many false prophets have gone out into the world" (1 John 4:1).

This section on the occult is here for one reason—to warn readers against pursuing it to achieve the peace-at-any-cost that some of the grief-stricken seek.

Therefore, as we discuss the "things that go bump in the night," keep in mind that Satan is a deceiver, a liar, and the father of lies. It is in his best interest to confuse people and to derail them from the truth.

Communicating with the Dead

The Bible strictly forbids *any* attempt to communicate with the dead: "There shall not be found among you anyone who burns his son or his daughter as an offering, *anyone who practices divination* or *tells fortunes* or *interprets omens*, or a *sorcerer* or a *charmer* or a *medium* or a *wizard* or a *necromancer*, for whoever does these things is an abomination to the LORD" (Deuteronomy 18:10-12a). This verse does not leave a lot of room for misunderstanding.

Psychic hotlines have become big business in the United States.

There is a societal thrust toward seeking "revelation" from so-called mediums, tarot card readers, psychics, and clairvoyants. A sign of the times? Perhaps. But in light of the strong passage quoted above, should we who are aligned with Christ seek these people out or try to glean information about our futures? Absolutely not.

When people try to contact the dead, they invite the fellowship of the agents of darkness pretending to be angels of light. Remember 2 Corinthians 11:14-15a: "[F]or even Satan disguises himself as *an angel of light.* So it is no surprise if his servants, also, disguise themselves as *servants of righteousness.*"

Isaiah, the great Old Testament prophet, issued a strong warning that to consult a medium was to turn one's back on God: "And when they say to you, 'Inquire of the mediums and the necromancers who chirp and mutter,' should not a people inquire of their God? Should they inquire of the dead on behalf of the living? To the teaching and to the testimony! If they will not speak according to this word, it is because they have no dawn" (Isaiah 8:19-20).

Pastor Erwin Lutzer states, "The point, of course, is that all information about life after death that comes from spiritists or channelers is unreliable. *Those who turn to the occult world for knowledge of death are misled.* Yes, there is life after death, but we cannot learn the details from *demons,* whose chief delight is to confuse and deceive."[17]

Also the Bible story of Lazarus and the rich man teaches that interaction between heaven and hell cannot occur:

The poor man died and was carried by the angels to Abraham's side. The rich man also died and was buried, and in Hades, being in torment, he lifted up his eyes and saw Abraham far off and Lazarus at his side. And he called out, "Father Abraham, have mercy on me, and send Lazarus to dip the end of his finger in water and cool my tongue, for I am in anguish in this flame." But Abraham said, "Child, remember that you in your lifetime received your good things, and Lazarus in like manner bad things; but now he is comforted here, and you are in anguish. And besides all this, between us and you a great chasm has been fixed, in order that those who would pass from here to you may not be able, and none may cross from there to us." *(Luke 16:22-26)*

Regularly we hear about someone on one TV show or another claiming to have a supernatural power to communicate with the "dearly departed." One man in particular has a television series depicting this kind of "communication." I feel sorry for the poor families waiting breathlessly, tearfully, for any word of comfort from this man or from any others who make such a claim. They are seeking comfort wherever they can find it. Hurting people sometimes defy their own discernment in order to stop the pain. Sometimes they turn to mediums for that elusive comfort and often end up sadly and bitterly disappointed.

Some of these so-called mediums are quacks, to be sure. (One even "talks" to dead pets, she claims.) There may be some, though, who do have the supernatural power to communicate with *demons*, but I don't believe they actually communicate with the *dead*.

Erwin Lutzer wrote about this subject:

[D]emons impersonate the dead to *create the illusion* that the living can communicate with the dead. These spirits have astonishing knowledge of the dead person's life since they carefully observe individuals while they are living. Through the power of deception, they can mimic a deceased person's voice, personality, and even appearance. The King James Version actually translates the word *medium* as those who have "familiar spirits" (Lev. 19:31; 20:6, 27; Deut. 18:11), suggesting the familiarity some demons have with individuals.[18]

Loraine Boettner also addressed this subject in his book *Immortality*:

Usually those who patronize the mediums are people whose Christian faith is weak, or who are not Christians at all. Instead of trustingly accepting and acting upon the information given in the Bible, which information is amply sufficient and clear for those who put their trust in God, they have undertaken to secure direct answers through the spiritualistic mediums. . . . The contact, if it is real, presumably is with evil spirits who impersonate the departed or who profess to give information from them.[19]

Attempting to talk with the dead is expressly and consistently condemned and forbidden by God. Therefore, we can rest assured that He does *not* use this particular vehicle for communication.

It has been suggested by some that demonic spirits may impersonate the dead. They may speak of wholesome things—love, religion, or goodness. They may even go so far as to make favorable references to Christ. Their schemes are designed to confuse and deceive the unwary. Don't fall for them. Beware.

As we'll see in an upcoming chapter, those who are in heaven are completely focused on Christ, continuously praising Him, and in such a blissful state that their memory of earthly things is dim. They would not have the *slightest* desire to spend their time with us in this place when they are there with Christ in the next life.

The Bible teaches that death causes a complete break with all that belongs to this world. In 2 Samuel 12:23, King David says about his son, who has just died, "But now he is dead. Why should I fast? Can I bring him back again? I shall go to him, but *he will not return to me.*" Job 7:9-10 says, "As the cloud fades and vanishes, so he who goes down to Sheol *does not come up*; he returns *no more* to his house, nor does his place know him anymore."

People in heaven will have no reason or desire to return to the earth. Heaven will be a place of perfect peace and rest. Those who have a spiritual appreciation for the blessedness of that state know it is *preposterous* to believe our loved ones would, even for an *instant*, desire the *distraction* of communication through a medium to those they loved on earth. Their complete trust in Christ in *all* matters would satisfy any concerns they may have for us. Their joy is directed instead to the source of all joy, God Almighty.

Near-Death Experiences

We've all heard about them, read about them, wondered about them. Near-death experiences can be defined as, "The account of their perceptions by persons who have experienced actually coming close to death. Some of these persons believe that they have had a glimpse of the situation of life after death."[20]

Most people who report these occurrences say they have somehow separated from their bodies, been transported into a dark tunnel, and seemed to travel toward a bright light at the end of the tunnel. What they see after that varies from person to person. Then, after a period of "revelation," they are transported back into their physical bodies where they live to tell about their experiences beyond death's door.

Pastor Erwin Lutzer warns, "Near-death experiences may or may not reflect the true conditions of life beyond death. They must be carefully evaluated to see whether they conform to the biblical picture of the hereafter."[21] Notice that Lutzer doesn't disregard these experiences completely. He leaves the door open to the *possibility* that some of them may be valid. But we judge these experiences the same way we judge accounts about angels. If someone, even someone trusted and sincere, tells us of an experience that occurred to him or her at death's door, and then came back into the body again, we should use spiritual discernment before believing the event could possibly be legitimate.

If the person tells us something that contradicts the clear truth of Scripture, we are duty bound to *disbelieve* the account. Remember Satan—the deceiver? His principal goal is to lure us away from the truth, and he's very crafty in the ways he pursues his goal. Any great liar knows that if you add some truth to the equation, the lie becomes more believable. Don't be confused and swayed by things that *sound* believable but contradict Scripture.

Lutzer affirms this advice as well:

> We know that at least some positive near-death experiences are demonic, for *they sharply contradict the teaching of the Bible.* First, some . . . tell us that the Jesus they met assured them that everyone will have an equally blissful welcome into the life beyond. Second, we are told that there is no judgment, no rigorous examination of a person's life. Several people explicitly mention that the "being of Light" they met gives everyone an unconditional welcome.
>
> One woman reported that when she crossed the line between

life and death she met Christ, who took her for a walk. He explained that all the religions of the world were paths to the same destination. There was a Buddhist path, a Hindu path, an Islamic path, and of course, a Christian path. But, like spokes in a wheel, all of them led to the central hub of heaven. In other words, everyone will be saved. This has always been Satan's most believable lie.[22]

These accounts absolutely contradict the truth of the Bible. That is how we can discern their error. *There is really only one reliable source of information about life after death—and that's God.* We can't do any better than to study what the Bible has to say about the hereafter. We can't give any validity to what others say—especially if it contradicts the Bible.

What happens to us when we die is a matter of great curiosity. No one on this side of death can claim ultimate reliability on the subject. In the next chapter, we'll discuss a few of the absolutes we *are* given about death.

As this world is constituted there must be shadows as well as light, night as well as day, pain as well as pleasure, a departure from life as well as an entrance into it.
LORAINE BOETTNER

9

DEATH

It becomes increasingly evident that the way we view death deter-mines, to a surprising degree, the way we live our lives.
BILLY GRAHAM

CROSSING OVER

When Paula drove up to the house, she noticed Laura sitting in the moonlight on the ornate iron bench in front of the house. The girl visibly straightened as Paula approached.

"Hey, Laura." Paula sat down next to her, setting her nursing bag down beside her. She put her arm around Laura's shoulders and looked up into the starry sky. Neither of them said anything for several long seconds.

"How's everything going in there?" Paula asked, nodding toward the house.

"Well, I tell you, everyone's going to be awfully glad to see *you*. We've all been waiting. The other nurse is nice, but I'm just glad you're here. My parents really depend on you, you know. Daddy just *adores* you."

Paula smiled. "The feeling's mutual."

"Yeah, I know."

"How are *you* doing, Laura?"

"Oh, I guess I'm okay. Daddy doesn't even know I'm there."

"Maybe he does. Maybe he just can't show it right now."

Laura shrugged and studied her shoes as she kicked at a leaf on the ground. "Whatever."

"I'd better get in there, I guess. I'm supposed to relieve Carrie at midnight. Will you be okay?"

"Yeah. Just thought I'd wait for you out here."

"If you need to talk, you know I'm here for you, don't you?"

"Yeah, I know. But I'm okay."

"Is Sarah here yet?" Paula asked.

"Nope. Probably be another hour or so. She and John had to come from Siloam Springs."

"I'm looking forward to meeting them. Are you coming in too?"

"Nah, I'll stay out here. I'll be in shortly, okay?"

"Sure."

Paula picked up her bag and went in through the kitchen door. When she stepped into the den, Carrie looked up, relief flooding her face. Carrie had been on-call when Penny had phoned hospice about Bachman's condition. She started packing up her equipment as Paula greeted Penny with a hug. An attractive, sandy-haired man also stood to meet her. Penny introduced him as Alex, their worship pastor from church.

"Alex." Paula shook his hand enthusiastically. "Bachman's best friend. He's told me so much about you. He says you've kept him sane through all of this—that you won't let him take himself too seriously."

"Funny, that's the same thing he's told me about *you*." He smiled.

One glance at her buddy, Bachman McNair III, told her how he was doing. However, she excused herself as she and Carrie walked into the kitchen.

"I've been here since 6:30 tonight," Carrie reported. "Mrs. McNair called at about 5:45 to say he had started to breathe irregularly, and his feet were cold and starting to mottle. So I came to assess him. She was right to call. I think this is it for him. His temp has been steadily climbing. His axillary temp is now 102.6. Respirations are at forty-eight. Seems to be Cheyne-Stoking some now. The periods of apnea are anywhere from twelve to fifteen seconds. Heart rate is 120."

"What's his BP?"

"The systolic BP has been running in the 80s since I got here, but the last pressure I got was 78/40."

"Is he responsive?"

"Well, I'm calling it 'poorly responsive' in my notes. He opens his eyes when he's moved, but there's no response otherwise."

"Okay. Well, thanks for being here with him. I'll take it from here."

"You know what? These people were as sweet as they could be, but I could tell they couldn't wait for you to get here. I know he's sort of your baby."

"Yeah, he is. Thanks for calling me. I wouldn't want to be anywhere but here tonight."

"Okay, I'll head on home now. Maybe I can get a little sleep before my pager goes off again."

Paula smiled and walked Carrie to the door. "Yeah, I hope so. Hope you have a quiet rest-of-the-night."

Paula started unpacking the things she would need to monitor Bachman's condition as she listened to Alex and Penny talking about some adventure he and Bach had experienced on the Buffalo River a couple of years ago.

She looked into Bachman's pale, drawn face and then leaned close to him and whispered, "I'm here, Bach. I'm right here. Can you hear me?"

He opened his eyes only a sliver, then tiring with the effort, closed them again. But Paula believed that he knew she was there. She kissed his bald head as she had done so many times before—this time choking back the tears that burned at the back of her eyes and nose.

Working quickly, she checked his vital signs and carefully gave him a head-to-toe assessment, noting every detail. His face had a creamy-yellow cast. The lights from the two lamps in the room cast shadows into the crevices of his eyes, under his cheekbones, and under his upper lip. His breathing was labored and irregular. Panting at a rate of about forty-eight breaths per minute for several seconds, he would stop breathing for a few seconds, take a couple of ragged, deep breaths, and then start the panting pattern again.

It was hard to hear his heartbeat because fluid was accumulating in his lungs, making too much noise for her to hear the heart sounds through the stethoscope. But according to a weak and thready pulse, she could tell that his heart was still racing at over 120 beats per minute. His blood pressure was too weak for her to hear clearly through the stethoscope; so she had to obtain it the old way—by palpation. She located a pulse at the inside of the elbow, pumped up the cuff until she couldn't feel the pulse anymore, and released the pressure, letting the gauge slowly fall. She felt the pulse again at seventy-four. Doing a pressure this way does not yield a bottom number; so she noted it as "seventy-four palp."

Even though Bachman was getting supplemental oxygen, his nail beds were purple. His hands, nose, and feet were cold. The appearance of the skin in his lower extremities was splotchy with purplish spots and speckles up to and including the knees.

After jotting down her findings, she turned to the anxious faces of the family. By this time Laura was back in the room, sitting next to Alex on the sofa, leaning into his shoulder like a little girl. Penny was sitting on the other side of Bachman's hospital bed watching every move, though she'd seen this assessment process many times before.

Moving to the other side of the room out of Bachman's hearing, Paula told them what they were waiting to hear. "Well, I guess you guys suspect that this is the end. I believe he's very close at this point. His blood pressure is very low; so his heart and lungs are compensating for it by going faster. His heart is pumping over 120 beats per minute. A normal heart rate is 60 to 100 beats per minute. Because his heart is pumping so fast, his lungs have to work overtime to keep up. But his temp is also elevated, and that causes the heart rate and respiratory rate to increase as well. The mottling has already risen to his knees. So he's really in his last few hours, I would think."

"Should we call an ambulance or something?" Alex asked.

Before Paula could answer, a response came from the person least likely to comment. Laura's clear, sweet voice said, "No. We don't have to call an ambulance. Since we've got hospice, he can just stay here. He wanted to die at home instead of in a hospital, didn't he, Mother?"

Penny blinked back tears as she looked at her youngest daughter in surprise. "Yes, that's right. He wanted to be right here with all of us."

They had expected a struggle with Laura over allowing her father to die at home. But tonight she was suddenly calm, composed, and accepting.

Good for Laura, Paula thought to herself. Then closing her eyes, she breathed a "thank you" to God.

"I wish Sarah would get here," Laura remarked as she looked out the kitchen window again. "I think I'll wait for her outside. Okay, Mother?"

"Sure, honey. Take a jacket. It's chilly out there. We'll come for you if anything happens."

Paula set to work bathing Bachman's face, throat, shoulders, arms, and chest with tepid water in an attempt to alleviate his fever. He opened his eyes. Penny, who was sitting right next to him holding his hand, told him quickly, "It's okay, sweetie. I'm right here." She held his frail hand to her cheek. "I'm right here."

Paula's own eyes filled as she saw the tears spill out of Penny's eyes, run down her cheeks, and then fall onto Bachman's hand. Penny pressed her quivering mouth to the back of his hand and then reached over to softly stroke his forehead, mustering a brave, regal smile.

Suddenly the door opened, and voices sounded in the kitchen. Laura entered the room with her sister, a beautiful girl with dark eyes that glowed with love for her father. Those eyes were riveted on him as she strode purposefully toward the hospital bed. John, her fiancé, bustled into the room after the girls, carrying a suitcase and a garment bag. Paula moved out of the way.

Sitting on the side of his bed, Sarah leaned over and held her father in her arms. She buried her face in his thin shoulder and wept. Paula could hear her saying over and over, "It's okay, Daddy. I love you. It's okay. You go on to Jesus if you need to, Daddy. It's okay." John stood behind his wife-to-be and placed both hands on her shoulders.

Sarah raised up slightly and, holding her father's hand, looked intently at his closed eyes. Laura crawled onto the bed and curled her slender body around Bachman's skeletal form. Penny sat in her chair beside the bed and patted Laura's leg comfortingly.

Paula memorized each face, each touch, and each tear. *I'll never forget this image as long as I live.* Alex moved over next to her, his eyes also moist with tears. Paula put her arm around his waist in a gesture of comfort.

"Alex," came Penny's soft voice, "will you say a prayer for Bach?"

"Certainly. I'd be honored."

Alex and Paula joined the circle around the bed. They all held hands—Sarah holding one of her father's hands and Laura holding the other.

"Our precious Lord," Alex began, his voice choked with emotion, "thank You so much for giving us the opportunity to know and love Bachman McNair. Thank You for what he's meant to all of us. We know You are in control of all things—even of the time of our deaths—and we thank You for that, knowing all things work according to Your perfect will.

"We also thank You, Lord, for providing this family with the hospice program, and thank You especially for sending Bachman a nurse who would love him and care for him as she would her own family. Thank You for the strength You've given to Penny, Laura, and Sarah through this time. Lord, You've given Bachman the courage and the insight he needed to trust You throughout his illness, and we know he trusts You even now at the time of his death.

"Continue to be merciful to him, Lord, and take him to be with You. Then, Lord, we ask that You would give us all a portion of Your strength and comfort in the next few days, weeks, and months, as we struggle to move on with our lives. We know that as Your children, we will one day be reunited with him as we take our places in heaven with You.

"Be with us now, Lord, as we commend Bachman's spirit to You. Amen."

"Thank you, Alex," Penny whispered. She resumed her watch at her husband's bedside. Sarah and John quietly moved to the sofa as Laura curled up in her father's leather chair. Alex strode into the kitchen, trailing a sniffle behind him. They could hear water running as he made a fresh pot of coffee.

Paula saw that it was almost 1:00 A.M. now; so she set about reassessing Bachman's condition, something she did once an hour. This time she was unable to even palpate a blood pressure. Bachman's heart had slowed to eighty-four beats per minute. His breathing had slowed to about twelve breaths per minute with long pauses in between. He was mottled to the groin now. She suspected he would not make it to

2:00. She sat back in her chair on the other side of the bed and watched him, remembering all the fun times, all the sweet times, all the sad times she'd experienced with him. She also thought about the others she'd taken care of. The special ones stood out in her mind.

She was jogged from her reverie by Alex's soft tenor voice singing, "Amazing grace, how sweet the sound . . ." They all joined in, singing slowly and softly in a melodic tribute to Bachman and to the God who had saved each of them.

At 1:43 A.M. Bachman opened his eyes once more and then went through the motions of taking a deep, deep breath, but no air actually moved into his mouth. Paula whispered, "This is it."

Penny bent over him, kissing his temple, and whispered, "Bach, I love you so much. Good-bye, my darling."

Moving again to the bedside, the girls watched their father take his last six breaths. Without tears now, Penny watched her husband close his eyes, wince once, relax, wince again, relax, and then as a long, slow breath escaped his lips, he crossed from one life into another. They all watched—waiting for another breath. But no breath came. After a full sixty-second count, Paula looked at her watch and pronounced death at 1:45 A.M. on October 5.

LET'S TALK ABOUT DEATH

What happens when we die? Why do we have to talk about it at all? How does death affect each one of us? What is its significance?

Dr. Loraine Boettner illustrated the way death sometimes touches us:

> We set out on the journey of life with high hopes and soaring ambitions. Life seems rosy and death seems far away. Year after year life runs its accustomed course, smoothly and serenely. We read of thousands dying from starvation in India, and other thousands that drown in China; but those places are far away and the people are not known to us. A neighbor down the street dies. That causes us to stop and think. We send flowers and feel sorry for the fam-

ily. But still it does not affect us directly, and we soon continue with our work and play. *There develops within us a sense of immunity to tragedy and death.* Then suddenly the bottom drops out of our world. Perhaps a mother or father, or some other relative or friend, is taken, leaving an aching void. Many of us have already had that experience. We have watched the changing face and have listened helplessly to the shortening breath. We have spoken or looked the last good-bye, and then, in an instant, the departing one has passed out of sight and out of hearing, into the world of the unknown. The body which, perhaps only yesterday, was so full of life and animation, now lies before us an insensate piece of clay. A short time ago the one we loved was here, going about his work or speaking to us; and now, perhaps in one moment, he is gone— gone so very, very far away. What baffling thoughts rush in upon the mind in those moments pressing for an answer. But there is no answer in either reason or experience. *The Bible alone has an answer for the thoughts that come with such perplexity and insistence.*[1]

How powerful is the concept of death to us? That depends on how *closely* it strikes us, doesn't it? Does it happen to the nameless, faceless thousands in faraway countries? A neighbor down the street? Your father, mother, son, or daughter? A husband or wife? Or will death score a direct hit on *you*?

In this chapter we'll discuss death—what it is, as well as what it isn't. From both physical and biblical perspectives we will describe what occurs when a person dies.

The Wages of Sin

Why does death exist in the first place? Death is the penalty for sin. When we die, we are receiving the wages of sin—our *own* sin. Romans 6:23 states, "For the wages of sin is death . . ." Death is the *consequence* of sin. Sin began with Adam and has been an "inherited" trait ever since. We are *born* into sin.

In his thesis titled "Christian Maturity" Doug Reed effectively explains this concept: "The word 'sin' is an old archery term from the

King James English. It means to miss the mark or target. Understanding this gives the concept of sin a whole new meaning. To sin is to miss the mark."[2]

What mark are we to aim for? Perfection. Christ is our standard. Once this is realized, one can easily affirm the truth of Romans 3:23, which says, "for all *have sinned* and *fall short* of the glory of God." Or Romans 3:10-12: "'None is righteous, no, not one; no one understands; no one seeks for God. All have turned aside; together they have become worthless; no one does good, not even one'."

When we understand the standard, how can we possibly claim to have attained such a level of righteousness? None of us can. Therefore, we are forced to admit that we are sinners. And our wage, according to God who created us, is death.

However, God did not leave us without hope. Instead, because of His love for us, He provided a way for us to be declared righteous after all. The means He used to accomplish this was to send His Son, Jesus Christ, to take on a fleshly body but also to live a perfectly righteous and sinless life among us. It is that perfect righteousness that accomplishes our salvation.

When Christ died, He received the punishment for the cumulative sins of His people. None of that sin was His own. He took our "badness" and gave us His "goodness" so that, by this substitution or transfer, we could be declared righteous before God. (See chapter 5 for a detailed discussion of God's sovereignty in salvation.)

This gospel message is not easy to accept for those who do not yet have a Spirit-infused understanding of such things. In fact, Dr. John MacArthur described the problems society might have regarding such teaching: "The gospel itself is disagreeable, unattractive, repulsive, and alarming *to the world*. It exposes sin, condemns pride, convicts the unbelieving heart, and shows human righteousness—even the best, most appealing aspects of human nature—to be worthless, defiled, filthy rags (cf. Isa. 64:6). . . . It comes as *bad news* to *those who love sin* and many who hear it for the first time react with *disdain* against the messenger."[3]

This is not a message easily embraced by the multitudes. In fact, only those who are given spiritual eyes to comprehend the truth of the gospel will come to accept it, to love it, and to attempt to share it in any way they can.

What does this have to do with death? Just this: Without the salvation that comes from the Lord, all mankind would be sentenced to an eternity separated from God in hell. But because of His mercy and lovingkindness, He has ordained that *some* of fallen humanity would be redeemed and share eternity with Him.

The typical response might be, "That's not fair. It's not fair that He chose some and not others." But it's not supposed to be "fair." Actually, we shouldn't desire fairness. If we were given what is "fair," everyone would be eternally condemned. So we should be forever thankful for His tender mercies to such undeserving sinners.

Let's put this concept of "unfairness" in a more familiar context to aid our understanding. At a Wal-Mart parking lot you see an elderly woman struggling to carry a huge bag of pine bark mulch to her car. You stop, take the load from her, carry it to her car, and deposit it in her trunk. She thanks you sweetly. A couple of minutes later you see someone else three aisles over also struggling with a load. But you're already in your car by now; so you go on home. You've done something nice for someone. You are pleased to have been able to help. The other person could say, "It's not fair that you helped the old lady, and you didn't help me." Would that be an appropriate allegation? Of course not. You see, fair doesn't have anything to do with it. You *chose* to help one person. You performed an act of kindness. That doesn't make you *unfair* because you didn't help the other. If God *chooses* to have mercy on one person and not another, that's His prerogative. It does not make Him *unfair*. It makes Him *gracious* because He shows mercy on *some* when *none* deserve it.

Here's another illustration of this grace of God. Imagine that every person in the world is caught up in a powerfully swift torrent of water that empties into hell. Through our own efforts there is no way we can escape this swirling current. Without God's direct intervention we would all rush into the yawning abyss. But God, in His mercy and lovingkindness, plucks *some* from the racing water, rescuing His children from certain destruction. There is nothing unfair about this. In fact, it demonstrates His power, love, and grace.

Paul deals with this attitude in Romans 9:14-16: "What shall we say then? Is there *injustice* on God's part? By no means! For [God] says to Moses, '*I will have mercy on whom I have mercy, and I will have compassion on whom I have compassion.*' So then it depends not on *human will or exertion*, but on God, who has mercy." The truth of the matter is that if our salvation were dependent on *our own* initiative, *no one* would *ever* be saved.

DEATH—THE COMMON DENOMINATOR

As Boettner has asserted, we tend to become *lulled* into a sense of immunity from death and its accompanying sorrows when we are not directly touched by its icy breath. However, when death comes closer to us, we begin to fret about it. We begin to feel helpless and hopeless against such an adversary. When that happens, we need to remember *who* is in charge. Death is not in charge. Our illness is not in charge. But the Lord God *is* in charge.

"Our future existence is not in the hands of doctors, nor in the hands of disease, nor in the hands of the drunk who runs into our car along the highway. *Our life is in the hands of the Almighty, who can use any means He wishes, including the above, to have us brought into the heavenly gates,*"[4] writes Erwin Lutzer.

That's not a bad thing. That is a very good thing. When we realize that God the Father Almighty holds us in His all-powerful hand, we can truly relax and find acceptance in a situation that otherwise makes no sense. "We must learn to live by His agenda if we are to trust Him."[5]

The why's threaten to overtake us otherwise. *Why* did my best friend develop cancer? *Why* did my baby boy have to die so young? *Why* do I have to suffer like this? *Why* is this happening to me? These questions stem from pain and bewilderment. Even the asking of them can cause us anguish and sorrow.

In the book of Hebrews we're told that Christ has defeated death and that death is under *His* control. Lutzer wrote about this truth:

Christ came, wrote the author of Hebrews, that "through death he might render powerless him who had the power of death, that is, the devil; and might deliver those who through *fear of death* were subject to slavery all their lives" (Heb. 2:14-15). Satan does not have the power of death in the sense that he determines the day a believer dies. But he has used the *fear* of death to keep Christians in bondage, unable to approach the curtain with a tranquility borne of the "full assurance of faith."[6]

Puritan Richard Baxter apparently was able to overcome his own fear of death, for he wrote these reassuring words: "Stir up then, O my soul, thy sincere desires, and all thy faculties, to do the remnant of the work of Christ appointed thee on earth, and then joyfully wait for the heavenly perfection in God's own time."[7]

One of my objectives in writing this book has been to comfort those going through the agony of facing death. It is my prayer and desire to help readers along the journey from bewilderment to acceptance of death or any other adversity, armed with the knowledge of God's sovereign control over all things. As Susan Hunt writes, "And such *acceptance* saves us a lot of emotional, mental, and physical energy. We experience *peace* rather than the exhaustion that comes when we argue with God, search for answers, or demand that He act the way we want Him to. With *acceptance* comes *calm*. We choose to *rest* in the fact that the Father possesses infinite and perfect wisdom and knowledge and that these are the basis for His judgments, however inscrutable they may be to us."[8]

The only way I know to make sense of it all is by utilizing the means Boettner earlier described: "The Bible alone has an answer for the thoughts that come with such perplexity and insistence." Remember 2 Timothy 3:16: "*All Scripture* is breathed out by God. . . ." The Bible is the *inspired* Word of God. In it we can read the things God deemed important for us to know. It is *entirely* reliable, and it is the *only* source of real *truth*.

"All flesh [mankind] is grass, and all its beauty is like the flower of the field. The grass withers, the flower fades when the breath of the LORD blows on it; *surely the people are grass*. The *grass withers*, the *flower fades*, but the *word of our God will stand forever*" (Isaiah 40:6b-8).

In God's Word, death is addressed on two levels—the physical aspect and the spiritual aspect. We'll begin with physical death.

Physical Death

The study, or science, of death is called *thanatology*. It is not my design to prepare a scientific thesis on this subject but only to provide necessary information before moving on to the spiritual implications.

Death has been defined as the "permanent cessation of all vital functions."[9] The body is unresponsive. There is no movement or breathing, and there are no reflexes.

Some deaths are sudden, traumatic, and devastating. Some are painful. Some are peaceful. Some are instantaneous. Others are drawn out, lingering, and seem to wear us down over time.

Usually people are more worried about the *act of dying* than they are about *death* itself. "I've never done it before." "I'm not really sure how I'm supposed to go about it." "What will it feel like?" "Will it hurt?"

In that sense, death is a little like giving birth for the first time. Many women worry about childbirth. They realize that their dreams are tied up in what happens *afterward*—the holding, loving, and caring for their baby. But to get from pregnant to holding your baby in your arms, you have to experience the actual *birth!* It is a necessary part of the experience. "But how do you do it?" "What does it feel like?" "Will it hurt?"

As with childbirth, dying people's hopes are fixed on what happens *afterward*. That's where they'll find their reward (if they are children of God). Their dreams may be tied up in the joys and blessedness of heaven, but to get from sickness to heaven you have to go through the act of dying. "Death rescues us from the endlessness of this existence; it is the means by which those who love God finally are brought to Him."[10]

The process of dying is not really something we need to worry about. Like childbirth, it just happens. It generally takes care of itself. You don't have to graduate from a class in order to achieve it.

I've heard that women used to give birth in the fields as they worked, bundle up the baby, and continue working. In the past, Indian women often went off by themselves, gave birth, and then came back into the village with babe in arms as a part of certain tribal customs. Childbirth occurs *naturally* in response to the body's timing.

So does death. The sovereign hand of God ultimately governs both events. But my point is this: When it's time, it will happen. You can't change your mind and chicken out of either event. There comes a time when you reach the point of no return. The outcome is inevitable.

I am speaking, of course, in general terms. I understand there are difficult cases of childbirth that require skilled medical expertise. I also understand that with a difficult death experience, it is sometimes helpful to have some medical intervention to ensure comfort. But in general our bodies will do what they were meant to do.

Spiritual Death

What happens spiritually when people die? What comes next? We will all die. Our bodies will go to the grave, but our spirits do not. Our spirits do not die. Some instantly reside with God in heaven. Some instantly reside in the torment of hell. You see, it's not the act of dying that really matters—it's the *destination* afterwards that counts.

The soul, or spirit, *immediately* separates from the body at death. The body becomes a mere shell without life, an inanimate object, a piece of insensate clay. The spirit is set free. But its destination differs, depending on whether the spirit belongs to God or not. The souls of believers go *immediately* into God's presence. "Yes, we are of good courage, and we would rather be away from the body and at home with the Lord" (2 Corinthians 5:8). To be absent from the body is to be present with the Lord. There is no mention of any stops along the way.

This separation of body and spirit is only temporary. At the resurrection, the body and spirit will be reunited. Only then the body will rise imperishable. It will be a changed, resurrected body. Each of us will face the Day of Judgment, now with body and spirit reunited. We will either "rise to live" eternally with Christ in heaven or "rise to be condemned" to an eternity without Him in hell (John 5:28-29).

According to Loraine Boettner, "'Life,' in Scriptural and theological language, means not primarily continuation of existence, but a rich spiritual existence in association with God; and likewise, 'death,' in Scriptural and theological language, means primarily not cessation of existence, nor separation of body and spirit, but separation from God."[11]

Psalm 9:13b says, "O you [God] who lift me up from the gates of death. . . ." Death is the gate, the doorway, from one life to the other. Charles Spurgeon, one of the nineteenth century's most brilliant preachers, said, "[T]hink not that heaven and earth are divided. They are but kindred worlds, two ships moored close to one another, one short plank of death will enable you to step from one into the other."[12] What a beautiful description of death—one short plank that enables us to step from this life into the eternal one. Or as Erwin Lutzer wrote, "Death is the chariot our heavenly Father sends to bring us to Himself."[13]

Death is the actual vehicle by which we can move from this place, this existence, this life into the next. For believers that next life will be far better, far happier, far more wondrous and precious than anything we can imagine. For unbelievers that next life will be one of eternal torment worse than anything they can imagine. (This will be explained in greater detail in the next chapter.)

COMMON MYTHS ASSOCIATED WITH DEATH

Let's discuss for a moment what *does not* happen after death. Here is what the Word of God declares.

Purgatory

The Bible does *not* teach the doctrine of purgatory. In Roman Catholicism, purgatory is perceived to be "a place where the souls of believers go to be further purified from sin until they are ready to be admitted into heaven."[14] But the Scriptures teach that Christ paid the total price for our sins *once for all*, and there is, therefore, no need of further purification. We are considered "not guilty" when Christ redeems us. We are not cleansed by purgatory but by the blood of Christ, our Savior. This blood sacrifice was given freely to those who love Him, and it paid the debt of sin *completely*. "[Christ] has no need, like those high priests, to offer sacrifices daily, first for his own sins and then for those of the people, since he did this *once for all* when he offered up himself" (Hebrews 7:27). "But if we walk in the light, as he is in the light, we have fellowship with one another, and the *blood of Jesus his Son* cleanses us from *all* sin" (1 John 1:7).

John MacArthur comments on purgatory in his book *The Glory of Heaven:* "The Roman Catholic doctrine of purgatory is nowhere taught in Scripture. It was devised to accommodate Catholicism's denial of justification by faith alone."[15] He says that Catholics view purgatory as the place where people gain whatever merit they may be lacking to enter heaven. He continues by saying, "No post-mortem suffering is necessary to atone for remaining sin; *all* our sins are covered by the blood of Christ."[16]

Let's look at just a couple of the many passages that teach that the spirit of a believer goes immediately into heaven, without *any* stops in between. "And [the thief on the cross] said, 'Jesus, remember me when you come into your kingdom,' And [Jesus] said to him, '*Truly, I say to you*, today *you will be with me in Paradise*'" (Luke 23:42-43). "I [Paul] am hard pressed between the two. My desire is to *depart and be with Christ*, for that is far better. But to remain in the flesh is more necessary on your account" (Philippians 1:23-24). You see, it is one or the other—in the body or with Christ. No intermediary destination is ever mentioned in the Bible.

Most Roman Catholics think that there are things we can do in this life to help those in purgatory reach heaven faster. They believe that prayer on behalf of the deceased persons, masses said for them, or offerings given for their benefit can help their loved ones attain the purity they will need. The Scriptures do not teach these things.

Loraine Boettner explained, "We believe that it avails nothing to pray for the dead. . . . Prayers for the dead imply that their state has not yet been fixed and that it can be improved at our request."[17]

That brings up a great point—why pray for the dead? When believers die, they enter into God's presence—a state of perfect happiness with Him. So why would anyone need to pray for them? When unbelievers die, they go to a place of punishment and separation from the presence of God. It does no good whatsoever to pray for them now. At the time of our death, our eternity is fixed. There are no second chances.

Second Probation

Simply put, this is a false doctrine stating that if a person dies in a lost state, he or she has a second chance to accept the Lord and thereby to inherit the kingdom of heaven.

> Almost universally the Christian Church has held that only those who are believers at death are saved, and that there is no second chance nor opportunity of any kind for repentance after death. . . . Support for the theory . . . is based more on general humanitarian conjectures or surmises of what God in His love and goodness might be expected to do . . . rather than on any solid Scriptural foundation. . . . The solemn reality is that all who die in unbelief pass beyond death to a lost eternity. . . . Scripture uniformly represents the state of the righteous and that of the wicked after death as fixed.[18]

Hebrews 9:27 supports this belief when it says, " . . . just as it is appointed for a man *to die once*, and *after that* comes judgment."

Here's the biggest problem I see to the theory of second probation (besides the fact that it is *completely* contrary to God's Word). If we all get a second chance at salvation, why wouldn't we just grab all the gusto we can get in this life and save the repentance until the next? Let's eat, drink, and be merry in this life. Who cares? We can *always* be saved after death. No, I'm afraid not!

What a frivolous and corrupted idea. Yet there are those who ignore the Bible's clear teaching and believe they will get a second chance. They will be very, very disappointed someday. (And that is a *monumental* understatement.)

Soul Sleep

Soul sleep is a theory holding that when the physical body goes to the grave, the soul is buried with it. Both body and soul sleep until Christ's return. This idea may have come from the way the body actually looks after death—like it's sleeping.

However, in reality the spirit is *freed* from its shell (the body). The spirit is fully conscious and active and *alive*. It is reunited with the body at the resurrection.

Here is the distinction. The *body* sleeps until the resurrection. Therefore, resurrection applies only to the body. The soul doesn't need resurrection because it doesn't die.

Remember the parable about Lazarus and the rich man? One was lost. One was saved. But both were fully awake and conscious immediately after death.

It's true that Scripture sometimes speaks of death as "sleeping," but it is important to realize that sleep is only used as a *metaphor* for death. The body does the sleeping. The spirit does not.

Reincarnation

This romantic notion appeals to many people and is shared by numerous religions throughout the world. It is the belief that when we exit this life, we are born into another earthly existence. This cycle, or what some call "the continuity of life," repeats until a certain level of purity and perfection has been achieved.

Belief in reincarnation *totally* contradicts the Bible, but it presents other problems as well. If people think they will come back as another person, their responsibility for this life would be less important. After all, they might think, they will get another chance . . . and another and another.

We've all heard the stories, some even from famous people, of those who claim to "remember" a former life. One explanation is that the story is rigged and bogus from the start. Another option is that they are misled. Their stories can be quite compelling. They may even appear to be in possession of facts that they could not *possibly* have known. In the way the stories are presented, there is (seemingly) no other explanation than that they actually did have a previous life. But that's leaving Satan out of the equation. Remember his purpose and his goal. He is the deceiver. He is crafty, and his goal is always to turn people from God and toward himself (whether they are aware of it or not).

If some supernatural knowledge has been imparted to the people who claim to have been reincarnated, how cleverly disguised is Satan's craftiness. He sometimes even uses children to convey these stories. People mistake the innocence of the child for authenticity. What better way for Satan to confuse and deceive. Beware!

Annihilation

Unfortunately, this may be one of the most popular theories. It is the belief that once the body dies, the spirit dies too. The spirit ceases to exist, and the body rots in the grave. There is nothing after death. We are just totally annihilated.

I have a friend who espouses this belief. It's the only option that makes sense to her. The whole idea of an all-powerful God, of Christ His Son, of a place called heaven or one called hell is beyond her comprehension.

She represents a huge portion of society today—and throughout all time, for that matter. She is a nice person—generous, intelligent, responsible, hard-working, and ambitious. We've been friends for many years, and she has always been there for me. But she is spiritually lost. She is the type of person the Bible refers to when it says, *"The natural person does not accept the things of the Spirit of God, for they are folly to him, and he is not able to understand them because they are spiritually discerned"* (1 Corinthians 2:14).

I have another friend who is a physician, a scientist, a scholar, and probably the most brilliant man I've ever met. He says he believes nothing he cannot prove scientifically. He, like many super-intelligent people, is more comfortable believing in the sufficiency of human reason than trusting in something he perceives as such "utter foolishness" as Christianity. Without God's gift of spiritual insight, human reason dismisses the truth of God as "foolishness."

First Corinthians 1:18-21, 25 states:

> *For the word of the cross is* folly *to those who are perishing, but to us who are being saved it is the power of God. For it is written,* "I will destroy the wisdom of the wise, and the discernment of the discerning I will thwart." *Where is the one who is wise? Where is the scribe? Where is the debater of this age? Has not God made fool-*

ish the wisdom of the world? For since, in the wisdom of God, the world did not know God through wisdom, it pleased God through the folly of what we preach to save those who believe. . . . For the foolishness of God is wiser than men, and the weakness of God is stronger than men.

My [Paul's] message and my preaching were not with wise and persuasive words, but with a demonstration of the Spirit's power, so that *your faith* might not rest *on men's wisdom, but on God's* power. *(1 Corinthians 2:4-5* NIV)

So if you take away all belief in a spiritual existence, you're left with a body that decays into nothingness and a spirit that is snuffed out by death. There would be no consequences for sin, no penalty at all. Not such a bad theory, is it? Except that it's not true.

There *is* eternal life after death. And what we hold to in this life determines where we'll spend the next. Those who believe their lives, body and soul, end at death will be in for a rude awakening. "What emotions other than terror can possibly possess a person when he finally is given an insight into the ultimate reality of things and who with his sins unforgiven goes out into a Christless eternity?"[19]

It saddens me to think of this. Some of those I love will experience this surprising revelation. One day they will come to understand that God is real—that He is the One to be praised and worshiped after all. But it will be too late.

Tragically, those people will be consigned to eternal torment. I don't like to think about that. Yet I know God is sovereign. Those who have been appointed to live with Him forever in heaven will do just that. Nothing can thwart God's plan. Things will work out *exactly* as He has ordained. Whether I love these people or not, they may not be part of God's elect. That is divine justice and is, therefore, perfect. But since we do not know who are the elect and who are not, we are commanded to preach Christ to *all* mankind.

John MacArthur says, "If the plain truth of the gospel doesn't penetrate the heart, no amount of cajoling or salesmanship on the part of the evangelist is going to bring a person to salvation."[20] Salvation does not depend on the eloquence of the preacher, special evangelistic techniques, or the persuasion of rational arguments. It depends entirely on election by the Father, redemption by the Son, and calling by the Holy Spirit who applies saving faith to our very hearts, changing us forever and enabling us to put our faith in Christ.

All I can do for my friends is to proclaim the truth as set forth by the Scriptures and continue to pray for them, as I have done for many, many years. I have also prayed for those of you who would someday come to read this book. The results, however, belong to God. It is up to Him to cause the seed that has been planted to grow and to become fruitful. My duty is just to plant the seed—and even that is in God's sovereign hand. The very fact that you are reading these words right now was guided and directed by God.

Boettner critiques annihilation: "Mere extinction of being would not be a sufficient penalty for the evil, nor a fit reward for the righteous."[21] His point is that annihilation would not be adequate punishment for those who have rejected Christ. There is no suffering in annihilation. On the other hand, there is no joy in annihilation either. Therefore, there would be no ultimate reward for those who have accepted Christ as their Lord and Savior.

However, we're told in the Bible that we *will not* be annihilated. Instead we will step from one earthly existence into an eternal one in heaven or hell. "And many of those who sleep in the dust of the earth shall awake, some to everlasting life, and some to shame and everlasting contempt" (Daniel 12:2).

Boettner reminds us that the Bible gives the only truly reliable information about the state of the soul after death. He continues by saying that "God does not annihilate the wicked . . . but makes them the means of displaying eternally His hatred for sin, as His holiness and justice are manifested in that punishment."[22]

When the Bible says the wicked will perish, it doesn't mean they will be reduced to the state of nonexistence. It means they will be in a *continuing* condition of suffering. Likewise, believers in Christ will enjoy a *continuing* state of blessing—experiencing joy and devotion to Him.

We are told in many places in the Bible that though man's body is mortal, his spirit is immortal. "*I [Christ] give them [the elect] eternal life, and they will never perish*, and no one will snatch them out of my hand" (John 10:28).

Compare what the Bible says regarding those who are *not* believers: "Then he will say to those on his left, 'Depart from me, you cursed, *into the eternal fire* prepared for the devil and his angels.' . . . And *these will go away into eternal punishment, but the righteous into eternal life*" (Matthew 25:41, 46).

As you can clearly see, annihilation is *not* taught in the Scriptures.

Conditional Immortality

This idea is very similar to annihilation. It significantly softens the doctrine of eternal punishment by saying, yes, the righteous will inherit the kingdom of heaven, but those who die in a lost spiritual state—apart from Christ—will be annihilated. Their bodies will decay, and their souls will be snuffed out of existence with death. That would be great news for those who die unrepentant. But conditional immortality is untrue, as demonstrated above.

Universalism

Universalists believe that eventually all people will arrive safely in heaven. Those who believe this haven't been paying attention. Many, many Scripture passages teach the doctrine of eternal punishment.

Here's a question: If we are *all* going to heaven, then what are we *saved* from? Why do the Scriptures make such a big deal about being declared righteous, about believing in the Son of God, about some being granted eternal life in Christ, and some being condemned to eternal misery without Him?

"Universalism has never been widely accepted by those who take the Scriptures seriously. Obviously if this teaching were true, there would be no pressing reason to fulfill the Great Commission or to urge unbelievers to accept Christ in this life."[23]

SUICIDE

What about suicide? People resort to suicide to escape their pain. Sometimes they have physical pain, sometimes emotional. Suicide is *never* the answer. Yet unfortunately some still find it preferable to living.

Erwin Lutzer comments, "Those who do choose suicide (for whatever reason) should remember that death is not the end, but a doorway to an eternal existence. Sad to say, some who find the pain of dying intolerable will waken in a realm that is even more terrible than earth could ever be."[24] Lutzer is speaking of unbelievers. Thinking they are putting an "end to it all," they immediately find themselves just at the beginning of a terror infinitely worse than *anything* they experienced on the earth. What a sobering warning this is.

He says, "[I]t is presumptuous to commit suicide on the premise that all will be well on the other side. For one thing, many people who say they are Christians aren't. Thus for them suicide is a doorway to eternal misery. For another, we forget that we are accountable to Christ for the way we lived (and died) on earth."[25]

Unfortunately some believers also contemplate or commit suicide. The last act these suicide victims perform on this earth is murder. But as tragic as that is, it does not rob them of their inheritance. It does, however, mean that they will have to give an account to Christ for what they've done. They have sinned against God, and they have sinned against the people in their lives. A moment of thoughtlessness leaves loved ones struggling with anguish, confusion, guilt, and pain. Suicide is the ultimate selfishness.

We've all heard the cliché that suicide is a *permanent* solution to a *temporary* problem. Cliché or not, that says it all. Especially when you realize that permanent equals eternal.

Let me encourage those of you contemplating such a horrible option to seek help from someone who can point you to the truth. Call your pastor if you have one. Or call someone else's pastor if you don't. Contact a doctor or a counselor, preferably someone who specializes in Christian counseling. Talk to someone you respect or someone you believe to be really "together," mentally healthy, and wise. Speak to *anyone* who might be able to help you face the situation you're in. Let the person minister to your grieving heart and spirit and lead you beyond the maze of obstacles you're facing to the open spaces where you can see Jesus. He is able to save to the uttermost all who seek His face. You owe it to yourself to try one last option before committing such a drastic act.

One of the goals of this book is to help prevent the broken hearts that can lead to such pain. The time to prepare for a broken heart is *before* it breaks. Arm yourself with the knowledge that can ease your pain and comfort your soul by reminding you of the answers to the questions that begin with "why."

We know that broken hearts will happen. We are told there will be trouble for us on this earth. We *will* get kicked in the teeth sooner or later. We *will* suffer. We *will* grieve. But we're also told to take heart. Christ has overcome the world. The victory is won! In Him we can place our trust, knowing that *whatever* happens to us in this life is either caused or allowed by the God who loves His people, and everything will work to the good of those who love God and are called according to His purposes (Romans 8:28). "I [Christ] have said these things to you, that *in me you may have peace*. In the world you will have tribulation [trouble]. But take heart; I have overcome the world" (John 16:33).

Remember the illustration in a previous chapter about jumping into the waiting arms of your father? Remember also that if we call on the name of the Lord, if we trust Him to save us, He will always be there to catch us when we fall. He doesn't exempt us from pain. He guarantees it, in fact. But He also gives us the solution—simply to trust in Him for all things. He is the only One worthy of our faith and trust.

I saw a sign on a church marquee once that I've never forgotten. It said, "God never promised smooth sailing. He promised a safe harbor." So don't fall prey to your emotions when dealing with a problem that seems too big for you to handle. Use your head. Think. And seek help immediately, especially if the only option you see to erase your pain is to put an abrupt end to your life.

Life does go on. Time does heal pain. A week from now you may be dealing with a completely different set of factors. A month from now you could be well on your way to recovery. A year from now your life may be more meaningful and blessed than you ever thought it could be. Five years from now this pain will be just a distant memory. Don't count yourself out. Don't turn your back on the goodness of God. Cry out to Him for deliverance. "Is not the way of life, through the valley of death, made safe by him that conquered death?"[26]

WHAT ABOUT EUTHANASIA?

Euthanasia is generally described as the deliberate killing of those who are suffering. It is sometimes referred to as "mercy killing." Is euthanasia wrong? In my opinion, it depends on what is specifically meant by the term. Dr. John T. Dunlop defines it like this: "Euthanasia can be categorized as active or passive, as well as voluntary or involuntary. Whereas active euthanasia involves willfully taking positive steps to terminate life, passive euthanasia entails deciding not to take positive steps to prolong life."[27]

Active euthanasia is sometimes called an act of commission, not omission. Something is done directly to *cause* another person's death. This is what Dr. Kevorkian has done in a misguided attempt to ease human suffering with his physician-assisted suicide.

The other type, *passive* euthanasia, Dr. Billy Graham defines as "to discontinue or desist from the use of '*extraordinary*' *life-sustaining measures* or *heroic efforts* to *prolong* life in cases judged *hopeless*. It is *refraining* from action that would probably delay death and instead permitting death to occur naturally."[28] It may be difficult for some to realize that even in this scenario, the time of death is under God's control, not ours. It is all intricately interwoven into His plan.

There is a big difference between killing someone and letting nature take its course. In the first example, *we* are the instruments of death. In the second, *the disease process* is the instrument of death.

When faced with this decision, think to yourself, *If we could somehow prolong his or her life, what would we be prolonging it for? Would we want to live in that condition? What would he or she have to look forward to? More pain and suffering? Greater and greater indignities to suffer? A few more weeks of lying in a bed, the skin breaking down here and there? Not able to enjoy even the smallest pleasure?*

Almost every other medical specialty has as its goal to help the patient get better. Hospice doesn't have that goal because by the time a patient is appropriate for hospice, it has been determined that he or she will not get better. So we change the goal to something we can and do achieve in most cases: "The patient will remain comfortable and free of suffering for the rest of his/her life."

It is not surprising then that most of the medical profession has a mind-set quite different from that of hospice advocates. Many of the family members I've worked with have told me about the guilt trips that medical personnel can sometimes place on them in a hospital setting. Sometimes they make the family feel that if they don't go along with the ventilator or the feeding tube or the dialysis or the surgery, they must not love the patient. So some families agree to these life-prolonging procedures even when they know that such interventions violate the patient's wishes.

When faced with these decisions, remember that some things are worse than death. To those able to put their own feelings aside, to stop thinking about what other people will think about them, and to put their loved one's wishes first, I say, "Good for you." I know it's a tough decision, but I applaud you for taking a courageous stand with the patient's good in mind. You're not "playing God" by doing so. No one can "play God" but God. He and He alone decides when each of us will take our last breath.

I had a patient who was placed on a ventilator against her wishes months before she was admitted to hospice. She spent three weeks on the machine. Before the medical staff removed it, they warned the family and the patient that she would likely die very quickly without it. They all nodded their understanding. Good-byes were tearfully said. The tube was removed, and guess what? The patient began to breathe on her own. She was still with us eight months later. Though she's since died, God decided her "graduation day," not a doctor, not a family member, not even the patient herself. (As an aside, this patient was *furious* with her family for putting her on the ventilator in the first place. She admonished them to respect her wishes if there was a next time. And they did.)

I cannot stress the importance of making your wishes known to your family in advance or of determining the wishes of your loved one who is ill. A living will is an important document to complete, and it is a significant part of "being prepared." It states that if you are in a condition from which you will most likely not recover, you do not wish to have extraordinary measures used to prolong your life artificially. A living will is a gift you give your family, as well as providing your own protection from unwanted resuscitation attempts.

A living will form may be picked up at any hospital, hospice office, law office, or doctor's office. Look it over. Think about it. Talk to an attorney if you'd like. This is one of those things you shouldn't put off. Without a signed living will, emergency personnel and healthcare providers must try to do everything in their power to sustain your life even if you are in a state from which you will never recover.

We have a right to make decisions about how we approach our own death. For example, Penny in my opening story decided to honor Bachman's request to be able to die at home with his family gathered around him. He didn't want to be placed on ventilator support or be "shocked" back to life by ER staff. He was prepared to meet God, and he did it in his own way.

The decision was one of love, not cruelty. The family wasn't "playing God." They were *honoring* God by trusting in Him and accepting the fact that Bachman was at the threshold of heaven, ready and waiting for his Master's voice to welcome him on the other side of death. "Trusting God for the grace to accept adversity is as much an act of faith as is trusting Him for deliverance from it."[29]

"YOU KNOW THE GOOD, THEY DIE YOUNG"

It seems generally accepted that the elderly will die, but when a young person or a child dies, some call it an "untimely death." I hear phrases like, "He was taken way before his time," or "What a waste. He had his whole life ahead of him."

I must strongly disagree with this mind-set. According to the Word of God, *there is no such thing as an untimely death.* "All the days ordained for me were written in your book before one of them came to be" (Psalm 139:16 NIV). There is no number of days we *could have had* if only we hadn't died so soon. *All* of our days will come to pass as the Lord has ordained. Nobody can thwart His will, even about the time of death. "God is Lord of death as well as life. He rules over pain and disease as sovereignly as He rules over prosperity."[30]

In a sermon preached by Dr. D. A. Carson about a godly response to adversity, he said he once heard someone say that losing a spouse at the age of eighty was one thing, but it wasn't fair to lose one at thirty. He told the man, "If you believe that, ask someone who has just lost his spouse at eighty and see if he shares your perspective. Death is always too soon. It always hurts."

People talk about the terrible pain associated with losing a baby. Does it hurt more to lose a baby than it does to lose a child at the age of five or ten or even at fifty? How can you possibly measure *degrees* of pain? When we lose someone we love, *at any age*, it is going to hurt. We are going to feel the anguish of saying good-bye. We are going to experience the emptiness their absence leaves in our hearts and in our lives.

One of the most comforting illustrations I've heard about losing a child came from Pastor Erwin Lutzer. He reminded us that Christ is often portrayed in the Bible as the Great Shepherd. Just as a shepherd at times will bend down to pick up and carry one of his little lambs cradled in his arms, so also the Great Shepherd has the right to do the same with one of His. "If the Almighty wants to reach down and take one of His little lambs, or if He wishes to take a servant in the prime of life, He has that right. We think it cruel only because we cannot see behind the dark curtain."[31]

I have heard it said that babies who die go immediately to heaven. I have also heard it argued that even babies are born into sin and must suffer the consequences of that sinful state. The truth is that the Bible is silent about the specifics of what happens to babies when they die. The bottom line is that *whatever* God has determined in regard to these little ones who die is perfect and just. We can place our complete trust in His decisions, even about such an emotionally charged issue as this.

"The death of an infant, however, causes us to struggle with the will and purpose of God. . . . But we can be sure that there is a purpose in such a life, even if it is not immediately discernible."[32]

Loraine Boettner also addressed this issue: "Even infants, who sometimes have been with their parents only a few days, or even hours, may leave profound influences that change the entire course of the life of the family. And undoubtedly, from the Divine viewpoint, the specific purpose for which they were sent into the world was accomplished."[33]

People speculate on the life of John F. Kennedy, about what he could have done if he had not been taken "so early." I found myself asking the same question when I first heard of the death of his son, John, Jr. After the initial shock and disbelief, I remembered that I could trust God—even in the midst of my sorrow. Those society says are taken "too soon" lived as long as they were ordained to live. They didn't die *one second* sooner than they were supposed to.

Of course, the ultimate example of a young, productive life being taken was that of our Lord and Savior Jesus Christ. He was only about thirty-three years old. And talk about charisma. He had it. And He had the *ultimate* ministry. He had the *ultimate* power to do good things. But He died much too soon. Right? Wrong! *He died* exactly *when He was destined to die.*

Loraine Boettner wrote, "The night before He was killed He said, 'I have glorified Thee on the earth, having *accomplished the work which Thou hast given Me to do,*' John 17:4. As He hung on the cross, dying for the sins of others, He said, '*It is finished.*' From the human viewpoint it looked as though His ministry had just begun. *But from the Divine viewpoint He had accomplished that which He came to do.*"[34]

Christ died at *exactly* the right time. So will we. "Our death is just as meticulously planned as the death of Christ. There is no combination of evil men, disease, or accident that can kill us as long as God still has work for us to do. To those who walk with faith in God's providence, they die according to God's timetable."[35]

EMBRACING DEATH—IS THAT POSSIBLE?

I have in this chapter tried to show that death for an unbeliever is a passageway into eternal torment—but death for a *believer* is the gateway into eternal bliss in heaven. I have argued that believers can face death without dread. Am I suggesting that we long for death? No. But we *can* and some *do* long for the life that comes afterward.

The apostle Paul certainly did. He wrote,

> *For we know that if the tent, which is our earthly home, is destroyed, we have a building from God, a house not made with hands, eternal in the heavens. For in this tent we groan, longing to put on our heavenly dwelling, if indeed by putting it on we may not be found naked. For while we are still in this tent, we groan, being burdened—not that we would be unclothed, but that we would be further clothed, so that what is mortal may be swallowed up by life. He who has prepared us for this very thing is God, who has given us the Spirit as a* guarantee. *(2 Corinthians 5:1-5)*

In *The Glory of Heaven*, John MacArthur said, "We, too, should long to be clothed with our heavenly form. We should look forward to being absent from the body and present with the Lord. We should become more preoccupied with the *glories* of eternity than we are with the *afflictions* of today."[36]

Henry Bast said that Paul "didn't face life merely with stoic courage, or death with resignation, but that he faced both with faith and hope."[37] So can we.

CASE STUDY

I was assigned an admission as I was preparing to leave the office for the day. The assignment fell to me because I was the nurse on call that night. I wasn't happy about having this sprung on me at the last minute and was muttering all the way out to the patient's home about having to skip the plans I had made for the evening. But it is just like God to teach me a lesson by something like this.

When I got to the house, I was greeted by two of the friendliest, kindest, most hospitable people I'd ever met. It was a couple who looked to be in their mid-sixties. They ushered me into the warmth of their home where we sat at the dining table to talk. After I finished explaining to them about the hospice program and its philosophy, they thanked me profusely for coming out at such an hour and told me that they believed I was truly sent by God to them. (Boy, did I feel ashamed about complaining.)

Mr. and Mrs. J. T. Black had been told earlier in the day that Mrs. Black's mother, Rebekah Pollard, was dying, and the doctor had recommended hospice care. Mrs. Pollard had made it absolutely clear to them after her last hospitalization that she was through with hospitals. She was ninety-one years old and ready to "meet her Maker," she told them. She knew what awaited her and was eager to go.

After all the papers for the admission process were signed, I had the opportunity to meet Mrs. Pollard. However, she was much too sick to respond to me. Her bedroom smelled of fresh flowers and baby powder. A Bible lay open on her bedside table. I actually thought she might die before I could finish the admission process. She was gurgling with every breath and would only respond to painful stimuli. I repositioned her in the bed in an attempt to maximize her respiratory effort. Her breathing eased, and the gurgling ceased.

I finished my physical examination and met with the family again to give them my assessment. I gently explained to them that she was very sick, that fluid was beginning to accumulate in her lungs and that she might not last through the night. They didn't shed a tear.

They shared the reason with me. Mrs. Pollard had lived in their home for the past twenty years, and J. T. loved her like his own mother. Mrs. Black told me the story of their relationship and spoke of the strong faith with which she'd been raised. In fact, Mrs. Pollard was instrumental in introducing J. T. to Christ several years ago. Mrs. Black continued by telling me that though it was breaking her heart to have to say good-bye to her mother, she knew without a shadow of doubt that her sweet mother would be face to face with her Savior soon and was joyous at the thought. She knew her mother was ready and eager to go to God.

Mrs. Black had cared for her mother tenderly. She had turned her every few hours, powdered her when she felt clammy, read the Bible to her, and prayed that her passing would be painless and merciful. She and J. T. inspired me that night. I had rarely witnessed such tender love for a parent mixed with such utter joy at the thought of her entering eternity with Christ. These people were putting their faith in action, where I could see it and appreciate it. I left with the promise that I would be back first thing in the morning to check on her.

She surprised me the next morning. She was awake and alert and said, "Hi. I'm Rebekah." I smiled at her and said, "Hi. I'm Deborah." We had a good visit that day.

She lived only a week or so, but it was enough time for me to become like one of the family. We shared the Scriptures and prayed together. I sang hymns to Mrs. Pollard one day even though I don't know if she was able to hear me. There was no despair or mourning in that home. This was simply, "So long for now. We'll see you soon, Mama."

I always try to be aware that I'm Christ's representative to the people I meet. I want to be a blessing to others and to reflect attitudes that honor Christ. My goal is to help others, to strengthen them, to comfort them, to minister to them in any way I can. But this time, I was the one ministered to. Being around these dear people and seeing such faith in action served to strengthen my own faith. I was so thankful I'd gotten that admission after all.

"For the Christian death should come as quietly as the twilight hour with its cool peace and its embracing rest."[38] If we cannot quite view death with this kind of optimism, maybe that's because we think of it as taking us *away* from home rather than bringing us *to* it. Adoniram Judson, the great Baptist missionary to Burma, stated that when Christ called him home, he would go with the gladness of a schoolboy bounding away from school.

One of our teachers at church, Bob Lepine, recently taught a lesson on death. He equated our physical lives with waiting in an airport terminal. Yes, we can have a grand time in the terminal. There are books to read, restaurants to enjoy, people to talk with, and games we can play. But no matter how enjoyable the terminal is, we'd all rather be at our destination, right? If we can catch an early flight home—GREAT. If not, we can just hang around the terminal until our flight departs. He said life should be like that. This life is not our home if we belong to Christ. It's a staging area of sorts. So if we are taken to our destination right away, then that's best. If not, we should enjoy our lives here on earth while we wait for Him to bring us to our eternal home.

I'm not suggesting that we can all immediately possess these exemplary attitudes toward death. But it's something for which we can *strive*. All I'm asking is that we examine our lives now. Ask yourself what your own beliefs are regarding life after death. How do those beliefs measure up with what the Bible teaches? Do some real soul-searching. It's always better to prepare in advance than to wait until the last minute to prepare for *any* undertaking—much less for eternity. I urge you to prepare *now* for what will happen to your spirit *then*.

If we are prepared for eternity, there is no reason for despair or bewilderment when our time comes. Is it wrong to experience apprehension when contemplating death? I don't think so. We'd be less than human if we didn't. Richard Baxter wrote, "Were I on the top of a castle or steeple, fastened by the strongest chains, or guarded by the surest battlements, I could not possibly look down without fear; and so it is with our prospect into the life to come."[39]

The point is this: No matter how secure we *actually* are, there are times we don't *feel* secure. *We feel fear instead, though we are quite safe*. That's the way it is with the death of a Christian. We are in a totally safe place, in the very palm of God's hand; yet we may *feel* fear.

Once, before surgery, I experienced a little of this kind of trepidation. I knew I was in God's hands, that the result of the surgery would be whatever He had ordained for me. I knew that if it were my time to die, I would die. I was okay with that, trusting Him with my life. I also knew that if it wasn't my time, *nothing* could happen to end my life prematurely.

Yet there was still a degree of fear as the surgery date approached, as I was prepped, and as I was wheeled into the operating room. There was even a period of time after the surgery when I wondered if I was going to die. But God was merciful. It was not time for me to go. (As an aside, that experience catapulted me into starting on this book. I had thought about it for a long time, but when faced with the possibility of my own demise, I decided that if I was going to write this book, it was time to start.)

If impending *surgery* can cast a shadow of fear over me, certainly impending *death* would give cause for concern—even fear. However, approaching death for a Christian is a win-win situation. If Christ decrees that we will be healed from our infirmity, we win. If He beckons us to come to Him through death, we still win.

I cannot say the same for unbelievers. If He decrees that they be healed of their infirmity, they win (at least temporarily), because it has bought them more time to prepare for eternity. However, if they die, it is definitely the ultimate loss for them. Eternal torment awaits them on the other side.

So if we are believers, should we *long* for our own deaths or the deaths of our loved ones? Not at all. We are "not to desire death, but that which is beyond it,"[40] according to Richard Baxter. He was writing about his own imminent death. He also encouraged his readers to make preparation *now* for what will await us *then*. He said that if he wasn't willing to die, he was obviously not sufficiently prepared. Once our preparation is complete, our willingness to obey Christ, even in death, is intact.

Yes, apprehension precedes many new activities and events—the first day on the job, surgery, the first day in a new school, flying in a plane, giving a speech in public, going on an extended vacation, performing on stage, or even going to a new dentist. Fear of the unknown is natural. But we need not *fear* death if we are in Christ. We can rest in His assurance. His arms are ready to "catch us" as we joyously "fall" into His presence.

Did Richard Baxter find acceptance in his death? You be the judge. He wrote,

> To thee, O my Savior, I commit my soul; it is thine by redemption, thine by covenant; it is sealed by thy Spirit, and thou hast promised

not to lose it. . . . Cause me to "draw near with a true heart, in full assurance of faith." Thy name is faithful and true. True and faithful are all thy promises. . . . I am weary of suffering, sin and flesh; weary of my darkness, dullness, and distance. Whither should I look for rest, but home to my heavenly Father and thee? . . . What have I to do with my remaining time, even these last and languishing hours, but to look up unto thee, and wait for thy grace and thy salvation? . . . My pains seem grievous. But love chooses them, uses them for my good, moderates them and will shortly end them.[41]

What an example he has given us to follow. The sweet thread of trust and faith in Jesus Christ is woven into the very fabric of his thinking.

Yes, we may fear the act of dying, but death should hold no terror for the true Christian. Here are several biblical passages that teach this important truth:

Precious in the sight of the LORD is the death of his saints. (Psalm 116:15)

For to me to live is Christ, and to die is gain. (Philippians 1:21)

For I am already being poured out as a drink offering, and the time of my departure has come. I have fought the good fight, I have finished the race, I have kept the faith. Henceforth there is laid up for me the crown of righteousness, which the Lord, the righteous judge, will award to me on that Day, and not only to me but also to all who have loved his appearing. (2 Timothy 4:6-8)

And I heard a voice from heaven saying, "Write this: Blessed are the dead who die in the Lord from now on." "Blessed indeed," says the Spirit, "that they may rest from their labors, for their deeds follow them." (Revelation 14:13)

One of the most compelling passages that teaches us to long for heaven is found in John 14:1-3. In this passage Jesus comforts His disciples as He prepares to go to the cross:

Let not your hearts be troubled. Believe in God; believe also in me. In my Father's house are many rooms. If it were not so, would I have told you that I go to prepare a place for you? *And if I go and prepare a place for you,* I will come again and will take you to myself, that where I am you may be also.

THE "GIFT" OF DEATH

Erwin Lutzer presented a thought about death that I had never considered before: Death *rescues* us from eternal sinfulness.

> No doubt you will vacillate between despair and hope, denial and determination. Perhaps you will have more concern for those you leave behind than you do for yourself. Not a one of us can predict how we might react when it is our turn to hear the dreadful news.
>
> And yet the Bible presents an entirely different picture of death that should give us hope. After Adam and Eve sinned, they died spiritually as well as physically. Sending them out of the garden, far from being an act of cruelty, was actually proof of God's kindness. We read, "Lest he stretch out his hand, and take also from the tree of life, and eat, and live forever—therefore the Lord God sent him out from the garden of Eden, to cultivate the ground from which he was taken" (Genesis 3:22-23).
>
> If Adam and Eve had eaten of the other special tree of the garden—the Tree of Life—they would have been immortalized in their sinful condition. . . . Imagine living forever as sinners, with no possibility of redemption and permanent transformation. Although they would never have had to face the finality of death, they would have been condemned to a pitiful existence.
>
> Thus God prevented Adam and Eve from eternal sinfulness by giving them *the gift of death*, the ability to exit this life and arrive safely in the wondrous life to come. . . . Only through death can we go to God (unless, of course, we are still living when Christ returns)."[42]

You see, God provided a *wonderful gift* by granting death to fallen mankind lest they stay in their fallen state forever. But the most wonderful gift of all is the one God granted to His children. That gift is redemption from our fallen state through the death of His beloved Son, Jesus Christ. Christ destroyed the "sting" of death for those who believe in Him: "'Death is swallowed up in victory.' 'O death, where is your victory? O death, where is your sting?' The sting of death is sin, and the power of sin is the law. But thanks be to God, who gives us the victory through our Lord Jesus Christ" (1 Corinthians 15:54b-57).

Several authors have used the following "sting" imagery in describing what Christ has done for His children. The illustration is that of a loving father. The dad is outside with his little child. A pesky bee flies around the child, landing here and there but not stinging yet. The child, not realizing his danger, seeks to capture the menacing bee. Once a bee stings, his stinger stays with the victim, rendering the bee completely harmless. Knowing this, the concerned parent moves in on the bee, allowing it to sting him to protect the child from this painful experience. The bee can no longer hurt the child. The threat is gone.

The same is true for a believer. Christ has taken the painful sting of death in our place, and in so doing, has rendered death harmless to us. It no longer has any power over us. What thanks and gratitude we should have for our Lord for the wonderful gift He has given those who love Him.

Thus, let me come to thee in the confidence of thy love,
and long to be nearer, in the clearer sight, the fuller sense,
and more joyful exercise of love forever.
Father, into thy hand I commend my spirit.
Lord Jesus, receive my spirit.
Amen.
RICHARD BAXTER

THE TRUTH ABOUT HEAVEN AND HELL

[F]or a time is coming when all who are in their graves will hear [Christ's] voice and come out—those who have done good will rise to live, and those who have done evil will rise to be condemned.

JOHN 5:28-29 NIV

LOOKING BACK

Sitting quietly in her car, Paula looked at the house she had visited so often. Had it really been over two months since Bachman had died? She'd visited Penny once since then, a couple of weeks after the funeral, just to check on her. She'd intended to visit more often, but with so many new patients it had been hard to find time.

Lying on the seat next to her was a little Christmas gift for Penny. She hoped Penny was ready for it. It was a picture of Bachman and Penny she'd taken on one of their afternoons in the backyard the previous spring. Paula had bought a lovely frame for it and was hoping it would be a comfort.

Gathering up the gift, Paula got out of the car and started for the kitchen door. Before she was halfway there, Penny rushed out to greet her with a warm and welcoming hug.

"Thank you so much for coming," she said. "I've really missed you. It was good to hear your voice over the phone yesterday, but it's really nice to see you again."

"I've missed you too," Paula responded, feeling a lump of emotion in her throat.

"Come in, come in," Penny said, taking Paula's hand and leading her into the kitchen. The room smelled of apples and cinnamon. Paula closed her eyes for a moment, enjoying the delicious aroma.

"Mmmm. What is that luscious smell?"

"I just baked some muffins."

Paula smiled appreciatively at her friend. She watched as Penny busily set the table with pretty Christmas china, a hot cup of coffee, and a basket of muffins wrapped in a bright red and green plaid cloth. Soft, creamy butter was placed before her along with the matching Christmas cream and sugar set.

She noticed that Penny was wearing one of Bachman's old golf shirts, a red one, with a Christmas necklace dangling over it. Seeing her gaze, Penny said, "I like wearing his things sometimes. Some of them still smell like him, you know. It helps me remember."

"That's fine. I didn't say a word." Paula smiled back at her.

"I know, but I saw that you noticed. You notice everything. That's one of the things I like about you, dear."

"Thanks. Penny, this is so beautiful—the dishes, the muffins, the napkins. You didn't have to go to all this trouble for me, but I certainly am enjoying it." She took a sip of the hot, rich coffee after stirring in two heaping teaspoons of coffee creamer. "Mmm. This hits the spot on a cold, wintry morning." Looking around the kitchen, Paula continued, "You know, this place just *feels* like home, doesn't it?"

Penny doctored her coffee too. "Well, I like it. But it's so quiet around here now. I miss the bustle of activity. It's really too big just for me. I doubt the girls will ever come back here to live. I've been thinking about buying a little condo—a nice one but smaller. Then I wouldn't have to worry about the yard and the upkeep and everything."

"I thought you loved working in the yard and digging in the dirt," Paula replied, buttering a steaming muffin. Her mouth watered with anticipation.

"Oh, I used to, but I don't think I can get into it this year. And I can't just let it go."

"The Christmas decorations are beautiful. You did a great job on those."

"Thanks. The girls helped me with them. It's not the same without Bachman here to enjoy it with me, but I do love this season of the year."

They munched on muffins for a few quiet moments. Then Paula looked over at her and asked, "How are you doing, Penny? Are you okay?"

Penny put her muffin back on the plate and dabbed at her mouth daintily with her napkin. "I'm okay most of the time. But then sometimes I miss him so badly I think I won't be able to make it. I feel like sitting in that recliner and just not getting up again. I feel old and tired and useless . . . like *my* life is over too. I guess I just start feeling sorry for myself. It doesn't happen a lot, but when it does, I just feel awful."

"I know. Bless your heart. What do you do to get yourself out of those moods?"

"I guess the most helpful thing I do is to pray. I know God has not abandoned me. He never abandoned Bach either. He took Bach home, that's all. But He's left me here for a reason. So I just pray He'll get me through the day—through the hour. He always does."

She heaved a deep sigh before continuing. "The most comforting part of it all is knowing Bachman is in heaven right now. He's experiencing more joy than he ever knew on earth. He's in the presence of Christ. He's with his mother and his brother. I don't know how people cope who don't know the Lord, who don't have that peace in knowing the one they love is in heaven. Do you?"

"Well, I've known a lot of people who have died without knowing Christ. The families comfort themselves any way they can. They have to find some way to cope, but usually their hope is unfounded. Personally, I couldn't make sense of death and dying at all without the hope I have in Christ." She paused for another bite. "You mentioned Bach's mom and brother. What about his father?"

"Oh, well, I don't think Bach's dad would be there. Bachman McNair II was a real . . . I'll say a *proud* man. Oh, he was brilliant and successful, but he'd never go to church with the family. He either worked or played golf every Sunday. He didn't mind if the rest of them went, but they'd better not pester *him* about attending. Bach told me he tried to talk to his father once about the Lord, but his dad became enraged and yelled at him, 'Don't you stand there and tell me about

Jesus. You believe what you want to, but don't push your fairy tales on me.' Bachman felt like he should have talked to him again, but he never did."

"Well, I know he would have if the opportunity had come up. Bach was no coward."

Penny laughed lightly. "Not with any of us, he wasn't, but with his dad, he may have been. We all were. His dad died about twelve years ago. He never showed any interest in spiritual things. He never gave a thought to Christ as far as we know."

"That's awful."

"Paula, I've got something to show you." Penny rose from her chair and motioned for Paula to follow her into the den.

The Christmas tree was in the corner by the French doors leading out onto the deck. It was beautifully decorated in gold and cream-colored ornaments. A large angel dressed in a flowing cream-colored dress topped the tree with five or six long ribbons of cream-colored satin streaming down to the base of the limbs. It was beautiful, with the tiny white twinkle lights covering the tree in the background.

"Oh! How gorgeous!" Paula exclaimed.

"Thanks. But that's not what I wanted to show you. See these gifts right here? They're from Bach."

Paula's head whipped around to look at Penny in surprise.

Penny returned her gaze with eyes moist with tears.

"That's right. Alex brought them over here last weekend. Apparently Bachman arranged with Alex's wife, Destra, to buy all these things. She told me he called her one day last summer. She came over. He gave her a list of things to buy and the cash she'd need to make the purchases. That way I wouldn't know about them. He wanted to surprise us at Christmas."

"Well, he succeeded in that, didn't he?"

"Yes, he certainly did. He had hoped he would make it to Christmas, you know. But . . ." She gently fingered the bows on one of the boxes.

"I can't believe that man," Paula said quietly, slowly shaking her head.

Penny picked up a small box wrapped in gold and red Christmas paper. "This one's for you." She held the gift out to Paula, who placed a hand over her chest in disbelief.

"For me?"

"He wouldn't forget you at Christmas, now would he?"

Paula was stunned—and touched more than she could say. Tears welled in her eyes as she read the gift card that had "Paula" scrawled over it. She picked at the tape on the box, unwrapping it without tearing the pretty paper. A tear spilled out onto the box. She wiped her cheeks and looked over at Penny, who was holding a tissue to her nose, watching Paula open the gift.

Inside the little box was an angel. It was small, delicate, and beautiful. Made from clear etched glass and silver, it reflected the lights from the Christmas tree. The tiny angel held a silver bell in front of her. The tiny bell tinkled as Paula picked the angel up, held it in her hand, and looked speechlessly at Penny.

Underneath the angel in the box, Paula saw a card with her name on it. She opened it to see Bachman's own shaky handwriting. Her heart ached as she envisioned him painstakingly writing to her: "To Paula. What would I have done without your TLC these past months? I'll never be able to thank you enough. You've been my guardian angel. Thought I'd leave you one to remind you of me. Yours in Christ, your 'boyfriend,' Bach."

She felt the sudden sting of tears as she passed the card over for Penny to read. Paula left the den, stifling a sob, and returned with the gift she'd brought to Penny.

"Okay," she sniffed. "It's your turn."

"Oh, Paula, you didn't need to get me anything."

"I know. But I wanted you to have this."

Penny opened the gift bag, digging into the tissue until her hand found the frame of the picture. Lifting it from the bag, she gasped as she saw the mischievous, smiling face of her husband. In the photo she was bending down behind him, pressing her cheek to his. Her smile was radiant as it reflected the love and happiness of the moment.

"Oh, Paula. I didn't have one of us together after he got sick. Thank you so much. I'd forgotten you even took this picture."

The two women hugged each other, crying as they remembered the man they loved so much.

"I'm not crying for Bach. I know where he is, and I wouldn't bring him back to this existence for anything. These tears are for me. I want you to understand that," Penny explained.

"I know that. I'm just so thankful God gave me the opportunity to help out and to get to know you guys." Paula closed her eyes and breathed a quiet "thank You" to God.

HEAVEN AND HELL: OUTDATED MYTHS OR EVERLASTING TRUTHS?

People smirk and eyes roll whenever someone mentions heaven and hell. Many consider those who actually believe such "antiquated notions" as simple and naïve. Like grownups who listen as their child tells them about an "imaginary friend," they say, "Isn't that cute?" From their perceived intellectually lofty perch, they feel sorry for us for believing in such fairy tales.

As one who *does* believe in heaven and hell, one thought enters my mind about them. I think of the horrible terror unbelievers will experience when they die and then realize the utter *reality* of these places.

The doctrines of heaven and hell have become dangerous stumbling blocks to those who do not believe the truth of Scripture. Please keep in mind that these doctrines were not developed by the Christian church, but are taught by God in the Bible. In fact, the vast majority of teaching regarding hell came from the lips of Jesus Christ.

It is my desire to show you a true and balanced view of both heaven and hell as described in the Bible—the God-breathed Word of God. It is up to the Holy Spirit to illumine these truths in a way you will not only *understand* but *believe.*

IS LIFE REALLY ETERNAL?

The bodies of the wicked and the righteous both go to the grave. The difference is that the wicked will dwell *eternally* in hell, whereas the righteous (made so by the blood of Christ—not by their own efforts) will dwell *eternally* in heaven. *All* will be resurrected at Christ's return. *Some* will rise to *live*. *Others* will rise to be *condemned*.

Loraine Boettner assigns three stages to human life:

- Birth to death
- Death to resurrection
- Eternity in the resurrected body[1]

After death we will all be immortal creatures. According to Boettner, "Immortality means the eternal, continuous, conscious existence of the soul after the death of the body."[2]

In the previous chapter we talked about the false doctrine of annihilationism—the idea that the body and soul cease to exist after death. Boettner tackles this idea head-on: "To deny the future life is to open wide the gate for all kinds of indulgence and crime. If death ends everything life in this world becomes a mockery, and the person who can secure for himself the most pleasure regardless of the means used is the most successful, the most to be envied."[3] Thus, this is a dangerous mind-set if left unchallenged by the truths of Scripture.

Annihilationism is a fast-growing belief in our society and other world cultures. I can understand why it would be comforting to think the hereafter does not exist—especially if I had no belief in Jesus Christ. That way, I could discount all the awful teachings about hell as myth. Of course, I'd also be missing out on the glories of heaven. The fact remains, though, that heaven and hell *are* real places. They exist despite the latest whims of society. Those who think they don't are quite simply . . . wrong.

But let's face it, the doctrine of hell has become an embarrassment to some churches and to some preachers, even those who claim to be evangelical. It is not a popular subject. Some mainline denominations that have held to the biblical teaching on hell for centuries have now *made the decision* that annihilation is what really occurs. They have departed from clear biblical instruction and adopted what seems best to *human reasoning* instead.

Theology is the study of God. It is God's explanation of the world, its origin, purpose, and destiny, given through an inspired book, the Bible. Philosophy is man's explanation. Its basis resides within the limitations of the human mind and the material world. John MacArthur wrote, "[U]nlike human wisdom, which exalts the sinner, divine wisdom glorifies God."[4]

What does the Bible teach about life after death?

For God so loved the world that he gave his only Son, that whoever believes in him should not perish but have eternal life. *(John 3:16)*

For the wages of sin is death, but the free gift of God is eternal life *in Christ Jesus our Lord. (Romans 6:23)*

And the smoke of their torment goes up forever and ever. *(Revelation 14:11)*

These are just a few of the many, many passages I could use to demonstrate the biblical instruction regarding eternal life. (See the previous chapter for a more detailed look at the doctrine of eternal life and the opposing doctrine of annihilation.)

Have you ever wondered why we were not told more about death and the life afterward? One reason may be because the topic is a little too *advanced* for us. It would be like teaching college courses to a kindergarten student. First Corinthians 13:12 says, "For *now* we see *in a mirror dimly,* but *then face to face. Now I know in part; then I shall know fully,* even as I have been fully known." Jesus said to His disciples, "I still have many things to say to you, but you cannot bear them *now*" (John 16:12).

So we have to be patient and *trusting* with the teaching we are given in the Scriptures regarding life after death. One thing we can be sure of is that the revelation we have been given is sufficient.

Jerry Bridges writes, "It is just as important to *trust* God as it is to obey Him. When we disobey God we doubt His sovereignty and question His goodness. In both cases we cast aspersions upon His majesty and His character."[5]

God doesn't take disbelief and doubting lightly. Psalm 78:19-22 says, "They spoke against God, saying, 'Can God spread a table in the wilderness? He struck the rock so that water gushed out and streams overflowed. Can he also give bread or provide meat for his people?' Therefore, when the LORD heard, *he was full of wrath*; a fire was kindled against Jacob; *his anger rose* against Israel, because *they did not believe in God* and did not *trust his saving power*."

Oh, the goodness of God. These people who spoke against Him were not His enemies. They were His beloved people, Israel. Though He could have punished their lack of faith or trust in Him, He went on to provide for them in miraculous ways.

We can trust in a most trustworthy God. We can believe what He has in His kindness shown us about death, heaven, and hell. For those who do not believe, who cannot trust, there awaits a time when they *will* see things as they are. By that time, though, it will be too late.

There are only two possible responses to Christ. You can either embrace Him or reject Him. There are no other options. You can't be neutral. If you aren't for Him, then you stand against Him. And if you stand against Him, that is the most dangerous place in the world. "Like the mouse who thinks it can stand against the farmer's plow or the rowboat poised to thwart the path of an aircraft carrier, it is insanity for man to think that he can oppose the living God, who is angry with sinners and is bent on taking vengeance on those who oppose Him."[6]

THE DOCTRINE OF HELL

"Hell disappeared, and no one noticed." Erwin Lutzer used that shocking quote to open a chapter in his book *One Minute After You Die*. He goes on to say, "With that terse observation, American church historian Martin Marty summarized our attitude toward a vanishing doctrine that received careful attention in previous generations. . . . Hell, more than any doctrine of the Bible, seems to be out of step with our times."[7] Another theologian, Harry Buis, said it this way: "[T]here is no other doctrine that is clearly taught in Scripture which is so generally denied or ignored in our modern theological world."[8]

To disavow such a doctrine, a person's confidence in his own human wisdom has to take precedence over God's teaching in the

Scriptures. What will we put our trust in—sinful man's ideas regarding our *eternal* well-being or the words of the *almighty, all-powerful, holy God of the universe*? Many, many people would rather depend on their own thinking, on their own theories, than on the actual Word of God. They create theories that sound good and fair to them, and in so doing, discard the clear teaching of the Bible: "[T]hey exchanged the truth about God for a lie" (Romans 1:25).

Revelation 20:14-15 gives some of that truth about God. In the final judgment the unbelieving dead of all the ages will stand before Him to be judged: "Then Death and Hades were thrown into the *lake of fire*. This is the second death [with physical death being the first], *the lake of fire*. And if anyone's name was not found written in the book of life, he was thrown into the *lake of fire*."

Matthew 25:41 says, "Then he will say to those on his left, 'Depart from me, you cursed, into the *eternal fire* prepared for the devil and his angels.'" A few verses down we read, "And these will go away into *eternal punishment*, but the righteous to eternal life" (v. 46). Dr. Wayne Grudem defines hell as "a place of eternal conscious punishment for the wicked."[9]

God's Word is eternal. It doesn't change to accommodate the changes in our culture or society. Mankind is also the same now as ever. We may like to believe we have evolved into enlightened beings, but our basic natures haven't really changed. "What has been is what will be, and what has been done is what will be done, and there is nothing new under the sun" (Ecclesiastes 1:9). If God said in His Word that unbelievers will be thrown into a lake of fire, then that is exactly what will occur.

Pastor Erwin Lutzer asserts that this doctrine is often disregarded because it is difficult to reconcile hell with the love of God. I often hear, "A loving God would not condemn anyone to hell." What is the evidence? And by what authority can people affirm such a belief? Certainly not by the Bible, for it teaches just the opposite. Do they put their own feeble human wisdom above the Word of Almighty God? Then it would be more appropriate for them to say, "I just don't *feel* that a loving God would send anyone to hell." Saying it that way points to the real authority behind such a statement—the person's own feelings. How reliable are our feelings? *Utterly unreliable* when it comes to biblical doctrine.

A text attributed to Martin Luther says, "Feelings come and feelings go, but feelings are deceiving. My warrant is the Word of God; nought else is worth believing." You might say, "Well, I just don't feel that way." And your feelings change what? Nothing. Truth is still truth—regardless of how you feel about it.

Yet many of us allow our feelings to control our lives, our thinking, and ultimately the destination of our souls. The only reliable information we are given about death and the life after comes to us from the pages of the Bible—God's holy Word.

Why does it feel so wrong to some people to believe in hell? Lutzer explains it this way, playing devil's advocate—so to speak:

> To put it simply, to us the punishment of hell does not fit the crime. Yes, all men do some evil and a few do great evil, but nothing that anyone has ever done can justify eternal torment. And to think that millions of good people will be in hell simply because they have not heard of Christ (as Christianity affirms) strains credulity. It's like capital punishment for a traffic violation.
>
> Thus millions of Westerners believe in some kind of afterlife, but it is one of bliss, not misery. Genuine fear of suffering in hell has vanished from the mainstream of Western thought. Few, if any, give prolonged thought to the prospect that some people will be in hell. Fewer yet believe they themselves will be among that unfortunate number.[10]

These people have problems in their thinking in at least two significant ways. They have forgotten or have never truly realized the vast gulf between the supreme holiness of God and the total depravity of mankind. Perhaps the reason they find hell so offensive is because of their insensitivity to sin. Also they have forgotten or have never truly realized that if we all got what we truly *deserved*, we would be headed toward eternal torment in hell.

That brings us to the root of the problem of reconciling hell with a loving God—whether hell is fair and just. "To us humans, everlasting punishment is disproportionate to the offense committed. God appears cruel, unjust, sadistic, and vindictive. The purpose of punishment, we are told, is always redemptive. Rehabilitation is the goal of all prison sentences. The concept of a place where there will be endless punishment without any possibility of parole or reform seems unjust."[11]

There again Lutzer reveals the thinking of a person who uses his own reasoning and wisdom as the standard and authority for denying the truths of Scripture. Our concept of fairness and justice is not always in line with God's. Whose concept is right—ours or God's? The Bible teaches us that God's decrees are perfect. I may not always understand them, but I know His judgments are perfect because He is perfect. It's a very dangerous thing to put ourselves in the place of God.

Dr. Wayne Grudem has a different explanation for why this doctrine of eternal punishment is so objectionable. His reason pertains more to *believers* who question the fairness of hell:

> The reason it is hard for us to think of the doctrine of hell is because God has put in our hearts a portion of his own love for people created in his image. . . . As long as we are in this life, and as long as we see and think about others who need to hear the gospel and trust in Christ for salvation, it should cause us great distress and agony of spirit to think about eternal punishment. Yet we must also realize that whatever God in his wisdom has ordained and taught in Scripture is *right*. Therefore we must be careful that we do not hate this doctrine or rebel against it, but rather we should seek, insofar as we are able, to come to the point where we acknowledge that eternal punishment is good and right, because in God there is no unrighteousness at all.[12]

He didn't say coming to that point in our spiritual maturity would be a simple thing. But this is a point toward which we should continually strive, asking God to enable us.

What's It Like in Hell?

People who interpret the Bible do not all agree on the physical descriptions of hell. We are told it is a place. This place is generally thought to be "below," whereas heaven is said to be "above." That can be the *baseline* from which to work.

The Bible describes hell in many ways. Most of the disagreements stem from the fact that some interpret verses as figurative rather than literal. Ultimately no one can be absolutely sure what form hell takes. But the bottom line is that *whatever* form it takes, you wouldn't want to go there.

First of all, hell is real. It is an actual place. Some choose not to acknowledge its existence. But that is as foolish as imagining, for example, that Chicago doesn't exist. You can try, and even succeed, in convincing yourself that Chicago is an imaginary place people talk about. But the people in Chicago *know* it's a real place. Pretending doesn't change a thing. Hell exists. Believe it.

Hell is described in many biblical passages as a place where eternal flames inflict never-ending suffering on its inhabitants. It is a conscious existence of eternal pain and agony in the flames. "[They] serve as an example by undergoing a *punishment* of *eternal fire*" (Jude 7b). Revelation 20:10 reads, "[A]nd the devil who had deceived them was thrown into *the lake of fire and sulfur* where the beast and the false prophet were, and they will be tormented day and night *forever and ever*."

Some say this fire is symbolic. If so, it is symbolic of the worst pain and torment possible. Perhaps fire is the clearest way of articulating the torments of hell. But if it is a symbol, then beware. Don Whitney, in a sermon preached at the Bible Church of Little Rock, said that a symbol is never as powerful as what it represents. Consider a wedding band, for instance. It represents a marriage but is not nearly as strong and as beautiful as a marriage. What about our country's flag? It is a symbol of the United States of America, but it is not nearly as powerful as the country itself. A road sign may have a symbol of a railroad crossing ahead. That symbol doesn't begin to reflect the potential danger of the crossing. So if fire is a symbol for something else in hell, whatever it represents is unimaginable in its torment.

Mark 9:47-48 brings us to another descriptive characteristic of hell: "And if your eye causes you to sin, tear it out. It is better for you to enter the kingdom of God with one eye than with two eyes to be thrown into hell, 'where their *worm does not die* and the *fire is not quenched.*'" Here hell is like the misery of being consumed by a worm that does not die. These worms are generally thought to be maggots, but nobody knows for sure. As long as there is flesh on the body, they will continue to eat it. And since the body doesn't die in hell, they can feast on it eternally. What an agonizing thought. "Drought and heat snatch away the snow waters; so does Sheol those who have sinned. The womb forgets them; *the worm finds them sweet*; they are no longer remembered, so wickedness is broken like a tree" (Job 24:19-20).

Hell is sometimes described as utter blackness like we have never experienced on this earth: "They [evildoers masquerading as and misleading genuine believers] are wild waves of the sea, foaming up their shame; wandering stars, for whom *blackest darkness* has been reserved *forever*" (Jude 13 NIV). Peter expresses the same verdict on these people: "These are waterless springs and mists driven by a storm. For them the gloom of *utter darkness* has been reserved" (2 Peter 2:17). Think of that. Hell is a place of total darkness. Those who are there will never see again. They will be completely, totally blind because of the darkness around them.

The "darkest dark" I've ever experienced was in Blanchard Springs Caverns in Arkansas. When we were in the belly of the cavern, the guide had us sit down. Warning us first, he switched the lights off for what seemed to be minutes but was only seconds. I placed my hand directly in front of my open eyes and couldn't even see the outline. I could sense the closeness but could see nothing. The space seemed to be closing in on me. Then the lights came back on, and I breathed a huge sigh of relief. Now *that* was dark. But that may have been nothing compared to the depth of the darkness of hell described in the Scriptures.

People believe many fallacies regarding hell. We've seen the illustrations showing Satan with his red suit, cape, horns, and pitchfork standing over the poor, wretched, sweating sinners in the furnaces of hell. Not so.

First of all, there is no indication Satan has ever looked like that. These pictures are total speculation based on human imagination. Secondly, Satan will be one of the "tormented," not a tormentor.

Revelation clearly points to that truth in this passage and others: "[A]nd the devil who had deceived them was thrown into the lake of fire and sulfur where the beast and the false prophet were, and *they will be tormented day and night forever and ever*" (20:10).

Now, as I mentioned before, the arguments regarding these descriptions center around whether the language is literal or figurative. Some think the flames are literal, the blackness figurative. The worm could be symbolic, the emptiness literal. Some assert that it is *all* literal; others that it is *all* figurative. No one can assert one way or the other with perfect certainty. But one thing *all* the trustworthy scholars I've read agree on is that hell is a place of unspeakable torment that goes on eternally, into infinity for those who die in their sins without Christ.

One of the most gruesome and painful characteristics of hell is the endlessness of it. If we were told that after a million years of suffering, there would be a chance for repentance, even that would provide the tiniest glimmer of hope. But hope is completely nonexistent in hell. After millions of years, there will still be no end to such torment. Instead, it will be as though just beginning. Hell is *inevitable* for those who have never come to Christ, and it's *inescapable* once you're there.

One criticism of the doctrine of hell is that it is downright rude and offensive to people. Some say that if we have to teach it at all, we need to find a way to teach it more *optimistically*. Talking about hell is a real "downer." But according to Pastor John MacArthur, "There is no way to declare the truth of God's wrath in an 'optimistic' tone."[13] Any attempt to convey the frightful wrath of almighty God in a light, humorous, nonthreatening, positive way would be ridiculous. There is just no other way to communicate such a deadly serious teaching except soberly, prayerfully, thoughtfully, and truthfully.

I am not trying to persuade anyone to make an uninformed commitment to Christ motivated purely by fear. However, fear of hell *can* be a powerful motivation to turn to the Savior. In fact, this fear of punishment can be the very means God uses to reach some people. And if that's what the Father uses to reach your heart, so be it, and praise Him for it. Boettner wrote, "Fear of punishment is not the highest motive to morality but it is an effective one, and where it is absent crime soon becomes rampant."[14]

The holiness of God demands that every sin be punished. Sin will either be punished in Christ, or it will be punished in those who remain unrepentant and unforgiven.

The love of God decrees that *some* of fallen humanity will be rescued from the prospect of hell and delivered into a heavenly kingdom to dwell with Him in continuous praise and adoration forever.

For us to come to Christ, we must understand His holiness, as well as our own sinfulness. We must realize that we cannot, on our own merit, attain to the kingdom of heaven. It is at this point that we finally identify our desperate need of a Savior and acknowledge Jesus Christ as that Savior. Only then can we genuinely repent of our sins and place our complete trust in Him to deliver us into the kingdom of God. "The depth of the riches of God's mercy will also then be revealed, for all redeemed sinners will recognize that they too deserve such punishment from God and have avoided it only by God's grace through Jesus Christ."[15]

That's the *good news* about hell. *Hell is avoidable* for all who repent and come to Jesus Christ. Sometimes the good news looks even better when placed in contrast with the "bad news." For instance, a doctor may tell you, "You look great." Now place that news in the context that your last chemo treatment has been administered, and the scans have finally come back negative—no cancer showing anywhere. When your doctor tells you, "You look great," how much better that news seems.

Erwin Lutzer wrote, "If God had not possessed love and mercy throughout all eternity, we might have been created by a malicious and cruel being who delighted in watching His creatures suffer perpetual torment. Fortunately, that is not the case. The Bible tells of the love and mercy of God; He does not delight in the death of the wicked. But it also has much to say about His justice. . . . To put it clearly, we must accept God as He is revealed in the Bible, whether He suits our preferences or not."[16]

In conclusion, let me say that all the horrors described above are nothing compared to that of being eternally separated from God. By the time people are condemned to hell, they will have comprehended the truth of God. Thus, this separation will be eternally crushing to them. Isaiah 45:22-24 says, "Turn to me [God] and be saved, all the ends of the earth! For I am God, and there is no other. By myself I have sworn; from my mouth has gone out in righteousness a word that shall not return: '*To me every knee shall bow, every tongue shall swear allegiance.*' Only in the LORD, it shall be said of me, are righteousness and strength; *to him shall come and be ashamed all who were incensed against him.*"

The New Testament has a similar passage. Philippians 2:10-11 says, "so that at the name of Jesus *every knee should bow*, in heaven and on earth and under the earth, and *every tongue confess* that Jesus Christ is Lord, to the glory of God the Father."

Hell is not complete separation from God. It is separation from the *blessings* of God. It is not, however, a separation from the *wrath* of God. Those who end up in hell will be surrounded on all sides by His awful wrath.

What does all this have to do with death and the dying of a loved one or even with your own impending death? When someone discovers that he is dying, he may begin to think about the hereafter. If a person is not saved and has no faith in Christ, he may experience more suffering, more pain, more anxiety, and more spiritual discomfort than those whose eternal destiny is secure.

Family members sometimes forbid the chaplain or the nurse from talking to the patient about spiritual matters. They presume that because the patient may not have expressed an interest in spiritual things in the past, he or she wouldn't want to talk about it now. But that's not always true. Sometimes even though the person never cared one whit about anything spiritual before, he or she may feel an urgency to talk about such things now and to resolve the spiritual issues with which he or she may be wrestling.

The hospice chaplain is not there to *push* anything on anybody. He or she works to support the patient and the family and to help them resolve the issues regarding their own spiritual readiness before dying. I urge well-intentioned family members to allow such conversations, especially if the patient is receptive to them. Just because the patient may not talk to the family about spiritual things doesn't mean he or she doesn't want to talk to *anyone* about such things.

I've personally seen these conversations make a significant difference in the overall peacefulness in dying—not to mention the eternal security of people's souls. And sometimes it's easier to talk to a stranger about spiritual matters. Remember that.

Some families try to hide the fact that they have admitted their loved ones into the hospice program. They don't want the patients to know they are dying. (Most of the time I believe the patients already know that anyway.) But I urge you not to keep the news from your loved ones. Dying people deserve to know the truth. If they have been informed of their impending death, they will have the opportunity to use whatever time is left to prepare for it.

Sometimes it is only in the face of death that people can have a true perspective. That may be when they begin to really see and appreciate life. They can distinguish what is good and valuable and truly important in life from what is unimportant and meaningless. When death forces a person to take a good look at life, it can also force that person to see God more clearly. At the very least, it gives them the *opportunity* to ponder these things.

Genuine deathbed conversions may be few, but the fact remains that some people *are* brought to Christ even on the very day of their death. Blocking such interaction will only add to your own frustration. With such an eternal issue at stake, I urge you to utilize the strong spiritual resources at hand.

The thief on the cross next to Christ was converted on the day of his death. Luke offers this account of the experience:

> *One of the criminals who were hanged railed at him, saying, "Are you not the Christ? Save yourself and us." But the other rebuked him, saying, "Do you not fear God, since you are under the same sentence of condemnation? And we indeed justly, for we are receiving the due reward of our deeds; but this man has done nothing wrong." And he said, "Jesus, remember me when you come into your kingdom." And he said to him, "Truly, I say to you, today you will be with me in Paradise." (Luke 23:39-43)*

Isn't that simple? "Jesus, remember me when you come into your kingdom." That's all it takes—not merely *saying* the words but *mean-*

ing the words. If you've never made that simple request, I pray you will before it's eternally too late. Call on the name of the Lord.

Warning people about hell is not an act of cruelty, but rather of mercy and love and compassion. I'll never forget the story Dr. Whitney used to close his sermon on this subject:

Imagine driving home at night through a horrible thunderstorm. The rain and hail are pounding your car. The streetlights are out. Limbs are down. The roaring, swirling wind is blowing so hard that it's difficult to hold the car on the road. Visibility is only a few feet.

There, in front of your car, you spot a figure in your headlights, soaked and bleeding, waving madly and shouting something you can't quite make out over the howling wind. *Man,* you think, *I don't want to stop for that guy. I'll get soaked. All I want to do is get home. No telling who he is. Might be some psycho or something.*

You swerve—only to find him there again, waving and shouting for you to stop. When you realize you either have to run him down or stop, you finally stop. You roll the window down a quarter of an inch.

He rushes to your window and shouts through the storm, "Thank God, you stopped. So many cars have rushed right by me, and now all those people are dead. The bridge up ahead has washed out, and they all plunged into the water."

This man's warning saved your life. It was an act of mercy. So is the warning of Christ about hell. He stands with His arms outstretched on a cross and speaks to our hearts, "Stop. Don't go past Me."

THE DOCTRINE OF HEAVEN

I have a sense of relief just being able to move on now to the subject of the blessedness of heaven. Now we come to *the good part.* Without heaven, there would be no comfort for the dying, no comfort for the grieving, no comfort for the suffering. Heaven is the reward, the prize, the dessert for the life of a Christian.

Heaven, and our nearness to Christ there, offers the only comfort we can gain from the hardship and adversity brought into our lives on earth. So it is supremely important that we understand what awaits us there.

Death would hold nothing but emptiness and horror without heaven. Instead, death is the means through which we enter that most blessed state of being. Erwin Lutzer wrote, "Our present body is like a tent where our spirit dwells; it is a temporary structure. . . . Death takes us from the tent to the palace; it is changing our address from earth to heaven."[17]

Imagine that. Our spirits are housed in flimsy, dirty, worn-out tents. And when we "move up," we move not into another temporary but sturdier dwelling, but into the palace of the King. To make our circumstances even more wonderful, we won't be there merely as guests but as His children. What a glorious thought.

John MacArthur said it like this: "Plainly, Scripture is teaching that all Christians will receive a full share of the inheritance of heaven. Every believer will 'inherit all things' (Rev. 21:7), so the inheritance isn't carved up and apportioned on the basis of worthiness. And when God says, 'I will be his God and he shall be my son'—He is saying that heaven will be not only our dwelling-place, but also our possession: We will be there not as boarders, but as full-fledged members of the family. What an inexpressible privilege that is."[18]

In my enthusiasm to begin to describe the beauty of heaven, let me not forget to offer a word of caution. There is a lot of misinformation out there about heaven. Just as the image of angels has been modified to fit society's whims, so also heaven has been "merchandised" to us. We hear a lot about it. Occasionally we even hear stories of how someone went to heaven and came back. They tell tales of heaven, write books about their experiences, and go on talk shows to describe what they went through. Beware.

John MacArthur correctly states, "Clearly, because Scripture is the Word of God, *we must reject every anecdotal account that contradicts what Scripture teaches*. Ultimately we are forced to conclude that *the Bible is our* only reliable *source of information about heaven*."[19]

I believe it is safe to say that more people believe in heaven than in hell. They are much more likely to believe that if heaven really exists, we will all somehow make it there. I hope I have shown from the Scriptures that this is not the case. It really does exist, but not everyone will go there.

In fact, the Bible says that only a few will go. Now that "few" consists of more than we can number, but the vast majority of the people who have ever lived and died on this earth will *not* inherit the kingdom of heaven.

Matthew 7:13-14 says, "Enter by the narrow gate. For the gate is wide and the way is easy that leads to destruction, and those who enter by it are *many*. For the gate is narrow and the way is hard that leads to life, and those who find it are *few*."

How many people are included in the "few"? The apostle John helps us here: "After this I looked, and behold, *a great multitude that no one could number*, from every nation, from all tribes and peoples and languages, standing before the throne and before the Lamb [Christ]" (Revelation 7:9).

Your question might be, "How can I find this 'gate' that leads to heaven? How can I make sure that I'm one of that 'multitude' of people there?" I'm glad you asked. Christ has—and is—the answer.

In the book of John, Jesus uses the analogy of a shepherd and his sheep to describe the relationship between the Great Shepherd and His spiritual sheep (those who believe and trust in Him):

"Truly, truly, I say to you, he who does not enter the sheepfold by the door but climbs in by another way, that man is a thief and a robber. But he who enters by the door is the shepherd of the sheep. To him the gatekeeper opens. The sheep hear his voice, and he calls his own sheep by name and leads them out. When he has brought out all his own, he goes before them, and the sheep follow him, for they know his voice. A stranger they will not follow, but they will flee from him, for they do not know the voice of strangers." This figure of speech Jesus used with them, but they did not understand what he was saying to them. So Jesus again said to them, "Truly, truly, I say to you, I am the door of the sheep. All who came before me are thieves and robbers, but the sheep did not listen to them. I am the door. If anyone enters by me, he will be saved and will go in and out and find pasture." (John 10:1-9)

And then in a better-known passage He says, "I am the way, and the truth, and the life. No one comes to the Father except through me" (John 14:6). That leaves no room for doubt. He is the gate through which we pass to reach the kingdom of heaven. There is no other way.

We are taught that those who enter through Christ will be saved. They will be numbered among the multitude in heaven. Salvation does not depend on our *own* effort, but on *Christ's* efforts. It is because of *His* righteousness and *His* death on the cross as the payment for our sins that we can walk through that gate into eternal life with Him.

This promise is seen in numerous passages in Scripture, but let's read the one in 1 Peter 1:3-9:

> *Blessed be the God and Father of our Lord Jesus Christ!* According to his great mercy, *he has caused us to be born again to a* living hope *through the resurrection of Jesus Christ from the dead,* to an inheritance *that is* imperishable, undefiled, *and* unfading, kept in heaven for you, *who* by God's power *are being* guarded *through faith for a salvation ready to be revealed in the last time. In this you rejoice,* though now for a little while, *if necessary, you have been grieved by various trials, so that the tested genuineness of your faith—more precious than gold that perishes though it is tested by fire—may be found to result in praise and glory and honor at the revelation of Jesus Christ.* Though you have not seen him, you love him. Though you do not now see him, you believe in him *and rejoice with joy that is inexpressible and filled with glory, obtaining* the outcome of your faith, the salvation of your souls.

What a beautiful passage. Now let's consider heaven and its wonders.

Where Is Heaven?

The word *heaven* can mean different things. In theological terms, we may occasionally read and hear of the first, second, and third heavens. This is not of vital importance, but just so you'll have a working understanding of the terms, let me describe what is meant by each.

The first heaven is generally considered to be atmospheric. It is the sky (troposphere), the region of breathable atmosphere that blankets the earth. The second heaven is generally considered to be planetary. It is made up of stars, moon, planets, earth, galaxies, etc. We refer to it as outer space most of the time. The third heaven is the place where God dwells with His holy angels and the spirits of believers who have died. According to Scripture, the other two heavens will eventually pass away, but this one is eternal.

When Will We See Heaven?

When we die, our bodies will go to the grave. The body is a shell that houses the spirit in this life. When the shell (or "temporary dwelling" as the Bible refers to it) dies, each person's spirit is released and goes directly into the presence of God if he or she is a Christian. There the spirit will exist until the time when the body will be resurrected from the grave as a changed, immortal, glorious body. The spirit and body then reunite, and it is in that new, perfected body that the believer will forever dwell with Christ in heaven.

The bodies of those who die without Christ will also go to the grave. But, according to the Scriptures, their spirits go into hell and exist there until the resurrection. At that time the bodies and spirits are joined together once more, but instead of spending eternity in heaven with Christ, they are condemned to spend it in hell without Him.

For the rest of this chapter, when I refer to the glories of heaven, I am speaking only in terms of those who die "in Christ," that is, as believers.

Here are just a few passages that support what I have said about the resurrection of the body and everlasting life or condemnation:

> *Do not be amazed at this, for a time is coming when* all who are in their graves *will hear his voice and come out*—those who have done good *[by trusting Him] will* rise to live, *and* those who have done evil *[by rejecting Him] will* rise to be condemned. *(John 5:28-29 NIV)*

> *But we do not want you to be uninformed, brothers, about those who are asleep [dead], that you may not grieve as others do who have no hope. For since we believe that Jesus died and rose again,*

*even so, through Jesus, God will bring with him those who have
fallen asleep [their spirits]. For this we declare to you by a word
from the Lord, that we who are alive, who are left until the coming of the Lord, will not precede those who have fallen asleep. For
the Lord himself will descend from heaven with a cry of command,
with the voice of an archangel, and with the sound of the trumpet
of God. And the dead in Christ [their bodies] will rise first. Then
we who are alive, who are left, will be caught up together with them
in the clouds to meet the Lord in the air, and so we will always be
with the Lord. (1 Thessalonians 4:13-17)*

This event is commonly called the Second Coming of Christ. At
the Second Coming something really unusual takes place. It's called the
Rapture. Christians who are living at that time will be supernaturally
changed. Their bodies change in a moment into an eternal form. These
people do not have to die a physical death. Instead, they are caught up
with Christ in the air.

What about those who have been cremated or had body parts
amputated or breasts removed? Are they going to be whole in heaven?
Boettner addresses this topic:

We do not believe . . . that in the resurrection there will be any difference between those who are buried in the graves of the earth and
those whose bodies were destroyed by fire, or devoured by wild
beasts or drowned in the sea, or blown to bits by the explosion of
bombs. Certainly the martyrs who were burned for the faith and
whose ashes were scattered by the winds shall arise in the resurrection, and their bodies shall be not one whit less glorious than
those of others who received burial. There is no limit to the power
of God. He who in the first place made the body from the elements
of the earth can bring again the body that has been disintegrated by
whatever means. The identical particles are not essential to a resurrection. A sailor buried at sea rises as surely as if he had been
expensively embalmed and buried in the family plot.[20]

Perhaps he draws his conclusions from Revelation 20:13, which
says, "And the sea gave up the dead who were in it, Death and Hades

gave up the dead who were in them. . . ." There is no limit to God's power. We will be whole in heaven.

Immediately after the dead are raised, those who are alive at the time will be raptured into heaven with Christ: "Behold! I tell you a mystery. *We shall not all sleep* [die], but we shall all be changed, *in a moment, in the twinkling of an eye*, at the last trumpet. For the trumpet will sound, and *the dead will be raised imperishable, and we shall be changed*" (1 Corinthians 15:51-52).

Jesus Himself gives a warning in Luke 17:34-35: "I tell you, in that night there will be two in one bed. One will be taken and the other left. There will be two women grinding together. One will be taken and the other left." He is describing what will occur when Christians are raptured out of the world.

You can imagine the chaos if all Christians miraculously are removed from the earth in the same instant, leaving those behind who have never known Christ as their Savior. At that time it will be too late for unbelievers to turn to Him for salvation. They will have missed their "window of opportunity."

Some scoff at this whole idea of the Second Coming, the Rapture, and the resurrection of the dead because these are all supernatural events. People say this all sounds like some weird fairy tale. This shouldn't surprise us. The first time Christ came to this earth, as God in the flesh, He came in a supernatural way—by the Virgin Birth. He came quietly, with little fanfare. Only a few shepherds and wise men knew of His birth.

But the second time He comes to the earth will be literally earth-shattering. He will come back with power and glory, and all people on the earth (living and dead) will know about it. "And then they will see the Son of Man coming in clouds with great power and glory. And then he will send out the angels and gather his elect [His chosen ones] from the four winds, from the ends of the earth to the ends of heaven" (Mark 13:26-27).

In fact, the apostle Peter anticipated that people wouldn't believe in the Second Coming:

[Y]ou should remember the predictions of the holy prophets and the commandment of the Lord and Savior through your apostles, knowing this first of all, that scoffers will come in the last days with scoffing, following their own sinful desires. *They will say, "Where is the promise of his coming? For ever since the fathers fell asleep, all things are continuing as they were from the beginning of creation." For* they deliberately overlook this fact, *that the heavens existed long ago, and the earth was formed out of water and through water by the word of God. (2 Peter 3:2-5)*

So, yes, some will have a hard time believing in such a dramatic and supernatural event. But those are the ones who also have a hard time believing in the dramatic and supernatural event of His first coming. They would rather believe in the lies they hear—that heaven and hell do not exist or that we'll all get to heaven sooner or later, if not in this life, then maybe in the next, or that if our good deeds outweigh our bad ones, we'll go to heaven. I tell you the truth: If they rely on anything but Christ to get to heaven, they will perish. "They perish because they refused to love the truth and so be saved" (2 Thessalonians 2:10b NIV).

I haven't answered the question about exactly *when* the Second Coming will occur. That's because no one can answer that question:

Therefore, stay awake [be on your guard], for you do not know on what day your Lord is coming. . . . *Therefore you also must be ready, for the Son of Man is coming* at an hour you do not expect. *(Matthew 24:42, 44)*

But concerning that day or that hour, no one knows, *not even the angels in heaven, nor the Son, but only the Father. Be on guard, keep awake. For* you do not know when the time will come. *(Mark 13:32-33)*

Now concerning the times and the seasons, brothers, you have no need to have anything written to you. For you yourselves are fully aware that the day of the Lord will come like a thief in the night. *(1 Thessalonians 5:1-2)*

Only God knows when the Lord will return, and He did not

choose to reveal that information. That Christ hasn't yet returned is a mercy. It allows those of us who have been given the grace to believe to do so. It will allow those who have not yet entered the fold to do so before it is eternally too late. "And count the patience of our Lord as salvation" (2 Peter 3:15a).

What Is Heaven Like?

We've reviewed what it takes to get to heaven. Now let's talk about what an indescribably beautiful and glorious place it is. What's so special about heaven?

A PLACE PREPARED FOR US

Heaven is a beautiful place God has prepared for those He has chosen. In John 14:1-3 Jesus told His disciples, "Let not your hearts be troubled. Believe in God; believe also in me. In my Father's house are many rooms. If it were not so, would I have told you that *I go to prepare a place for you*? And if I go and prepare a place for you, *I will come again and will take you to myself,* that where I am you may be also."

These verses speak not only of His second coming, but also they let us know that He is the One preparing a place for us in His Father's "house"—heaven. No, He's not taking two thousand years to get it ready. Christ can create our place in heaven in a moment in time.

OUR HOME

I enjoy my earthly home. It brings me great comfort and contentment. I'd rather be here than anywhere in the world. I enjoy working in my garden and the yard. I love to entertain and to share my home with others. In other words, I feel completely comfortable here. I confess that I've wondered how well I will fit in heaven. So when I read the following by John MacArthur I was excited and encouraged: "If you're worried about feeling out of place in heaven, don't. Heaven will seem more like home than the dearest spot on earth to you. It is uniquely designed by a tender, loving Savior to be the place where we will live together for all eternity and enjoy Him forever—in the fullness of our glorified humanity."[21]

Also encouraging is the concept that our heavenly home will be shared with those we love. When we think about home, don't we think of our family? Don't we associate home with those we love? In fact, that's the most distinctive feature about it. In heaven we'll be with those we love. That includes not only our family and friends (if they were Christians), but we're told we will have a perfect love for all the inhabitants of heaven. That is the place where our love is perfected.

We will love others without the corrupting influence of sin, but *the main reason heaven will be our home is that we will be with our Father, our Brother, our Lord.* God is the very essence of love. "Without question, the most marvelous thing of all about heaven—heaven's supreme delight—will be unbroken fellowship with God Himself. . . . The presence of Christ is what makes heaven heaven."[22]

Thomas Boston, a seventeenth-century Scottish Presbyterian scholar, agrees: *"The Blessing of the Divine Presence.* Here lies the chief happiness of the saints in heaven, without which they could never be happy."[23]

Puritan Richard Baxter also affirms this idea: "God himself will be the full and everlasting object of my love. Perfect joyful complacency in God is the heaven which I desire and hope for. In God there is all that love can desire for its full everlasting feast."[24]

We will not have to face the grief of saying good-bye anymore. No one dies there. There are no barriers between people. We will all understand the same language. We will love each other without regard to race, sex, age, size, or social status. Those things are irrelevant there. "It is a city that never changes its inhabitants. None of them shall ever be removed out of it; for life and immortality reign there, and no death can enter into it."[25]

CASE STUDY

James Franklin was a patient I loved dearly. He was a minister of the gospel of Christ in a small rural town in Arkansas. He had been a pas-

tor for over forty years. In fact, he had been known for so long as Rev. Franklin that everyone just called him "Reverend," even his lovely wife, Lexa.

When I met Reverend, he was dying from prostate cancer that had metastasized to the bone. He was such a cute old man—gentle and soft-spoken. I fell for him instantly. He searched my face with his soft, brown eyes and told me he was happy to meet me. But his speech came slowly because he was hurting so badly. There was pain in those brown eyes.

My first priority was to find the right combination of drugs to stop the pain while allowing him to still function optimally. His doctor was cooperative and willing to try what I suggested. Between the two of us, we initiated and implemented a plan. Within a day or so, Reverend was comfortable again for the first time in months.

On my frequent visits to his house, I would talk with him about the Bible, sharing stories with him when he didn't want to talk, listening to his stories when he did. Lexa and I became very close. She depended on me to be truthful with her, to tell her exactly what was going on with her husband and what she could do to make his life better. We worked together as a team to make his last few months as enjoyable as we could.

He loved to sit next to the bay window in his bedroom, slouching into his big chair, watching the goings-on out on the street. Then as the disease progressed, he was confined more and more to his bed. Finally, we brought in a hospital bed for him. By that time, he was spending all his time there, too fragile to get up, too weak to talk much anymore.

Early one evening Lexa couldn't wake him. She called hospice. I'd previously offered to go sit with him when it was time to place him on continuous care. It was time.

When I arrived, he was conscious but very, very weak. Lexa was handling the crisis calmly, serenely. We had talked about this event many times. Because of her deep faith in God and in His promises, she was relaxed and accepting. The whole family was in the home that night as well as some of their church members. Everybody loved

Reverend. They were there to honor him and to lend their loving support to Lexa.

She sat next to him hour after hour. Once an hour I would check his vital signs and monitor his pain status. He seemed comfortable, but his breathing was becoming more labored. I elevated the head of his bed. His breathing evened out and came easier. He lingered on into the night, exceeding my expectations. When I'd first assessed him, I didn't think he had more than an hour or two to live. But here it was almost 3:00 in the morning.

Lexa was struggling to stay awake at his bedside. Members of the family were sleeping in the other rooms in chairs and on sofas, and some of the kids were on the floor on pallets of quilts. I offered to sit by Reverend's side for a while so Lexa could get a few hours' sleep. Reluctantly she offered up her chair. She gave me a big hug and asked me to wake her "if anything happened." I assured her I would.

The house was quiet and warm. The only sound was the ticking of the big clock in the living room. The smells of supper still lingered in the air, filling the room with the aroma of "home."

I picked up Reverend's cool hand and held it between my two warm ones. I marveled at the way my white hands looked, entwined with the dark, rich color of his. Leaning over him, I planted a soft kiss on his forehead and told him I loved him and that it was okay to go if he needed to. To my surprise, he opened his eyes and looked up toward the ceiling.

"Reverend?"

"Yes, child." His soft voice sounded tired and weak.

"Are you hurting anywhere?"

"No." He closed his eyes for a moment and then opened them again.

"I love you. You know that, don't you? I'm so glad I got to know you. You've been such a blessing to me."

He merely nodded his head slowly, his eyelids heavy as he struggled to stay awake.

"When you get to heaven, who do you want to see first?"

Expecting him to say something like "Jesus" or "the apostle

Paul," I was mildly surprised when he said, so softly I could barely hear him, "My mother."

Quick, hot tears filled my eyes as I heard the unexpected desire of his heart and watched his eyes close again. This time they stayed shut.

How about that? I thought. As much as he knows about the glories of heaven, it's still his mother who will be the most precious first sight for him there. I was touched and moved by his answer. I'll never forget his expression or the sound of his voice when he uttered those last two words.

I just sat next to him, holding his hand, crying quietly. I prayed, "Thank You, Lord, for sending me to this wonderful home, for allowing me the privilege of getting to know this dear family. Continue to be merciful to Your servant James and bring him into Your kingdom in Your perfect timing. Send the blessing of Your strength and comfort to the family and allow them to humbly and graciously submit to Your will in Reverend's life and in all things." Then I settled back into the chair and wondered at the turn of events that brought Reverend's life and mine together. God had planned this intersection of our lives.

Reverend settled back into a deep sleep, but his breathing remained slow, regular, and unlabored.

While the whole house was quiet, I sang hymns to him softly. Suddenly he let out one ragged breath, paused, another breath, paused. And then . . . nothing.

"Reverend? Reverend?" I whispered to him. No response. With my stethoscope, I listened to his tiny birdcage of a chest. No heartbeat.

"Go with God, Reverend. Go with God."

Bodies That Never Die or Break Down

What will our resurrected bodies look like? Will they still have human shape? Will they radiate light? Will they be larger or smaller than our bodies are now? Will they appear young or old?

The answer to these and other such questions no one knows. We are not told specifically what these new and improved bodies will look like. But we are told other things about them. According to 1 Corinthians 15, they will be imperishable, powerful, spiritual bodies. After all, "you can't have a decaying body in a permanent home."[26] So these bodies will be immortal. Whatever form they take, they will bear a resemblance to Christ. "Just as we have borne the image of the man of dust [Adam], we shall also bear the image of the man of heaven [Christ]" (1 Corinthians 15:49).

John MacArthur affirms the point by writing, "So the best picture of what we'll be like in heaven is the resurrected body of Jesus Christ. We will have a body fit for the full life of God to indwell and express itself forever. It can eat but won't need to. It will be a body that can move at will through space and matter. It will be ageless and not know pain, tears, sorrow, sickness, or death."[27]

If we use Christ's resurrected body as a guide to what ours will be like, we must remember that He was not subject to material forces. After the Resurrection the apostles convened in an upper room in Jerusalem. "On the evening of that day, the first day of the week, the doors being locked where the disciples were for fear of the Jews, Jesus came and stood among them and said to them, 'Peace be with you'" (John 20:19). Notice that they were behind locked doors. Then suddenly Jesus appeared in the room.

Luke tells of the same event with a little different slant: "As they were talking about these things, Jesus himself stood among them, and said to them, 'Peace to you!' But they were startled and frightened and thought they saw a spirit" (Luke 24:36-37). The doors were locked, but there He stood among them. No one knows exactly how that happened. Perhaps He materialized in the room because He is God. But perhaps our resurrected bodies will also be able to travel through space and matter.

Pastor Lutzer says, "Evidently we too shall be able to travel effortlessly . . . we shall still eat, not because we are hungry, but because we will delight in the fellowship it affords. After the resurrection, Christ ate fish with His disciples on the shores of Galilee. And, of course, believers will be present at the marriage supper of the Lamb (Rev. 19:7)."[28]

And what about our minds? Will we be little robots in heaven? Absolutely not. Boettner wrote, "The mind loses none of its power or knowledge at the death of the body. On the contrary, it enters on a much higher plane of existence. The first and immediate result is that the soul, freed from the limitations of the earth and cleansed of the last vestiges of sin, finds its mental and spiritual faculties heightened and is more alive and active than it ever was before."[29]

Many of the writers I've been reading say that we will be engaged in heavenly "occupations" there. Did you think we wouldn't have to do another lick of work when we get to heaven? Well, you were wrong. But that work will be pure bliss to us. "Each job description will entail two primary responsibilities. First, there will be the worship of God; second, there will be the serving of the Most High in whatever capacity assigned to us. . . . But just as there are varied responsibilities in the palace of an earthly king, so in heaven some will be given more prominent responsibilities than others. Of this we may be certain: heaven is not a place of inactivity or boredom."[30] Centuries ago Puritan Richard Baxter wrote, "Activity will be my perfection and my rest. Though now I know not fully what service I must do, I know it will be good, and suitable to the blessed state I shall be in."[31]

The bottom line? God has prepared for us an eternal dwelling place. The very body we'll inhabit will be eternal and without blemish. Then the immortal body will dwell in an eternal place, bathed in the light and love of the Father.

The "No Mores" of Heaven

NO MORE DEATH, SORROW, TEARS, OR PAIN

Some of the joy in heaven will result from the absence of certain things. There will be:

No more death
No more sorrow
No more crying
No more pain

"He will wipe away every tear from their eyes, and death shall be no more, neither shall there be mourning nor crying nor pain anymore, for the former things have passed away" (Revelation 21:4). Henry Bast wrote, "The state of the dead in Christ is blessed because they are delivered completely and finally from all sorrow, sin and suffering."[32]

A most beautiful and encouraging comment came from the pen of J. C. Ryle:

> Blessed be God. There shall be no sorrow in heaven. There shall not be one single tear shed within the courts above. There shall be no more disease and weakness and decay; the coffin, and the funeral, and the grave and the dark-black mourning shall be things unknown. Our faces shall no more be pale and sad; no more shall we go out from the company of those we love and be parted asunder—that word, *farewell,* shall never be heard again. There shall be no anxious thought about tomorrow to mar and spoil our enjoyment, no sharp and cutting words to wound our souls; our wants will have come to a perpetual end, and all around us shall be harmony and love. Oh, Christian brethren, what is our light affliction when compared to such an eternity as this? Shame on us if we murmur and complain and turn back, with such a heaven before our eyes. What can this vain and passing world give us better than this?[33]

NO MORE SIN

"But nothing unclean will ever enter [heaven]" (Revelation 21:27). God's children should look forward to such a place with eagerness. Recently, during a sermon by Todd Murray at the Bible Church of Little Rock, I was deeply convicted. He asked this question: "If I could do absolutely anything I wanted to do, what would it be?" Thoughts immediately flew into my head—like travel the world, or act in a movie, or chat with Streisand . . . you get the picture. But Todd continued by saying, "I'd never . . . sin . . . again." *Oh, yeah.* I confess that idea didn't even enter my mind.

But it should have.

When we sin, the Bible says that we *grieve* the Holy Spirit. "And do not *grieve the Holy Spirit of God,* by whom you were sealed for the day of redemption" (Ephesians 4:30). In the New Testament, it appears that He is *grieved* by the sins of His own people. But the sins of unbelievers provoke His *wrath.*

When we once realize how much Christ suffered when He took

upon Himself our putrid, corrupt, filthy sins and paid the penalty for every last one of them in His own perfect, righteous body, we should *yearn* to throw off the sin we continue to commit. But the good news for all believers is that in heaven sin will not exist. We will at last be free from its influence. The desire to sin will no longer be a part of our being. Hallelujah!

NO MORE HUNGER, THIRST, OR TEARS

"They shall hunger no more, neither thirst anymore; the sun shall not strike them, nor any scorching heat. For the Lamb in the midst of the throne will be their shepherd, and he will guide them to springs of living water, and God will wipe away every tear from their eyes" (Revelation 7:16-17).

NO MORE MARRIAGE

Now don't get me wrong. I'm not saying we'll be more joyful in heaven because there will be no more marriage. Here begins the rest of the "No Mores" that will neither add to nor take away from our joy. This is just the way it will be in heaven; so we're told. "For in the resurrection they neither marry nor are given in marriage, but are like angels in heaven" (Matthew 22:30). No, there will be no such bonds in heaven. Or actually there will be *multitudes* of bonds there because we will love *each other* purely, completely, and perfectly. But keep in mind that the primary object of our love will be the Lord, our God.

NO MORE SUN, MOON, NIGHT, OR SEA

"And the city [heaven] has no need of sun or moon to shine on it, for the glory of God gives it light, and its lamp is the Lamb" (Revelation 21:23). And then in Revelation 21:1 we read, "Then I saw a new heaven and a new earth, for the first heaven and the first earth had passed away, and the sea was no more." Revelation 22:5 says, "And night will be no more. They will need no light of lamp or sun, for the Lord God will be their light, and they will reign forever and ever."

Precious Promises Fulfilled

J. C. Ryle listed some of God's beautiful promises to us in this section from his excellent book, *Holiness*:

> To every believer belong exceeding great and precious promises . . . promises sure to be fulfilled, because made by One who cannot lie, and has power as well as will to keep His word. "Sin shall not have dominion over you."—"The God of peace shall bruise Satan under your feet shortly."—"He that has begun a good work will perform it until the day of Jesus Christ."—"When thou passeth through the waters I will be with thee, and through the floods, they shall not overflow thee."—"My sheep shall never perish, neither shall anyone pluck them out of my hand."—"Him that cometh unto me I will in no wise cast out."—"I will never leave thee, nor forsake thee."—"I am persuaded that neither death, nor life, nor things present, nor things to come, shall be able to separate us from the love of God, which is in Christ Jesus." (Rom. 6:14; 16:20; Philip. 1:6; Isa. 43:2; John 10:28; 6:37; Heb. 13:5; Rom. 8:38)[34]

Because of promises such as these, our future is secure. Our "investments" in heaven are protected, never to depreciate, never to be devalued, and never to become obsolete. They are "an inheritance that is imperishable, undefiled, and unfading, kept in heaven for you" (1 Peter 1:4). God's promises are truly wondrous and absolutely faithful. You can stake your life on them.

Ceaseless Worship of God as the Object of Our Love

This will be our primary occupation in heaven. We must beware of any other views or "revelations" regarding heaven that do not focus on God and our praise of Him. Heaven is totally God-centered, unlike some of the anecdotal accounts I've read that seem to make heaven exist for us instead.

God is not here for us. We are here for Him.

We do find incomprehensible glories and pleasures there, but the chief focus in heaven will *always* be the worship and glorification of God. "Scripture repeatedly makes clear that heaven is a realm of unsurpassed joy, unfading glory, undiminished bliss, unlimited delights and unending pleasure. . . . It will be a perfect existence."[35] Paul understood this truth when he wrote in Philippians 1:21, "For to me to live is Christ, and to die is gain." He knew that through death we will finally achieve a union with Christ for eternity, and comprehending the joy of that relationship, Paul yearned for what lay on the other side of death.

I believe that Solomon, the writer of Ecclesiastes, realized that the day of our death is our glorification. He said, "A good name is better than precious ointment, and the *day of death than the day of birth*" (Ecclesiastes 7:1).

A seventeenth-century pastor echoed this wisdom of Solomon when he wrote, "But in God we shall have all our desires, and we shall desire nothing without Him. . . . God will be all in all to the saints: He will be their life, health, riches, peace and all good things."[36] He continues by using the example of Noah's ark to demonstrate our secure state: "When they were living on earth with the rest of the world, He opened the doors of their hearts, entered into them, and shut them again, so that sin could never re-enter, to reign there as formerly. Now He opens heaven's doors to them, draws His doves into the ark, and shuts them in so that the law, death and hell can never get them out again."

Notice that in this passage God does all the work. "His doves" do nothing. He opens the spiritual doors to their hearts, then seals them unto Himself for as long as they live, as well as bringing them into His fold, sealing out everything but what is pure and good and pleasant in His sight. Then by His sustaining hand, they will live with Him through all eternity, loving and praising Him forever.

"God accomplishes everything on behalf of those He saves. They contribute nothing. He chooses them, draws them, and enables them to believe. . . . No aspect of salvation hinges on anything good in the believer."[37]

As Jerry Bridges said, "How shall we respond to the fact that God is able to and does in fact move in the minds and hearts of people to accomplish His will? Our first response should be one of trust."[38]

In fact, we cannot trust Him completely until we understand just how much He is continuously at work in every aspect and every moment of our lives. When we realize how fully trust*worthy* He is, we can relax and place our trust in the only One who is deserving of such faith. But in heaven our eyes will be opened, and our hearts will be purified so that we will finally comprehend the *extent* of His greatness and glory. "One minute after we die, our minds, our memories will be clearer than ever before . . . in heaven there will be intuitive knowledge for our minds will be redeemed from the limitations sin imposed upon them."[39]

This freedom from sin's limitations is one of the things we should long for about heaven. But then there are *so many* things about heaven to long for. John MacArthur's book *The Glory of Heaven* really brought that home to me in a fuller sense. He takes snippets of information about heaven here and another passage there and weaves them together into a glorious tapestry. From this tapestry we can better see a *biblical* view of heaven. I must confess I never longed for heaven before, but now I'm looking forward to it with greater anticipation. My thoughts focus much more on *heavenly* things than they ever used to.

Colossians 3:1-2 says, "[S]eek the things that are above, where Christ is, seated at the right hand of God. Set your minds on things that are above, not on things that are on earth." And as Henry Bast wrote, "The desire for heaven is one of the marks of a child of God."[40] Then he goes on to warn us that if this desire is morbid, or if it is made an avenue of escape from the problems and responsibilities we have here on earth, it is not biblical or Christian.

The Holy City—Our Home Town

What is the Holy City? We are told in the Bible that the old heaven and earth will pass away, and a new city will take its place. "Then I saw a new heaven and a new earth, for the first heaven and the first earth had passed away, and the sea was no more. And *I saw the holy city, new Jerusalem, coming down out of heaven from God*, prepared as a bride adorned for her husband" (Revelation 21:1-2).

We know much detail about this new city of our habitation. Here is a summary description:

> Everything we know will be made perfect. Evil will be purged from the universe. Death and sin and sadness and pain will be entirely done away with. The new heavens and new earth that take the place of the old will be the glorious realm in which the people of God will dwell eternally. . . . Scripture doesn't tell us what the new earth will look like, but we have reason to believe it will in many respects be familiar. Jerusalem will be there—albeit an all-new Jerusalem. John's description concentrates on the Holy City, which has streets and walls, and gates. John also mentions a high mountain, water, a stream and trees. Best of all it is populated with the people of God—real people we will know and with whom we will share eternal fellowship.[41]

So let's talk about what it will be like there. First of all, the city will be laid out as a cube. This cube, according to Revelation 21:15-16, will be close to 1,500 miles in length, in width, and in height.

I liked the way MacArthur chose to illustrate this size: "How far is 1,500 miles? It is about the same as the distance between Maine and Florida. Imagine such an area squared off, then cubed, with multiple levels and millions of intersecting golden avenues. New Jerusalem is a place of immense size and unearthly majesty and beauty."[42]

On the outside boundaries of this cubed city will be twelve gates in a massive wall. This implies that we will be able to come and go. We won't be *prisoners* of the city. It will be home to us. "It had a great, high wall, with twelve gates, and at the gates twelve angels, and on the gates the names of the twelve tribes of the sons of Israel were inscribed—on the east three gates, on the north three gates, on the south three gates, and on the west three gates" (Revelation 21:12-13).

This imposing wall has twelve foundation stones, we're told. The names of the New Testament apostles are inscribed on them. The height of the wall is given as seventy-two yards. That's really not very high when you consider the enormous size of the city.

John describes the city like this: "And he carried me away in the Spirit to a great, high mountain, and showed me the holy city

Jerusalem coming down out of heaven from God, having the glory of God, its radiance like a most rare jewel, like a jasper, clear as crystal" (Revelation 21:10-11). So it will be more beautiful than we can imagine. He continues his description in verses 18-19a, 21: "The wall was built of jasper, while the city was pure gold, clear as glass. The foundations of the wall of the city were adorned with every kind of jewel. . . . And the twelve gates were twelve pearls, each of the gates made of a single pearl, and the street of the city was pure gold, transparent as glass."

Revelation 22:1-2a continues to describe the beauties of the place: "Then the angel showed me [John] the river of the water of life, bright as crystal, flowing from the throne of God and of the Lamb through the middle of the street of the city; also, on either side of the river, the tree of life with its twelve kinds of fruit, yielding its fruit each month."

This passage is another area of disagreement among Bible scholars. Some see all of these descriptions as *literal*. They believe the Holy City will look exactly as depicted here. Other scholars believe that all or part of this description is *symbolic* of the glories of the Holy City. If it is symbolic, remember that the symbol always pales in comparison to whatever it represents. So then heaven would be even more beautiful than John's descriptions illustrate. In either case, it will be a breathtakingly glorious sight and a place of unsurpassed joy.

A Place of Perfection and Unimaginable Joy

Even the best living situation here on earth is far from perfect. Ask any homeowner. Something always seems to need repair, attention, or a "fresh look." Even in the nicest homes you may have trouble with pests. Maybe someone flushes the toilet and scalds the person in the shower. We had a house like that once. And that's just talking about our homes.

What about our jobs? Can any of us say we have the perfect job? Never too boring or too frustrating? Never too taxing or too sedentary? Of course not.

What about the members of our family? our friends? our fellow church members? Are they all perfect? Hardly. Even the purest part about us—our spiritual worship of God—is tainted by the imperfection of sin.

In a wonderful sermon by Don Whitney a couple of years ago, he said it had been suggested once, just for the sake of illustration, that everything touched by sin was the color blue. His point was that everything in our world would be some shade of blue; some things would be loud, bright blues; others only blue-tinged.

In heaven there will be no sin and, therefore, no "blue" in any part of it. Heaven will be a place of the purest beauty and perfection. Not only that, but *we* will be perfected there too. No more sin. What a lovely, lovely thought.

We Will Have Perfect Knowledge

Even though God has chosen to reveal *some things* about this place He's prepared for us, we still cannot fathom the infinite perfection of the place, the inhabitants, the relationships, the worship, the occupations, or especially the God around whom all things center. "For now we see in a mirror dimly, but then face to face. Now I know in part; then I shall know fully, even as I have been fully known" (1 Corinthians 13:12).

We Will Be Perfectly Christlike

On earth it is impossible to be completely sinless, completely righteous, and completely good. In heaven we will be. Our focus will be on service to God and that alone. Christ came to earth to obey the Father. His focus was in fulfilling His service to God. Just before Jesus was arrested, He gathered His disciples around Him and prayed in their hearing: "I glorified you [God] on earth, *having accomplished the work that you gave me to do*" (John 17:4).

In heaven we will be likewise focused on completing the work God will give us to do—to worship and glorify Him. Our hearts will finally be purged of sinful desires. We will look to Him as our "all in all." We are commanded to do that now. We will accomplish that perfectly there. "[B]ut Christ is all, and in all" (Colossians 3:11).

A place of Perfect Pleasure

Imagine for a moment a time when you have experienced the most exquisite sense of pleasure. Every pore of your being may have seemed to be saying, "Ah, this is bliss." In heaven those ecstatic moments in time will not exist—the delight will be even better. That will be the very nature of our existence there. The reason for such ecstasy may be different because we will be focused on Him instead of on ourselves, but we'll live in a state of perfect pleasure. "Since nothing is better or greater than God, the pure enjoyment of Him must be the very essence of bliss."[43]

> You make known to me the path of life; in your presence there is fullness of joy; at your right hand are pleasures forevermore. (Psalm 16:11)

> His master said to him, "Well done, good and faithful servant. You have been faithful over a little; I will set you over much. Enter into the joy of your master." (Matthew 25:21)

We Will Experience Perfect Love

Here on earth even the purest love is tainted with sin. In loving others, even sacrificially, isn't there a subtle little voice in the back of your mind saying, "I will look better to others for doing this," or, "Maybe this person will think better of me for this," or even, "I hope this will increase my rewards in heaven"? That tiny voice of pride or selfishness that resides even in the biggest and best of hearts is enough to turn our love a "bluish tint."

However, in heaven we will experience pure, undefiled love. We will bask not only in the transfusion of love from one heart to another, but also in the tender love of the Father for His dear children. We can read of Christ's love in John 13:1: "Now before the Feast of the Passover, when Jesus knew that his hour had come to depart out of this world to the Father, having loved his own who were in the world, he loved them to the end."

He showed us the full extent of His love when He died on a cross to pay the penalty for our sins, when He suffered that moment of separation from His Father. It is this same love for us that was described in John 3:16, where it says, "For God so loved the world, that he gave his only Son, that whoever believes in him should not perish but have eternal life." That's love, folks. That's the kind of love that awaits us in a place of perfect bliss.

Only on this side of the curtain is death our enemy. Just beyond the
curtain the monster turns out to be our friend.
ERWIN LUTZER

11

COMFORT

Blessed be the God and Father of our Lord Jesus Christ, the Father of mercies and God of all comfort, who comforts us in all our affliction, so that we may be able to comfort those who are in any affliction, with the comfort with which we ourselves are comforted by God.

2 CORINTHIANS 1:3-4

COMING FULL CIRCLE

"Come on in. I'm sorry the house is such a wreck. They just delivered the hospital bed a little while ago. My husband is trying to get some sleep right now. Let me go check on him, and I'll be right back. Go ahead and have a seat."

Penny McNair looked around as Mrs. Wilcox scurried out of the room. Penny chose to sit at the dining table, hoping Mrs. Wilcox would take the seat across from her when she came back.

Soon she heard quick, heavy steps as the woman bustled back into the room. Every move she made was abrupt and desperate, as if she were in a race against time. Mrs. Wilcox hurried on into the kitchen, calling back over her shoulder, "May I get you a cup of tea? I think I'll pour one for myself."

"Yes, please," Penny answered.

In a moment her hostess hurried back into the dining room, setting the cups down and reaching for napkins—in constant motion. She fell heavily into the chair across from Penny and began to fan herself with one of the envelopes from the mail she'd brought in earlier.

"Oh, my. I really am sorry for all this mess," she repeated, looking around her.

Realizing that Mrs. Wilcox was becoming more and more flustered, Penny reached out and placed her hand over the other woman's chubby, pink hand. "It's okay. Why don't you take a minute and relax? Just stop and breathe for a second."

"Stop and breathe, huh?" Mrs. Wilcox shook her head. "No. I can't afford to do that. If I stop, I'll just . . ."

"Fall apart?" Penny volunteered.

Mrs. Wilcox paused, looked into Penny's kind eyes, and burst into tears. "I'm so sorry. I don't know what's gotten into me today," she sobbed.

"It's okay. Please don't apologize for anything. It's okay to cry. I've certainly done my share."

Mrs. Wilcox dabbed at her puffy eyes with the napkin. She took in a deep breath and let it out. "I don't know exactly why you're here, you know. I don't know what I'm supposed to say to you," she offered. "I know the hospice nurse sent you here, that's all."

"Well, let me answer some of your questions. I don't actually work for hospice. I'm a volunteer for them. I'm here because I know things are really tough for you right now, and I just want to help you in any way I can. Sometimes it helps to talk to someone else who's gone through this before—just to be able to talk about what's going on inside."

Mrs. Wilcox leaned forward. "You might not want to know what's going on inside me right now. Sometimes I'm so mad at Cecil I could spit! Isn't that awful? He's in there dying of a brain tumor, and all I can think about is how mad I am that he's leaving me like this." She sat back in the chair, looking away. "Aw, you just wouldn't understand."

"Wouldn't I?" Penny asked. "My husband died from cancer just a little over a year ago. I didn't think I would ever survive it. I'm sure that I don't know exactly how you feel, but I do know about pain and anger. I've already been through this. So I think if anyone can come close to understanding what you're feeling, I can."

"Oh. I'm sorry. I didn't know."

"Yes. In fact, when I first found out he was dying, I used to keep myself so busy I didn't have time to think. I knew if I ever sat down and allowed myself to think about everything, it would all finally sink in, and I didn't think I could handle that."

"Yes, that's how I feel," Mrs. Wilcox agreed. "I just don't want to think about anything."

"I know. But then again, it helps to figure out why you're feeling what you're feeling. And you can't do that unless you give yourself the time and the permission to do so," Penny explained. "One thing I learned through the whole experience is that you have to make time for yourself every day. You can't focus your complete attention on your husband. He needs you, yes. But he needs you to be strong and healthy and calm. You can't be any of those things if you allow yourself to become exhausted. You need to take time to replenish your energy and to refresh your mind. No one else can do that for you."

Mrs. Wilcox said, "I just feel guilty unless I'm right there with him all the time."

"Have you ever thought that he might not want you right there all the time? Maybe he'd like some privacy too."

"Really? Maybe—I hadn't thought of that."

Penny continued, "All I'm saying is, you can't keep being there for him if you don't stop to *refuel* every now and then. You won't be of any use to him if you allow yourself to get so run down that you end up sick too."

"Yes, I see what you mean," Mrs. Wilcox replied. Her eyes were dry now, though still red-rimmed. She blew her nose loudly into her napkin.

"Today has been awful so far. I didn't want them to bring that hospital bed here. But the nurse said it would help keep him from hurting himself since it has side rails and all. He keeps trying to get up out of our bed by himself, and he's fallen several times already. I just couldn't get to him in time. So I guess it was the right time to bring it in."

"What does he think about it?" Penny asked.

"Oh, I think he likes it. He's sleeping like a baby. It's just that . . ." She took a sip of tea.

"Go on. It's just that what?" Penny urged.

"Well, I've slept with that man right there beside me every night for fifty-seven years except for times when we were in the hospital. I just wish I'd realized that last night was going to be the last time that I'd ever have him there next to me. I would have tried to remember it better or something."

She held the soggy napkin to her eyes as the sobs surged through her body again. Penny got up and moved to the chair next to Mrs. Wilcox. She sat down and put her arm around the older woman's shoulders.

Neither said a word. But a moment of shared understanding passed between them. Afterward they were able to have a good talk. Penny told her about Bachman, making her laugh several times in the process. Mrs. Wilcox told her about her husband, his illness, and a little about their life together.

By the time Penny left, she felt that they were friends. Penny hugged Mrs. Wilcox (Emma now) and promised to come back soon. When she reached her car, Penny turned to wave. Then, gazing heavenward, she offered a word of thanks to God for allowing her to be an instrument of His love. As she got into the car, she thought about Emma and knew she had given the woman real support. Penny's experience had come full circle. It was her turn to be there for someone else, as others had been there for her.

THE GOD OF ALL COMFORT

When I initially planned to write this book, I intended it to be a little book of comfort for those who were losing a loved one to death or trying to make sense of their own approaching death. Through the *journey* of writing, I realize I have modified my original purpose.

The change has been in the way I now view life and death in the light of God's total sovereignty. In the beginning, it seems I believed I could be a source of comfort for those who were hurting. It was subtle; yet it was clear that I thought that by writing about some of my experiences or by repeating some of the words of comfort I offer my patients and their families, I could help people find the comfort and the answers they were looking for.

The book too has come full circle. As I write this last chapter about comfort, I realize with renewed fervor that if there is any comfort to be gained from the reading of this book, it certainly does not come from me. Now I truly understand that the source of all comfort is God. Without Him there will be no comfort. Without Him we are lost, helpless, and hopeless.

With Him, though, all things are possible. Through an understanding of His Word we can obtain comfort in all things. The reason? Because through His Word we realize that regardless of what happens to us or to our loved ones on this earth, we are still held safely in the palm of God's hand. When we realize the utter faithfulness and lovingkindness of the Father, we can handle any crisis with assurance that every moment of our lives is being shaped and molded by the One on whom we can totally depend, the One we can trust *completely*.

The more we realize that, the more we can say with the psalmist, "When I am afraid, I put my trust in you. In God, whose word I praise, in God I trust; I shall not be afraid. What can flesh do to me?" (Psalm 56:3-4). The more our heads and hearts are filled with the sweet truths of God's Word, the more assuredly we can say with Paul, "I have learned the secret of being *content in any and every situation*, whether well fed or hungry, whether living in plenty or in want. *I can do everything through him who gives me strength*" (Philippians 4:12-13 NIV).

God is the source of all comfort. However, in His infinite wisdom and kindness He allows us the privilege of being able to comfort others with the same comfort we ourselves have received from Him. In that way we, like Penny, can come full circle.

Unless we know what it feels like to hurt, we may be insensitive to the pain of others. God's kindness in allowing us to share in such pain enables us to become sensitive to the suffering around us. In that sense we are His "delivery service," distributing comfort to others. Comfort may come *through* us, but it does not come *from* us. It comes from God.

Writing this book has improved my understanding and appreciation of the significance of our role as a *conduit* for comfort. My prayer is still that the book may provide comfort to those dealing with pain, loss, separation, hopelessness, isolation, or bewilderment. But I know that any comfort you may receive from the pages of this book comes not from me but from God, to whom all praise is due.

"He will cover you with his feathers, and under his wings you will find refuge; his faithfulness will be your shield and rampart" (Psalm 91:4 NIV). In what safer place can we be found? In what promises can we take greater comfort or find more peace than in the promises He makes to protect and keep us?

Isaiah 49:13b says, "[F]or the LORD has comforted his people and will have compassion on his afflicted." Then in Isaiah 66:13 we read, "As one whom his mother comforts, so I [God] will comfort you." What more do we need?

"[I]n truth we may be confident that nothing bad will ever happen to us if we belong to Christ. This does not mean that nothing painful will ever happen. Our hearts may be broken a thousand times in this world, and our bodies wracked with pain. But these things are part of the Refiner's fire, the crucible of the kingdom of God."[1]

NO EXEMPTIONS FOR BELIEVERS

Some Christians believe they should somehow be exempt from pain and suffering because of their status with God. They are surprised when adversity comes into their lives. They ask, "Why me?"

Perhaps a better question would be: "Why not me?" There is nothing about Christianity that makes us immune from the pain and suffering others experience. In fact, we're told to *expect* adversity. Read the Bible. Men and women of God throughout the ages have experienced trial after trial, suffering beyond the wildest imaginings. Why should we be any different?

The famous nineteenth-century preacher Charles Spurgeon wrote:

Have not you, dear sick friend, often wondered how your painful or lingering disease could be consistent with your being chosen, and called, and made one with Christ? I dare say this has greatly perplexed you, and yet in very truth it is by no means strange, but a thing to be expected. We need not be astonished that the man whom the Lord loves is sick, for *he is only a man*. The love of Jesus does not separate us from the common necessities and infirmities of human life. Men of God are still men. The covenant of grace is not a charter of exemption from consumption, or rheumatism, or asthma.[2]

CARING FOR THE CAREGIVER

In a chapter devoted to comfort, I cannot overlook the importance of those who take a primary role in caring for others. Being responsible for the well-being of others may place us under a tremendous strain. Caregivers are generally sleep-deprived, exhausted, and easily distracted. They often are "on duty" twenty-four hours a day, seven days a week. With people depending on them, they frequently find themselves with very few moments alone, and even then they may feel that they are "on call." Does this description sound familiar?

In hospice we are trained to be watchful of the condition of caregivers. We are there to support them, not to take over for them. Support means that we look for caregiver burnout. We must teach them how to care for themselves as well as for the patient.

Some tips I can offer are:

• Allow others to sit with the patient in order to give yourself a break.

• When people ask how they can help, give them a specific assignment.

• Find a quiet spot in the home. Visit it daily.

• Admit that there will be times when you are helpless. Just being there is sometimes more important than doing anything.

• Do something good for yourself every day.

• Try to find a few minutes to exercise daily, even if you only walk around the block.

• Share the concerns of your heart with someone safe. It can be a freeing experience just to get the worries, the hurts, and the problems out in the open.

Spurgeon wrote, "Man's heart is never big enough to hold either its joys or its sorrows. You never heard of a man whose heart was exactly full of sorrow, for no sooner is it full than it overflows. The first prompting of the soul is to tell its sorrow to another. The reason is that our hearts are not large enough to hold our grief; we need to have another heart to receive a portion thereof."[3]

The Scriptures teach that this sharing of hearts is a primary function of the body of Christ. "If one member [of the body of Christ] suffers, all suffer together; if one member is honored, all rejoice together" (1 Corinthians 12:26).

The most valuable advice I can give you, though, is to get to know the Lord. If you know Him already, then get to know Him better. Develop a personal relationship with Him, and then talk to Him often. Ask Him to equip you with whatever it takes to care for your loved one. Study His Word to find the comfort only He can provide. He says in Psalm 50:15, "[C]all upon me in the day of trouble; I will deliver you, and you shall glorify me." Learn to trust His promises.

Writer Jerry Bridges says we must embrace three truths if we are really to trust God:

- God is completely sovereign.
- God is infinite in wisdom.
- God is perfect in love.

"Someone has expressed these three truths as they relate to us in this way: 'God in His love always wills what is best for us. In His wisdom He always knows what is best, and in His sovereignty He has the power to bring it about.'"[4] As Colossians 1:17 says, "[Christ] is before all things, and in him all things hold together." He's the only One who can truly help. It may not come in the way you desire, but if you are one of His children, it will come in the way that is best. "It is God's strength, not ours, that enables us to persevere. But we lay hold of His strength through faith."[5]

The more we understand the Word of God, the greater comfort we will be able to find in its pages. Knowledge of the Scriptures is a wonderful thing. But knowledge in and of itself can do nothing to bring us comfort. We must *apply* the knowledge. Therefore, we have to understand not only what the verse is saying but also what it really means to us. "We have only begun when we have mastered the 'what?' of the text. We complete our duty when we have served the 'so what?'"[6]

Todd Murray's "I Am Not Alone" (partially quoted earlier) is one of the most comforting songs I know. We can identify with it because it speaks of not knowing all the answers, of being confused and full of doubt at times. But it also shows us how to think biblically through a crisis and to trust God *completely.*

I AM NOT ALONE

I find myself in a chapter I had not anticipated
and one that I would just as soon was not part of my story.
I'm standing at a crossroads without a single sign to guide me.
I'm not lost, but I'm unsure what my next step should be.

Chorus:
And I refuse to fear, when the future is unclear,
Knowing You are here close beside me.
When I haven't got a clue, what it is that You're up to,
Even then I know that You have not abandoned me.
'Cause faith is believing in things that are yet unseen.
Faith is believing God will intervene.

But when I look, when I look only with my eyes,
I'm tempted to believe the lies that say I'm all alone.
When I perceive only with my darkened mind,
then I am sure to find a God who's cold like stone.
So when the heaven seems like brass,
and Your nearness a thing of the past,
I am not alone. With the eyes of faith I see
that You are here with me.

I will not resist You, when You move Your hand to mold me.
I will not insist *You show me all Your plans today.*
I will not despise the tools You're using now to shape me.
I will not require understanding *to obey.*

Chorus:
So I will not look, I won't look only with my eyes.
I won't believe the lies that say I'm all alone.
I won't perceive only with my darkened mind,
And I refuse to find a God who's cold like stone.

So when the heaven seems like brass,
and Your nearness a thing of the past,
well, I am not alone. With the eyes of faith I see
that You are here with me.
TODD MURRAY

Powerful words to express a powerful message. May God grant us the grace to trust Him in this way. The message is that we don't have all the answers, but He does. He's got it all under control. He is making us better by bringing this crisis into our lives. And we *don't* have to fear. We are not alone.

THE POWER OF PRAYER

God is right here with us; so talk to Him. That's all prayer really is, you know—talking to the Lord. It doesn't have to be a formal affair. There are no rules. You don't have to close your eyes. You don't have to kneel. You don't have to fold your hands a certain way. You don't have to say long, eloquently worded prayers. Just *talk* to Him.

Sometimes I pray in a more formal manner. Those prayers often start with "Dear Lord" and end with "Amen." But then I offer prayers up to Him all through the day. I talk to Him as I clean house or go for a walk. I talk to Him in the car or while waiting in line at the grocery store. These prayers are just a running conversation with my Friend, my Savior, Jesus Christ.

Why should we pray? The main reason is that it pleases Him. We're told to pray. "The Lord is at hand; *do not be anxious about anything*, but *in everything* by prayer and supplication with thanksgiving *let your requests be made known to God*. And the peace of God, which surpasses all understanding, will guard your hearts and your minds in Christ Jesus" (Philippians 4:5b-7).

Prayer is an expression of trust and dependence. It implies that we believe God is sovereign and that He is able to actually hear our prayers and will respond to them. Why would we pray to a God who is helpless to accomplish anything? If we pray *without* believing God can do anything He desires, then all we're doing is wishing, not praying.

Prayer is not like making wishes to a genie in a bottle. Some prayers will not be answered in the way we desire, but they will be answered in a better way—according to the wisdom of God our Father. "We must not expect in every case that prayer for recovery will be answered, for if so, nobody would die who had friend or acquaintance to pray for him. . . . We pray that they may remain with us, but when we recognize that Jesus wants them above, what can we do but admit his larger claim, and say, 'Not as I will, but as thou wilt' (Matthew 26:39)?"[7]

"Prayer does not change God's mind . . . ever. Why not? Precisely because He can learn nothing new from us and because He never has a plan that is less than perfect."[8] We can't *improve* on His plans. I hear you asking, "Well, if our prayers don't change God's mind, and He intends to do what He set out to do anyway, then why pray at all?"

That's a fair question. The first reasons are because He told us to do so and because it pleases Him. A friend of mine used to say that praying was like asking for a cookie. He said to imagine that one of my boys came into the kitchen as I was taking a pan of cookies from the oven. Even though I have every intention of giving my son a couple of cookies, I still teach him to ask, "May I have a cookie, please?"

My friend said, "Why do you teach him to do that?"

"Because it's polite to ask," I replied.

He said, "Does it please you when he asks?"

"Yes."

"Does it show you that he views you as being in authority over him?"

"Yes."

He summarized, "So even though you intended to give him cookies anyway, it pleased you for him to ask permission. It pleases God for us to ask as well. That should be enough reason to do it." I had to agree.

But here is a third reason. We are to pray because prayer does effect a change. What? Didn't I just say that prayer never changes God's mind? Now am I saying that prayer changes things?

"[W]e can conclude that prayer really does change things. Again, what it changes is not the eternal plan of God or the perfection of His knowledge. Most importantly, prayer changes *us*. Why else would Jesus instruct us to pray for those things that God already knows we need? Again, it is surely not for His instruction. . . . When we are engaged in prayer, something happens to *us*. We are changed by the experience. . . . In prayer God learns nothing new about us, we are ever learning about Him."[9] I love this conclusion: "No believer can spend much time in the adoration of God without being changed by the experience."[10]

Some may ask, "If suffering and adversity are allowed or actually brought about by God, is it right for me to pray that He take them away?" I do not believe it is wrong to pray for deliverance from adversity. We see it throughout the Bible. We're told to do it. However, part of our prayer should be for His will, not ours, to be done. Spurgeon comments: "In all trouble send a message to Jesus, and do not keep your misery to yourself. In his case there is no need of reserve, there is no fear of his treating you with cold pride, or heartless indifference, or cruel treachery. He is a [confidant] who never can betray us, a friend who never will refuse us."[11]

Ask Him for the grace to humbly and graciously accept and submit to His will—whatever that will be. Sweet submission always honors God.

MAN'S RESPONSIBILITY VERSUS GOD'S SOVEREIGNTY

One of the questions people have wrangled with throughout history has been an attempt to reconcile God's sovereignty with human responsibility. Yes, God is totally and completely sovereign. He rules and reigns over all things. He is all-powerful and all-knowing. He is actively working in every aspect of our lives. We know these things from the teaching of Scripture.

However, we are not little puppets waiting for our strings to maneuver us into mindless action. The Scriptures also teach us that we are responsible for our actions, thoughts, and sinful choices. We are given the standard for living our lives—Jesus Christ. It is our duty and obligation and joy to follow Him, and to live a life pleasing to Him.

So how can people be held responsible for their own actions and

God be totally sovereign at the same time? Such a proposition is called an antinomy. Both parts of the statement are true and correct but *seem* to contradict each other. It is unclear how they could both be true. Yet we know they are. They are both intertwined into God's design for our lives.

We must *know* that *all things* depend on God but *act* as though they depend on us. That way, we live our life responsibly while at the same time acknowledging that God is doing it all—working all things out according to His perfect plan.

ANGRY WITH GOD?

Many of you may bristle when you think God may have directed the painful suffering you are undergoing. Lots of people have gotten angry with God over things that have hurt them. Even understanding that God is in control is reason enough in their minds to be angry. If God is in control, then why did He let this happen? Why is He causing me such pain? How could He have taken the person from me that I loved the most?

Though God doesn't owe us an explanation, He answers us nonetheless. As discussed in detail in chapter 6, there are many purposes in suffering. The bottom line is that if we are believers, God causes or allows suffering in our lives for good purposes. It doesn't *feel* like it's for good at the time because it hurts. Later we may be able to see the benefits that come from suffering.

Left to our own understanding of the big picture, we are usually perplexed. We can't see the world as God sees it. We can't understand the complexities as He does. Our minds are finite and therefore can perceive only an infinitesimal portion of our world.

I like the illustration Jerry Bridges used in *Trusting God*:

[H]istory is like a giant piece of fabric with very intricate and complex patterns. During the limited span of our lifetimes we see only a tiny fraction of the pattern. Furthermore . . . we see the pattern from the underside. The underside of a weaving usually makes no sense. Even the upper side makes little sense if we view just a tiny piece. Only God sees the upper side, and only He sees the entire fabric with its complete pattern. Therefore, we must trust Him to work out all the details of history to His glory, knowing that His glory and our good are bound up together.[12]

D. A. Carson, in an absorbing sermon preached at the Bible Church of Little Rock in 1999, said, "When you confess God's sovereignty, do not misunderstand God's motives. Many times when confronted with any situation that causes us pain or discomfort or even inconvenience, we may be tempted to be angry with God."

He told a story about a young woman who had lost her best friend to leukemia. The woman was angry with God and accused Him of not loving her. Dr. Carson, in an attempt to comfort her, told her this: "You lost your best friend. God lost His Son—in fact, He didn't *lose* Him, He *gave* Him. And He didn't have to. Before you become too convinced that God doesn't care for you, measure things in terms of a little hill outside Jerusalem."

Remember the words of the apostle John: "In this the love of God was made manifest among us, that God sent his only Son into the world, so that we might live through him. *In this is love, not that we have loved God but that he loved us and sent his Son to be the propitiation for our sins*" (1 John 4:9-10).

When we believe the Scripture's promises that God superintends every event in our lives—past, present, and future—we can then experience peace instead of worry. Nothing will happen to us that God does not already know about. So in an ultimate sense there are no "mistakes" or "accidents" (Psalm 139:4, 16). God's power and grace will equip us to handle anything He brings into our lives (2 Corinthians 12:9-10). Nothing will happen to us, if we are His children, that will not eventually be used by God for some good purpose (Romans 8:28). And through everything, we are assured of His continual presence in our lives (Matthew 28:20).

Read what Richard Baxter wrote regarding this subject: "To say or hear that it is far better to be with Christ, is not enough to make us willing. . . . That is best for me which my heavenly Father's love designs and chooses for my good. I hope I shall never dare to say or think that he is mistaken, or that I could have chosen better for myself. Many a time hath the wise and good will of God crossed my foolish, rebellious will, and afterward I have perceived it was best."[13]

COMFORT FOR THE SORROWING

Many of you may have read this book to find help in comforting those who are sorrowing. The most important way you can comfort someone is just to "be there." You don't have to say anything profound. You don't have to do anything spectacular. For them, just knowing you care enough to be present with them is enough.

Be careful not to utter meaningless phrases such as, "Well, it's God's will," or "It could be worse." Perhaps we've even been guilty of saying, "I know just what you're going through. I went through it myself." That may be true but not necessarily helpful to someone who is hurting, regardless of how well-intentioned you are.

"Let those of us who wish to comfort the sorrowing remember that words can have a hollow ring for those who are overwhelmed with grief. Let us by our presence 'weep with those who weep' (Romans 12:15). We must say we care much louder with our actions than with our words. Our presence and our tears can say more than words could ever communicate."[14]

"The breaking heart wants none of your logic. It wants comfort and peace."[15] Later there may be a time for logic and sensible counsel, but not while a heavy heart feels like it is breaking in two.

If you are searching the Scriptures for a passage of comfort for your sorrowing heart and troubled mind, some find it in the beautiful, trusting words of Psalm 23.

The LORD is my shepherd; I shall not want.
He makes me lie down in green pastures. He leads me beside still waters.
He restores my soul.
He leads me in paths of righteousness for his name's sake.
Even though I walk through the valley of the shadow of death,
I will fear no evil, for you are with me;
your rod and your staff, they comfort me.
You prepare a table before me in the presence of my enemies;
you anoint my head with oil; my cup overflows.

Surely goodness and mercy shall follow me all the days of my life,
and I shall dwell in the house of the LORD forever.

DRAWING TO A CLOSE

Our lives are filled with such incredible beauty. Sometimes we get too busy to notice how gorgeous our world really is. We focus on the things that *demand* our attention, the squeaking wheels of our jobs, money matters, and family responsibilities. Happiness, contentment, appreciation for beauty—those things rarely *demand* our attention. So we tend to push them to the back of our lives so we can attend to the things in the forefront. It's human nature.

Fight it. We can *consciously* decide to retrieve truly significant things from their cobwebbed existence, take them out, dust them off, and enjoy the sense of comfort they can provide. We don't have to remain enslaved to the negativity that surrounds us. Wake up. Look around you. Study the colors, the smells, the sounds, the breeze, and the way the sun feels on your skin. Appreciate the world around you and the people in your path. Show those dear to you how much you love them as if this were your last day on earth.

You may have precious little time to do that. You may think there is not a free moment in your day. After all, this is the age of over-flowing day-timers and schedules. Well, schedule yourself thirty minutes somewhere in that busy day. Write it in your day-timer in ink. Then take those precious few moments to think about the good parts of your life, the parts you ignore because you've got more urgent things to take care of. Maybe those good parts of your life are your spouse, your children, or your parents. Maybe it's your God. They deserve more than just the dregs of your day—whatever's left over after all the activity. They deserve YOU.

Yes, our lives are filled with sorrow and pain. People will always be sick and dying around us. Some of them will be faceless names to us. Some will be precious to us. When someone we love becomes ill, especially terminally ill, we usually find a way to stop all the busyness in our lives. We learn to pare our activities down to only absolutely essential things.

Well, if we can do this in times of crisis or emergency, we can do it routinely. It's not too late to make the changes that can add hope, happiness, and contentment to your existence. Hopefully, you will have the time to change your priorities and to spend some quality time with those you love. Include some quality time every day with God, too. Don't forget Him. Don't abandon His Word. Don't turn away from Him.

When you're sitting at your mother's bedside, holding her hand as she lies dying, you realize that all those deadlines and meetings and appointments and reports mean so little in the overall scheme of things—compared to this.

Oh, the pain and agony of grief! Being a Christian doesn't mean it won't hurt anymore. But we learn through the Scriptures that these things are a valuable part of our lives. We learn to trust in One who controls all things and is sufficient to care for us, to preserve us, to keep us safe, and to bring us at last to our reward—an eternal life with Him. For He says, "I will never leave you nor forsake you" (Hebrews 13:5b).

Note the words of Charles Spurgeon: "If you do not know that Jesus loves you, you lack the brightest star that can cheer the night of sickness. I hope you will not die as you now are, and pass into another world without enjoying the love of Jesus: that would be a terrible calamity indeed. Seek his face at once, and it may be that your present sickness is a part of the way of love by which Jesus would bring you to himself."[16]

If you're not a believer, please take the time to examine the arguments set forth in this book. Look up the Scripture passages. Talk to someone who understands the Bible. Read through it, or at least the New Testament. If you just read one book in the New Testament, read John or Romans. Read it over again. It's amazing how many things you discover the second time that you missed the first.

Perhaps you will do as I suggest. You still may not believe it. There may be no tugging at your heart to accept Jesus Christ as your Lord and Savior. Reading the Bible doesn't guarantee salvation. After all, we are not saved by doctrine. We are saved by Jesus Christ. But there is one thing that *is* a guarantee. You will *not* find salvation *apart* from the Word of God. That is the means by which He will draw you to Himself.

In reading the Scriptures, you will come across passages like these:

Blessed be the God and Father of our Lord Jesus Christ, who has blessed us in Christ with every spiritual blessing in the heavenly places, even as he chose us in him before the foundation of the world, that we should be holy and blameless before him. In love he predestined us for adoption through Jesus Christ, according to the purpose of his will, to the praise of his glorious grace, with which he has blessed us in the Beloved. (Ephesians 1:3-6)

All that the Father gives me will come to me, and whoever comes to me I will never cast out. (John 6:37)

No one can come to me unless the Father who sent me draws him. (John 6:44)

This is why I told you that no one can come to me unless it is granted him by the Father. (John 6:65)

I have loved you with an everlasting love; therefore I have continued my faithfulness to you. (Jeremiah 31:3b)

These passages clearly indicate that it is God the Father who does the choosing. He applies salvation to those He has chosen. Jesus Christ secured that salvation by His life of perfect righteousness and His substitutionary death on behalf of His children. The Holy Spirit calls us and draws us to the Father. And it is the Holy Spirit who indwells believers from the moment of salvation until the moment we step into heaven.

Are you one of His children? Did God choose you to have salvation? Is He drawing you close to Him? Talk to Him. Call on Him to save you.

If you are not one of His children, you probably won't feel a genuine need to turn to Him for salvation. You will more than likely continue in your sins, undisturbed by their consequences. You will remain, in your mind, the master of your own life.

In either case, prepare yourselves for heartache and suffering. Adversity will happen. Pain is a by-product of being alive. Illness, injury, aging, financial setbacks, work-related issues, conflicts in relationships—all these things and more may appear in your life.

Remember that the adversities of life cause us to get bitter or to get better. They can be hurtful—that's true. But in the grand scheme of things, they are for our good if we are Christians. Adversities and trials cause us to grow, to change, and to mature in ways that could not otherwise be accomplished. Godly character traits are developed through adversity, which teaches us by capturing our focus and turning us to God, the true Source of all comfort.

The same adversities that motivate some to move forward are the ones that cause others to fall back. Facing the same circumstances, one person may decide to turn away from God—to be angry and bitter. The other may remember that trials come from the hand of God to help us and to make us stronger, to cause us to persevere through any hardship to the end. That person, though crushed by the weight of grief, can still rejoice in God's provision. He keeps his focus on the eternal.

"God is at work in a proactive, not reactive, fashion. That is, God does not just respond to an adversity in our lives to make the best of a bad situation. He knows before He initiates or permits the adversity exactly how He will use it for our good."[17]

Second Corinthians 4:16-18 says, "So *we do not lose heart.* Though our *outer nature* is wasting away, our *inner nature* is being renewed day by day. For this slight momentary affliction is preparing for us an eternal weight of glory beyond all comparison, as we look not to the things that are seen but to the things that are unseen. For things that are seen are transient, but the things that are unseen are eternal."

We are never alone if we are in Christ Jesus. "God the Holy Ghost daily teaches, leads, guides and directs [us]. God the Father guards [us] by His almighty power. God the Son intercedes for [us] every moment. . . . A threefold cord like this can never be broken."[18]

In closing let me quote once more from Dr. D. A. Carson's sermon to the Bible Church of Little Rock. It succinctly puts into perspective the question of why suffering is such an integral part of our lives:

> Remember, God is more interested in your *holiness* than in your *happiness*. He's more interested in your *faithfulness* than in your *financial success*. He's more interested in your *purity* than in your *power*. . . . He's more interested in your *eternal life* than in your *external wealth*. He's more interested in your *long-term joy* than in your *short-term fun*. And He's more interested in your *good* than in your *desires*.

My desire, from the outset of this project, has been to offer ways to better understand the relationship between the lovingkindness of God and the suffering we encounter in our lives. My hope is that the book has achieved that purpose and will be an instrument of comfort. My prayer is that you may experience the peace of God in the midst of any adversity.

> Consider it pure joy, my brothers, whenever you face trials of many kinds, because you know that the testing of your faith develops perseverance. Perseverance must finish its work so that you may be mature and complete, not lacking anything. . . . Blessed is the man who perseveres under trial, because when he has stood the test, he will receive the crown of life that God has promised to those who love him. . . . Every good and perfect gift is from above, coming down from the Father of the heavenly lights, who does not change like shifting shadows.
> JAMES 1:2-4, 12, 17 NIV

> *The grace of the Lord Jesus Christ*
> *and the love of God*
> *and the fellowship of the Holy Spirit*
> *be with you all.*
> 2 CORINTHIANS 13:14

APPENDIX

Frequently Asked Questions Regarding Hospice

Is hospice a place or a service?

Hospice is a service. That service can take place in many locations. Though there are several residential inpatient facilities throughout the country, hospice services usually take place in a private residence—either the patient's home or that of a family member. Hospice can also provide services in nursing homes and hospitals for end-of-life care. One of our brochures explains:

> Most people do not want to die alone in sterile, impersonal surroundings, hooked up by tubes to machines and cut off from their family and friends and everything that's familiar. Nor do they want to die in pain. They would prefer, if possible, to spend their last days at home . . . alert and free of pain . . . among the people and things they love. Hospice is dedicated to making this possible.

Isn't hospice only for cancer patients?

No. Unfortunately, there are many life-threatening diseases in the world today. Though the majority of our patients have cancer, we also have those who meet criteria for end-stage cardiac disease, end-stage respiratory disease, ALS, end-stage kidney or liver disease, stroke, AIDS, and even end-stage Alzheimer's disease or dementia. Basically hospices open their doors and their hearts to *all* terminally ill persons.

How much will hospice cost me financially?

Nothing. There is usually no out-of-pocket expense for hospice care. (A few hospices require the patient to pay a 5 percent or a five-dollar co-payment on medication and a 5 percent co-payment for respite care. And some of the residential centers apply a daily charge to the patient. You should find out about any charge or co-payment before choosing a hospice.) Medicare, Medicaid (in thirty-eight states), and most private insurances have hospice coverage in their plans. Even when they have no pay source, patients are not turned away as long as they meet the criteria.

Does hospice pay for all medications?

No. Hospice is responsible to pay for and to provide all the medications *that pertain to their terminal diagnosis or to the patient's comfort.* For instance, if a patient is admitted to the program with a diagnosis of end-stage COPD (chronic obstructive pulmonary disease), we would pay for all the medication the patient takes to make his breathing better, as well as any medication that would make the patient more comfortable. But in this case, hospice would not be required to pay for medications to decrease the patient's cholesterol, for example. That would not relate to the respiratory diagnosis. The patient would still be responsible for paying for the medications we do not cover.

Will I need any special equipment in my home before hospice care begins?

No. When we come to your house, we will assess your needs and recommend *and provide* any necessary equipment. Hospice will assist in any way it can to make home care as convenient, clean, efficient, and safe as possible. Hospice also provides any medical supplies you may need (gloves, adult diapers, dressings, etc.).

Does someone have to be with the patient at all times?

That depends on each situation. Many times a patient does not require constant supervision, especially in the early weeks or months of care. As the disease progresses though, a time usually comes when someone needs to be available continuously to meet the patient's ongoing needs.

How much time does hospice provide for each patient?

That depends on the individual situation. The more stable the patient, the fewer visits are needed from the hospice nurse. Most nurses see their patients an average of once or twice weekly. However, the frequency of visits increases as the patient's needs increase. There are also visits from home health aides, the social worker, the chaplain, volunteers, and in some cases a bereavement counselor. Some hospice organizations provide a physician who will visit the patients at home as needed. The bottom line is that we try to be there as much as is needed by the patient at any given time. However, we also do teaching and training in the home with the caregivers so they will feel confident and comfortable caring for their loved one between hospice visits.

Does hospice do anything to make death come sooner?

No. Hospices do nothing to speed up or to slow down the dying process. We know we can't add days to patients' lives, and so we try to add life to their days. We are there to support the patient and the family. We try to ensure that the patient does not suffer in the dying process, but we do nothing to hasten death or prolong life. By the time we are called, the patient and family have usually decided to let nature take its course. Our goal is to ensure a peaceful, painless death.

How does hospice manage pain?

Hospice personnel are pain and symptom control specialists. We are up-to-date on the latest medications, devices, and techniques to control pain and other symptoms such as restlessness, anxiety, shortness of breath, nausea, and vomiting. The goal is to find what we call "the lowest effective dose." That dose is the smallest amount of medication the patient needs to manage the pain and still keep functioning at the maximum potential.

Is hospice affiliated with any religious organizations?

No. We do not require patients to adhere to any particular set of beliefs but try to support the patient's own beliefs.

The best way I can explain what hospice actually does is to talk about the members of the hospice team and explain their functions.

NURSE

The first member of the team, and the most important one to the patient, is the hospice nurse. He/she is the team leader in the sense that it is the nurse's responsibility to identify and address the needs of the patient or to channel the information to the appropriate person to meet those needs. (There are wonderful male nurses in the hospice program, but since the majority of the nurses are female, I will refer to the hospice nurse as "she" from here on.)

The nurse usually carries a patient load of between four and fifteen patients, with an average of about ten. She sees her patients a minimum of once every two weeks (the Medicare requirement) but may see them on a daily basis—depending on the patient's condition. The *average* frequency is once weekly.

What does the nurse do? She is responsible for the patients' medical management for the duration of their lives. This role would be better understood if it were broken down into tasks.

The hospice nurse assesses the patient's physical condition with each visit. That entails taking vital signs, doing a brief physical examination, obtaining a history of what has occurred with the patient since the last visit, assessing the effectiveness of any medical interventions on an ongoing basis, and assessing the spiritual/emotional needs of the patient and family. The nurse records and interprets those findings to accurately determine the patient's condition at every visit.

She becomes the mediator between doctor and patient. She is an extension of the doctor. Whenever something needs to be brought to the physician's attention, she calls him/her and obtains the orders appropriate for that particular patient. She then implements those orders and evaluates their effectiveness.

The nurse is the "coach" of sorts for the dying experience. She teaches the patient and family about the disease process, alerting them to signs and symptoms they should watch for. She will let them know what to expect every step of the way and how to respond when/if it happens. It is my strong belief that if people understand what they're dealing with, they can handle those situations with greater confidence, calm, and efficiency. That is one of the goals of hospice care—to replace *chaos* with *calm*. Hospice takes a situation that seems unmanageable to the patient and family and turns it into one that is "doable."

In hospice we realize that, in all likelihood, our patients are not going to recover. Instead of setting an impossible goal, such as: "The patient will get well," we set an attainable one: "The patient will be free of suffering and discomfort for the duration of his or her life." That's an achievable goal in most cases and one the family can believe in and participate in as well.

The nurse, in a sense, becomes a part of the family while she takes care of the patient. While it's possible for a hospital nurse to develop closeness with patients, a hospice nurse usually experiences greater intimacy and caring relationships with them. This role gives her the opportunity to spend quality time with patients and their families in their own homes, sharing cups of coffee, seeing family pictures on the wall, exploring their feelings and personal goals with them, or meeting the grandchildren and friends. That's why I believe being a hospice nurse is such a great *privilege*. The relationship that develops between the nurse and her patient and the family becomes trusting and rewarding. It puts joy in *my* heart to walk into a room and see the patient's eyes light up because I'm there. My extended "family" is growing constantly.

This closeness and the love and appreciation derived from the relationships are the rewards that motivate hospice nurses to continue in this field. A nurse doesn't get into hospice for the "fun" of it because sometimes it's not much fun. Nor do they get into hospice for the money because in most cases they can make more money working in a hospital or for a successful medical clinic. They come to this particular field of nursing because they long to make a *real difference* in the lives of patients. They choose to offer their hearts to those who are dying—to be there for them when others may not want to. There is a sign in our office that reads, "Hospice nurses are not hired . . . they're called." That sums it up.

CERTIFIED NURSING ASSISTANT

Another very important team member is the Certified Nursing Assistant (CNA), sometimes called the home health aide (HHA). This person has received specialized training in providing personal care to the patient. Accustomed to caring for very sick patients, the CNA knows what signs to look for and when to contact the nurse for specific problems observed.

Personal care includes bathing, dressing, and sometimes feeding the patient as well as changing bed linens and keeping the patient's environment clean and safe. CNAs are not to be used as maids or housekeepers. All their tasks must be directly related to the patient.

I believe one of the most valuable roles performed by CNAs is to provide some relief for the caregiver. Their presence in the home allows exhausted family members to take a nap, go to the grocery store, or have lunch with a friend—much-needed downtime free from worry about the patient's care.

How much time do the aides give each patient? That depends on the policies of the individual hospice organization, on the availability of the staffing, and on the condition of the patient. Some hospices can offer up to eight hours a day. Others give just the amount of time it takes to do the personal care. Some see the patients two or three times a week; others visit daily. Most allow the aides to stay for the length of time actually needed by the patient. There is usually a coordinator in the office who works closely with the home health aides, the patients' families, and the nurses to establish the appropriate schedule for each patient depending on individual needs.

SOCIAL WORKER

Another valued member of the hospice team is the social worker. This person makes an initial visit to the patient upon admission to the program. He or she assesses the patient's coping skills, takes a brief social history, and gives vital information as needed. The social worker is a great sounding board, as are all the hospice staff members, for the patient's and/or families' feelings and concerns about the impending death. This team member will also have information about helpful resources for the family. The social worker is a tremendous help in assisting them along that road from denial to acceptance.

CHAPLAIN

The next team member is the chaplain. What a special person the chaplain can be. He or she provides for the patient's spiritual needs. Most hospice patients are not well enough to attend church anymore; so in a sense the chaplain brings church to them. The chaplain prays with them, talks to them, gives devotionals when desired, and even sings hymns to or with patients. He or she supports the patient's beliefs and provides services accordingly. Sometimes chaplains just sit with patients and observe a time of silent meditation or prayer. Whatever the patient needs, he or she is there to provide spiritual comfort and counsel in a nonjudgmental manner.

BEREAVEMENT COUNSELOR

Some hospices are fortunate enough to have a full-time bereavement counselor. Others utilize a member of their psychosocial team for this position. The bereavement counselor works to ensure that the family is dealing well with their loss. She provides much-needed information and counseling in an attempt to aid with the family's transition into daily life after the loss of a loved one.

VOLUNTEERS

Hospice volunteers are called "the heart of hospice." They play an important role in the overall program. Without them, in fact, many hospices would not be able to carry on their work. They provide assistance at all levels of skill. Many are relatives and friends of former patients. Having experienced the benefits of hospice firsthand, they now want to contribute to its good work. Volunteers must first undergo a training program to meet the requirements for making patient contacts. A volunteer coordinator is responsible for placement and scheduling of the volunteers as well as for recruitment and training.

Though the volunteers do not give *medical* care, they augment the support the hospice program gives to these families. They may sit with the patient to allow the family time to get away. Some come regularly to read to the patient, to help with a scrapbook, or just to hold a hand and talk. Others provide shopping services for families who are not able to get out to buy groceries or other items they need. Some build wheelchair ramps or install shower bars. They use their own strengths and capabilities for the benefit of the patient.

MEDICAL DIRECTOR

Each hospice office must also have a medical director, a physician who oversees the medical management of each patient enrolled in the program. Some medical directors make house calls on an as-needed basis. Others monitor the patients through close communication with the nurses and aides involved in their care. The hospice team benefits from the medical director's ongoing teaching regarding specific problems and disease processes encountered.

In addition to these staff members are the unsung heroes of the hospice organization—the secretary, the medical records clerk, the marketing director, the clinical nursing director, and executive director—who all work together toward building and operating an excellent program.

NOTES

Introduction

1. Jerry Bridges, *Trusting God Even When Life Hurts* (Colorado Springs: NavPress, 1988), 11.

Chapter 1: Denial

1. Billy Graham, *Facing Death and the Life After* (Nashville: W Publishing Group, 1987), 16.

Chapter 2: Why Me?

1. J. C. Ryle, *Ryle's Expository Thoughts on the Gospels* (Grand Rapids: Zondervan, n.d.), 2.
2. Ibid, 26.
3. Erwin Lutzer, *One Minute After You Die* (Chicago: Moody Press, 1997), 58.
4. Kahlil Gibran, *The Prophet* (New York: Alfred A. Knopf, Inc., 1923), 29.

Chapter 3: Options

1. Philip Yancey, *What's So Amazing About Grace?* (Grand Rapids: Zondervan, 1997), 266-267.
2. Susan Hunt, *Spiritual Mothering* (Wheaton, Ill.: Crossway Books, 1992).

Chapter 4: The Sovereignty of God

1. *The American Heritage Dictionary of the English Language* (Boston: American Heritage/Houghton Mifflin, 1973).
2. Jerry Bridges, *Trusting God Even When Life Hurts* (Colorado Springs: NavPress, 1988), 36.
3. Ibid., 36-37.
4. Charles Colson and Nancy Pearcey, *How Now Shall We Live?* (Carol Stream, Ill.: Tyndale House Publishers, 1999), 62.

5. Bridges, *Trusting God*, 84.
6. R. C. Sproul, *The Invisible Hand* (Waco, Tex.: Word Publishing, 1996), 107.
7. Charles H. Spurgeon, "The Sympathy of the Two Worlds," in John MacArthur, *The Glory of Heaven* (Wheaton, Ill.: Crossway Books, 1996), 239.
8. Richard Baxter, *Dying Thoughts* (Grand Rapids: Baker Book House, 1976), 110.
9. Sproul, *Invisible Hand*, 44.
10. Erwin Lutzer, *One Minute After You Die* (Chicago: Moody Press, 1997), 123.

Chapter 5: The Sovereignty of God in Salvation

1. *The American Heritage Dictionary of the English Language* (Boston: American Heritage/Houghton Mifflin, 1973).
2. Ibid.
3. Millard J. Erickson, *Concise Dictionary of Christian Theology* (Grand Rapids: Baker Books, 1986), 147.
4. David N. Steele and Curtis C. Thomas, *Romans: An Interpretative Outline* (Phillipsburg, N.J.: Presbyterian and Reformed Publishing Co., 1963), 37.
5. Erwin Lutzer, *One Minute After You Die* (Chicago: Moody Press, 1997), 42.
6. Doug Reed, "Christian Maturity" (Eureka Springs, Ark.: Thorncrown Chapel, 1997), 10.
7. Steele and Thomas, *Romans*, 84.
8. Loraine Boettner, *Immortality* (Phillipsburg, N.J.: Presbyterian and Reformed Publishing Co., 1956), 13.
9. David Steele, *God's Saving Work* (unpublished), chapter 9.
10. John MacArthur, *Ashamed of the Gospel* (Wheaton, Ill.: Crossway Books, 1993), 155.
11. Jerry Bridges, *Transforming Grace* (Colorado Springs: NavPress, 1991), 27.
12. Reed, "Christian Maturity," 18.
13. Henry Bast, from a sermon titled "The First Five Minutes After Death," in *Eager to Preach: Selected Sermons of Henry Bast* (Grand Rapids: Bethany Reformed Church, 1987), 122.
14. Lutzer, *One Minute After You Die*, 138.

15. Jerry Bridges, *Trusting God Even When Life Hurts* (Colorado Springs: NavPress, 1988), 99.

16. J. I. Packer, Introduction, in John Owen, *The Death of Death in the Death of Christ* (Edinburgh: Banner of Truth Trust, repr. 1967), 10.

17. Lutzer, *One Minute After You Die*, 139.

18. Richard Baxter, *Dying Thoughts* (Grand Rapids: Baker Book House, 1976), 10.

Chapter 6: The Purposes of Suffering

1. Erwin Lutzer, *One Minute After You Die* (Chicago: Moody Press, 1997), 120.

2. Henry Bast, from a sermon titled "How a Christian Faces Life and Death," in *Eager to Preach: Selected Sermons of Henry Bast* (Grand Rapids: Bethany Reformed Church, 1987), 117.

3. Jerry Bridges, *Trusting God Even When Life Hurts* (Colorado Springs: NavPress, 1991), 195.

4. Wayne Grudem, "Death and the Intermediate State," in *Systematic Theology* (Grand Rapids: Zondervan, 1994), 811-812.

5. Bridges, *Trusting God,* 52, 101.

6. Ibid., 209.

7. Ibid., 192.

8. Doug Reed, "Christian Maturity" (Eureka Springs, Ark.: Thorncrown Chapel, 1997), 12, 19.

9. Bridges, *Trusting God,* 173-174.

10. Susan Hunt, *Spiritual Mothering* (Wheaton, Ill.: Crossway Books, 1992), 161.

11. Reed, "Christian Maturity," 14.

12. J. C. Ryle, *Ryle's Expository Thoughts on the Gospels* (Grand Rapids: Zondervan, n.d.), 180.

13. Richard Baxter, *Dying Thoughts* (Grand Rapids: Baker Book House, 1976), 113.

14. Bridges, *Trusting God,* 155.

15. Ibid., 19.

16. Reed, "Christian Maturity," 18.

17. Hunt, *Spiritual Mothering*, 160.

18. Ibid., 161-162.

19. Billy Graham, *Facing Death and the Life After* (Nashville: W Publishing Group, 1987), 66.

20. Charles Spurgeon, sermon titled "Beloved, and Yet Afflicted" (Dominica: Metropolitan Press, n.d.).
21. John MacArthur, *The Glory of Heaven* (Wheaton, Ill.: Crossway Books, 1996), 100.
22. Bridges, *Trusting God*, 32.
23. John MacArthur, *Ashamed of the Gospel* (Wheaton, Ill.: Crossway Books, 1993), 131.
24. Charles H. Spurgeon, "The Sympathy of the Two Worlds," in MacArthur, *Glory of Heaven*, 239.

Chapter 7: Preparing for Approaching Death

1. Loraine Boettner, *Immortality* (Phillipsburg, N.J.: Presbyterian and Reformed Publishing Co., 1956), 9.
2. Billy Graham, *Facing Death and the Life After* (Nashville: W Publishing Group, 1987), 196.
3. Ibid., 105.
4. Crossroads Hospice brochure.
5. Erwin Lutzer, *One Minute After You Die* (Chicago: Moody Press, 1997), 25.
6. John MacArthur, *The Glory of Heaven* (Wheaton, Ill.: Crossway Books, 1996), 69.
7. Boettner, *Immortality*, 43.
8. Ibid., 47.
9. Wayne Grudem, "Death and the Intermediate State," in *Systematic Theology* (Grand Rapids: Zondervan, 1994), 816.
10. Lutzer, *One Minute After You Die*, 79.
11. MacArthur, *Glory of Heaven*, 62.

Chapter 8:
The Truth About Angels and Things That Go "Bump" in the Night

1. John MacArthur, *The Glory of Heaven* (Wheaton, Ill.: Crossway Books, 1996), 149.
2. Ibid., 150-151.
3. Wayne Grudem, "Angels," in *Systematic Theology* (Grand Rapids: Zondervan, 1994), 397.
4. MacArthur, *Glory of Heaven*, 153-154.
5. Grudem, "Angels," *Systematic Theology*, 402.

6. MacArthur, *Glory of Heaven*, 159.

7. Grudem, "Angels," *Systematic Theology*, 397.

8. MacArthur, *Glory of Heaven*, 156.

9. Ibid., 157.

10. Ibid., 152.

11. Grudem, "Angels," *Systematic Theology*, 407.

12. MacArthur, *Glory of Heaven*, 159.

13. Grudem, "Angels," *Systematic Theology*, 400.

14. Erwin Lutzer, *One Minute After You Die* (Chicago: Moody Press, 1997), 61.

15. Ibid., 62.

16. MacArthur, *Glory of Heaven*, 158.

17. Lutzer, *One Minute After You Die*, 20.

18. Ibid., 18.

19. Loraine Boettner, *Immortality* (Phillipsburg, N.J.: Presbyterian and Reformed Publishing Co., 1956), 137-138.

20. *Tabor's Cyclopedic Medical Dictionary* (Philadelphia: F. A. Davis Company, 1989), 1185.

21. Lutzer, *One Minute After You Die*, 25.

22. Ibid., 25-26.

Chapter 9: Death

1. Loraine Boettner, *Immortality* (Phillipsburg, N.J.: Presbyterian and Reformed Publishing Co., 1956), 9.

2. Doug Reed, "Christian Maturity" (Eureka Springs, Ark.: Thorncrown Chapel, 1997), 6.

3. John MacArthur, *Ashamed of the Gospel* (Wheaton, Ill.: Crossway Books, 1993), 128.

4. Erwin Lutzer, *One Minute After You Die* (Chicago: Moody Press, 1997), 136.

5. Jerry Bridges, *Trusting God Even When Life Hurts* (Colorado Springs: NavPress, 1988), 72.

6. Lutzer, *One Minute After You Die*, 46.

7. Richard Baxter, *Dying Thoughts* (Grand Rapids: Baker Book House, 1976), 16.

8. Susan Hunt, *Spiritual Mothering* (Wheaton, Ill.: Crossway Books, 1992), 189.

9. *Tabor's Cyclopedic Medical Dictionary* (Philadelphia: F. A. Davis Company, 1989), 457.

10. Lutzer, *One Minute After You Die*, 77.

11. Boettner, *Immortality*, 123.

12. Charles Spurgeon, sermon titled "The Sympathy of the Two Worlds," in John MacArthur, *The Glory of Heaven* (Wheaton, Ill.: Crossway Books, 1996), 243.

13. Lutzer, *One Minute After You Die*, 60.

14. Wayne Grudem, "Death and the Intermediate State," in *Systematic Theology* (Grand Rapids: Zondervan, 1994), 817.

15. MacArthur, *Glory of Heaven*, 72.

16. Ibid., 75.

17. Ibid., 49.

18. Ibid., 104-106.

19. Ibid., 37.

20. MacArthur, *Ashamed of the Gospel*, 129.

21. Boettner, *Immortality*, 66.

22. Ibid., 120.

23. Lutzer, *One Minute After You Die*, 101.

24. Ibid., 121.

25. Ibid., 122.

26. Baxter, *Dying Thoughts*, 37.

27. John T. Dunlop, *Dignity and Dying: A Christian Appraisal*, ed. John F. Kilner, Arlene B. Miller, and Edmund D. Pellegrino (Grand Rapids: Eerdmans, 1996), 43.

28. Billy Graham, *Facing Death and the Life After* (Nashville: W Publishing Group, 1987), 128.

29. Bridges, *Trusting God*, 213.

30. R. C. Sproul, *The Invisible Hand* (Waco, Tex.: Word Publishing, 1996), 8.

31. Lutzer, *One Minute After You Die*, 129.

32. Ibid., 75.

33. Boettner, *Immortality*, 35.

34. Ibid., 34.

35. Lutzer, *One Minute After You Die*, 130.

36. MacArthur, *Glory of Heaven*, 55.

37. Henry Bast, "How a Christian Faces Life and Death," in *Eager to Preach: Selected Sermons of Henry Bast* (Grand Rapids: Bethany Reformed Church, 1987), 115.

38. Boettner, *Immortality*, 37.
39. Baxter, *Dying Thoughts*, 43.
40. Ibid., 104.
41. Ibid., 114, 106, 129.
42. Lutzer, *One Minute After You Die*, 44.

Chapter 10: The Truth About Heaven and Hell

1. Loraine Boettner, *Immortality* (Phillipsburg, N.J.: Presbyterian and Reformed Publishing Co., 1956), 95.
2. Ibid., 59.
3. Ibid., 65.
4. John MacArthur, *Ashamed of the Gospel* (Wheaton, Ill.: Crossway Books, 1993), 116.
5. Jerry Bridges, *Trusting God Even When Life Hurts* (Colorado Springs: NavPress, 1988), 18.
6. Erwin Lutzer, *One Minute After You Die* (Chicago: Moody Press, 1997), 109.
7. Ibid., 97.
8. Harry Buis, *The Doctrine of Eternal Punishment* (Phillipsburg, N.J.: Presbyterian and Reformed Publishing Co., 1957), ix.
9. Wayne Grudem, "Hell," in *Systematic Theology* (Grand Rapids: Zondervan, 1994), 1148.
10. Lutzer, *One Minute After You Die*, 98.
11. Ibid., 105.
12. Grudem, "Hell," in *Systematic Theology*, 1152.
13. MacArthur, *Ashamed of the Gospel*, 133.
14. Boettner, *Immortality*, 84.
15. Grudem, "Hell," in *Systematic Theology*, 1151.
16. Lutzer, *One Minute After You Die*, 108.
17. Ibid., 51.
18. John MacArthur, *The Glory of Heaven* (Wheaton, Ill.: Crossway Books, 1996), 102.
19. Ibid., 40.
20. Boettner, *Immortality*, 50.
21. MacArthur, *The Glory of Heaven*, 140.
22. Ibid., 141-142.
23. Thomas Boston, "The Kingdom of Heaven," in MacArthur, *Glory of Heaven*, 214.

24. Richard Baxter, *Dying Thoughts* (Grand Rapids: Baker Book House, 1976), 83.

25. Boston, "The Kingdom of Heaven," in MacArthur, *Glory of Heaven*, 214.

26. Lutzer, *One Minute After You Die*, 77.

27. MacArthur, *Glory of Heaven*, 134.

28. Lutzer, *One Minute After You Die*, 71.

29. Boettner, *Immortality*, 94.

30. Lutzer, *One Minute After You Die*, 86, 89.

31. Baxter, *Dying Thoughts*, 72.

32. Henry Bast, "The Dead Who Die in the Lord," in *Eager to Preach: Selected Sermons of Henry Bast* (Grand Rapids: Bethany Reformed Church, 1987), 134.

33. J. C. Ryle, "Home at Last," in MacArthur, *Glory of Heaven*, 255.

34. J. C. Ryle, *Holiness* (Cambridge: James Clarke & Co., repr. 1956), 62.

35. MacArthur, *Glory of Heaven*, 68.

36. Boston, "The Kingdom of Heaven," in MacArthur, *Glory of Heaven*, 214.

37. MacArthur, *Ashamed of the Gospel*, 116.

38. Bridges, *Trusting God*, 69.

39. Lutzer, *One Minute After You Die*, 63.

40. Bast, "A Better Country," in *Eager to Preach*, 134.

41. MacArthur, *Glory of Heaven*, 91, 95.

42. Ibid., 108.

43. Ibid., 127.

Chapter 11: Comfort

1. R. C. Sproul, *The Invisible Hand* (Waco, Tex.: Word Publishing, 1996), 174.

2. Charles Spurgeon, sermon titled "Beloved, and Yet Afflicted" (Dominica: Metropolitan Press, n.d.).

3. Charles Spurgeon, "The Sympathy of the Two Worlds," in John MacArthur, *The Glory of Heaven* (Wheaton, Ill.: Crossway Books, 1996), 239.

4. Jerry Bridges, *Trusting God Even When Life Hurts* (Colorado Springs: NavPress, 1988), 18.

5. Ibid., 186.

6. David L. Turner, "The Structure and Sequence of Matthew 24:1-41:

Interaction with Evangelical Treatments," *Grace Theological Journal* 10, no. 1 (Spring 1989): 27.

7. Spurgeon, "Beloved, and Yet Afflicted."
8. Sproul, *Invisible Hand*, 203.
9. Ibid., 205-206.
10. Ibid., 207.
11. Spurgeon, "Beloved, and Yet Afflicted."
12. Bridges, *Trusting God*, 90.
13. Richard Baxter, *Dying Thoughts* (Grand Rapids: Baker Book House, 1976), 66.
14. Erwin Lutzer, *One Minute After You Die* (Chicago: Moody Press, 1997), 58.
15. Loraine Boettner, *Immortality* (Phillipsburg, N.J.: Presbyterian and Reformed Publishing Co., 1956), 10.
16. Spurgeon, "Beloved, and Yet Afflicted."
17. Bridges, *Trusting God*, 207.
18. J. C. Ryle, *Holiness* (Cambridge: James Clarke & Co., repr. 1956), 61.